'How much water do we really use, as individuals an[...]
we didn't really know, but the concept of the "water footprint" – developed and
analyzed by Arjen Hoekstra (and his colleagues) – has revolutionized our understanding of our water use. Hoekstra's compelling and informative book is a vital
contribution to the desperately needed public debate over how best to move to
sustainable water management, use, and policy. It deserves to be read by anyone
concerned about the planet's freshwater resources.'

Dr Peter H. Gleick, president and co-founder of the Pacific
Institute and creator of *The World's Water* book series

'Over the next 20 years the global demand for water is expected to exceed supply
by 40% with dire consequences for our planet. Professor Hoekstra's meticulously
researched book uses the concept of water footprinting – in ways that make it easy
to understand just how much water plays a central part in our everyday lives – as a
means of helping to manage and reduce water consumption. It is a timely contribution to an increasingly urgent debate.'

Paul Polman, CEO Unilever

'No concept has done more to show the role of water in our lives. For too long,
water has been mismanaged because it was invisible. The water footprint concept
has helped us see how water flows through our lives and economies – and what we
value, we protect.'

Stuart Orr, Freshwater Manager, WWF International

'This contribution by Professor Hoekstra advances our understanding of the role
of water in the consumer goods sector and can move us closer to addressing water
scarcity and sustainable consumption and move towards a Circular Economy.'

Will Sarni, Director and Practice Leader, Enterprise
Water Strategy, Deloitte Consulting LLP

# THE WATER FOOTPRINT OF MODERN CONSUMER SOCIETY

Water is not only used in the domestic context, but also in agriculture and industry in the production of commercial goods, from food to paper. The water footprint is an indicator of freshwater use that looks at both direct and indirect use of water by a consumer or producer. For example, it takes 15,000 litres of water to produce 1 kg of beef, or 8,000 litres of water to produce a pair of jeans.

This book shows how the water footprint concept can be used to quantify and map the water use behind consumption and how it can guide reduction of water use to a sustainable level. It shows that imports of water-intensive products can benefit water-scarce countries, but also that this creates a dependency on foreign water resources.

The book demonstrates how water-scarce regions sometimes, nevertheless, use lots of water for making export products. It raises the issue of sustainable consumption: how can consumers, businesses and governments get involved in reducing the water footprints of final consumer goods?

**Arjen Y. Hoekstra** is Professor in Water Management at the University of Twente in the Netherlands, creator of the water footprint concept and co-founder of the Water Footprint Network. He specializes in integrated water resources planning and management, river basin management and policy analysis.

# THE WATER FOOTPRINT OF MODERN CONSUMER SOCIETY

*Arjen Y. Hoekstra*

Routledge
Taylor & Francis Group

LONDON AND NEW YORK

from Routledge

First published 2013
by Routledge
2 Park Square, Milton Park, Abingdon, Oxon OX14 4RN

Simultaneously published in the USA and Canada
by Routledge
711 Third Avenue, New York, NY 10017

*Routledge is an imprint of the Taylor & Francis Group, an informa business*

*British Library Cataloguing in Publication Data*
A catalogue record for this book is available from the British Library

*Library of Congress Cataloging-in-Publication Data*
Hoekstra, Arjen Y., 1967–
The water footprint of modern consumer society / Arjen Y. Hoekstra. --
First edition.
pages cm
Includes bibliographical references and index.
1. Water consumption--Measurement. 2. Industrial water supply.
3. Water-supply--Accounting. I. Title.
TD345.H557 2013
333.91'13--dc23
2012045046

ISBN13: 978-1-84971-303-0 (hbk)
ISBN13: 978-1-84971-427-3 (pbk)
ISBN13: 978-0-203-12658-5 (ebk)

Typeset in Bembo by
GreenGate Publishing Services, Tonbridge, Kent

MIX
Paper from
responsible sources
FSC
www.fsc.org   FSC® C018575

Printed and bound in Great Britain by MPG Printgroup

# CONTENTS

# ILLUSTRATIONS

## Figures

## Tables

# PREFACE

How much is your water bill each month? Few people are able to answer this question. And if people have some idea, generally they will know the cost in dollars, euros, pounds or yen but not the amount of litres used. For most households in developed countries, the water bill is not large enough to remember it. Thus, most people just open the tap and have little idea about the total volume of water they use per day at home, for activities like drinking, cooking, cleaning, washing and gardening. Generally, people have even less of an idea about their *indirect* water use, the hidden water use behind the goods and services they consume. For many households, this indirect water use is 50–100 times larger than the water use at home. Particularly things like food, paper and cotton take a lot of water in their production process. This water use is 'hidden' for consumers, because for many commodities supply chains are stretched out across the globe. Today, of the seven billion people on Earth, 50 per cent live in urban areas, in the more developed regions even 75 per cent (UNFPA, 2011), while most of the water is used in agriculture and to a lesser extent in industrial and mining activities that take place elsewhere and are thus practically hidden from view. In daily life, one cannot see the water consumption and pollution that relates to the commodities consumed. A bunch of flowers bought in the European Union may have been imported from Kenya, Ethiopia, Colombia, Ecuador or Israel, where it took a substantial volume of water to grow the flowers. A pair of jeans bought in the USA may have been manufactured in China, where dyeing of the textile polluted the local streams. The cotton may have been imported into China from India or Pakistan, where many rivers are overexploited because of abstractions for irrigating cotton fields. Most of the time, the price of water consumption and pollution is hardly or not at all included in the price of the commodities produced. As a result, consumers throughout the world use water without having the slightest idea about their global water footprint.

The underlying thought of this book is that broad public awareness of the water footprint of our daily commodities is a precondition for sustainable water allocation and use worldwide. The book aims to contribute to increasing this awareness by reviewing the water footprint of a variety of commodities, from bread and beef to fuel and flowers. For most people, even professionals working in the water sector, the water footprint is a new concept. Many have heard about the carbon footprint of goods and services, and some may know the ecological footprint concept. The water footprint is similar to the other footprint concepts (Hoekstra, 2009; Galli *et al.*, 2011). The basic idea is that we look at the use of natural resources and the use of the assimilation capacity of the environment along the full supply chain. The ecological footprint quantifies the amount of bioproductive space required, measured in hectares. The carbon footprint measures the emission of greenhouse gasses, in carbon dioxide equivalents. Likewise, the water footprint quantifies the consumption and pollution of freshwater resources, measured in cubic metres of water. The water footprint of a commodity is the total volume of freshwater used – that is consumed or polluted – to produce the commodity, measured over the whole production chain. The water footprint of an individual or community refers to the total volume of freshwater that is used to produce the various goods and services consumed by the individual or community.

I introduced the water footprint concept in 2002 and have continued to work on the idea until 2005 at the UNESCO-IHE Institute for Water Education, and since then at the University of Twente, the Netherlands. The concept and methods have now been firmly established in scientific literature. Since 2007 the interest in the concept among other researchers, companies and governmental and non-governmental institutions is growing rapidly. With reports in newspapers like *The New York Times*, *The Wall Street Journal*, the *Guardian* and *The Times* and in popular magazines like *National Geographic*, the water footprint concept has found its way to a broader audience. The interest can also be monitored online. In the two-year period 2010–2011, the water footprint website of the Water Footprint Network (WFN) attracted 1.2 million unique visitors. The growing interest in the concept of the water footprint is rooted in the recognition that human impacts on freshwater systems can ultimately be linked to human consumption and that issues like water shortages and pollution can be better understood and addressed by considering production and supply chains as a whole. It is increasingly acknowledged that local water depletion and pollution are often closely tied to the structure of the global economy. Many countries have significantly externalized their water footprint, importing water-intensive goods from elsewhere. This puts pressure on the water resources in the exporting regions, where, too often, mechanisms for wise water governance and conservation are lacking. Not only do governments acknowledge their role in achieving a better management of water resources, businesses and public-service organizations also increasingly recognize their role in the interplay of actors involved in water use and management. Relevant questions posed nowadays by an increasing number of professionals are: How to implement proper water footprint accounting in the context of my country or organization?

How to identify the spots where water footprints have the largest impact? How to reduce the water footprint in those places?

This book is a successor to *Globalization of Water*, the book that I wrote with Ashok Chapagain, published in 2008 by Blackwell. In that book we made the argument that freshwater is a global resource and that wise water governance has a dimension that goes beyond the level of a river basin. We received a large variety of positive but also critical comments. Some colleagues in the field still don't like the idea of freshwater as a global resource and stick to the idea that water resources management is a local or at most national issue, whereby international cooperation is needed only in the case of trans-boundary river basins. Some don't like the phrase 'freshwater is a global resource' because it would ignore the fact that both supply and demand of water resources vary greatly from place to place. The debate sometimes overlooked that we had argued that freshwater scarcity has a global dimension *on top* of its local dimension. Anyway, there is no reason to change the thesis that there are global aspects in protecting our freshwater resources, so the current book builds on that. This new book adds various case studies that have been carried out in the years after the appearance of *Globalization of Water*. I will discuss in depth the water footprint of a number of specific commodities. Since most of the water consumption in the world relates to the agricultural sector, most attention will go to commodities that are agriculture based. Examples are cola, bread, pasta, meat, cotton, biofuels and cut flowers. However, I will also examine the water footprint of different forms energy and paper. In the latter case we consider the water footprint in paper processing, but also the water footprint in the forestry stage. It would have been nice also to include elaborate examples of some industrial products that are generally based on natural resources that are obtained in mining, but such cases are not yet available. To some extent this relates to the fact that industrial products usually contain a large variety of components, each with its own supply chain, so that a water footprint assessment becomes very elaborate, but a greater problem is the lack of good data on water consumption and pollution in industrial and mining activities. I am sure, however, that this will change in due time; it will have to.

The present book can be seen as a companion of *The Water Footprint Assessment Manual* (Hoekstra *et al.*, 2011). The latter is a rather technical book, containing the Global Water Footprint Standard, and includes precise definitions and calculation methods. It discusses all stages of what is called a 'water footprint assessment'. The four main stages are: setting the goals and scope of the assessment; water footprint accounting (which is about getting the numbers right); sustainability assessment (which addresses the 'so what' question); and response formulation (which addresses the 'what to do' question). In the present book, I neatly follow the definitions and calculation methods in accordance to the standard, without repeatedly saying that in every single chapter. For technical details I refer the reader to the manual and the scientific papers underlying the various chapters.

When writing this book, I have made use of a number of publications, many of which were co-authored with colleagues. I owe a lot to the indirect contributions that various members of my research team have made to this book. In particular, I thank Mesfin Mekonnen, Ertug Ercin, Maite Aldaya, Winnie Gerbens-Leenes and Pieter van Oel. Let me give an account of how the various chapters of this book build on earlier materials published by myself and my co-researchers. Chapter 1 is largely original, but I made use of one section of an earlier paper (Hoekstra, 2011b). Chapter 2, about the water footprint of beverages, is largely based on a paper that was published in *Water Resources Management* (Ercin *et al.*, 2011). For Chapter 3, on the water footprint of bread and pasta, I made use of an article about the water footprint of wheat in *Hydrology and Earth System Sciences* (Mekonnen and Hoekstra, 2010) and another article about pasta in *Agricultural Systems* (Aldaya and Hoekstra, 2010). Chapter 4, on the water footprint of meat, is based on a chapter written by me in the Earthscan book *The Meat Crisis* (D'Silva and Webster, 2010) and a more recent paper published in *Animal Frontiers* (Hoekstra, 2012). It leans heavily on the figures published in an article published in *Ecosystems* (Mekonnen and Hoekstra, 2012a). For Chapter 5, on the water footprint of cotton, I have made use of an article in *Hydrology and Earth System Sciences* (Mekonnen and Hoekstra, 2011a) and a report published by UNESCO-IHE (Aldaya *et al.*, 2010b). Chapter 6, on the water footprint of energy, draws on a number of articles: in *Ecological Economics* (Gerbens-Leenes *et al.*, 2009a), in the *Proceedings of the National Academy of Sciences* (Gerbens-Leenes *et al.*, 2009b), in *Energy and Environmental Science* (Gerbens-Leenes and Hoekstra, 2011) and in *Hydrology and Earth System Sciences* (Mekonnen and Hoekstra, 2011a, 2012b). Chapter 7, on the water footprint of cut flowers, is based on an article published in *Water Resources Management* (Mekonnen *et al.*, 2012). Chapter 8, on the water footprint of paper, is partly based on another article published in *Water Resources Management* (Van Oel and Hoekstra, 2012). Chapter 9, about the concept of a 'maximum sustainable water footprint' in a river basin, is largely new material. It includes, however, some of the main results of an article on blue water scarcity levels in the world's major river basins that was published in *PLoS ONE* (Hoekstra *et al.*, 2012). Chapter 10, on water-use efficiency and the rebound effect, and Chapter 11, on the need to address consumption patterns and the question on what is a wise allocation of our limited freshwater supplies, present mostly new material. Chapter 12, on the relation between trade and water, is based on a chapter in Edward Elgar's *Handbook on Trade and the Environment* (Hoekstra, 2008), a working report for the World Trade Organization (Hoekstra, 2010b) and a paper in the proceedings of an expert workshop on accounting for water scarcity and pollution in the rules of international trade, which was held in November 2010 in Amsterdam (Hoekstra, 2011b). Chapter 13, on the need for product transparency, and Chapter 14, on the question of who is responsible for change, present mostly new material.

I would like to thank everyone in my research group at the University of Twente for the stimulating working environment: Eelco van Beek, Martijn Booij, Caroline Bosire, Marcela Brugnach, Hatem Chouchane, Mehmet Demirel, Rianne van Duinen, Ertug Ercin, Winnie Gerbens-Leenes, Marjolijn Haasnoot, Ronald van den Hoek, Ying Huang, Maarten Krol, Zhuo La, Anne Leskens, Mesfin

Mekonnen, Marjolein Mens, Markus Pahlow, Mireia Romaguera, Anne van der Veen and Donghai Zheng. Thanks to the Faculty of Engineering Technology and the Institute for Innovation and Governance Studies, for giving me ample resources to hire staff and follow my aspirations. The University of Twente has been a key player in establishing the Water Footprint Network (WFN) and in providing funds to give it a strong impulse in its pioneering phase. I also thank the other founding partners of the WFN: the WWF, the global conservation organization, the UNESCO-IHE Institute for Water Education, the World Business Council for Sustainable Development, the International Finance Corporation, the Netherlands Water Partnership and the Water Neutral Foundation. The establishment of the WFN has been very instrumental in streamlining and enhancing the global interest in water footprint assessment and in helping it develop into a useful tool in freshwater conservation. I am grateful to all partners of the WFN, for the inputs provided in advancing the water footprint concept over the past few years. I thank the staff and associates of the WFN, who have made the network into a dynamic and productive international learning community: Derk Kuiper, Ruth Mathews, Ashok Chapagain, Erika Zarate, Maite Aldaya, Guoping Zhang, Michiel van Heek, Nicolas Franke and Kurt Unger. Thanks to Joke Meijer and Joshua Waweru for the secretarial support throughout the years, and René Buijsrogge for the support in maintaining the water footprint website. I would also like to thank Tim Hardwick from Earthscan, part of the Taylor & Francis Group, for stimulating me to start writing this book and for motivating me to finish it.

I thank my parents, Jaap and Wik, for remaining so driven and energetic, and for showing continued interest in my life and work. I express my thanks and love to my wife, Daniëlle, for the love, patience and support throughout the years and for the creativity that you bring into our home. Finally, thanks to my children – Joppe, Lieke and Mette – for the fun we have.

Arjen Y. Hoekstra
Enschede, the Netherlands

# 1

# INTRODUCTION

The invisible hand of Adam Smith will not make sure that the world's scarce freshwater resources will be allocated in a way that creates the highest value to mankind. Leaving freshwater allocation to the market, be it in the time of Adam Smith or be it in our time, is not a good idea. It's one of the worst ideas. I do not intend here to upset economists, but I think we should be fair and acknowledge that wise use of natural resources is not the private territory of the market. Freshwater is essential for life. Water is public health. Water is food. Water is energy. Freshwater allocation is primarily politics. The phenomenon of free-rider behaviour, the consumption and pollution of water by some at the expense of others, is material for the social scientist. Understanding the way in which water abstractions and pollutants change water flows and quality is part of the natural sciences. The relation between the quantity and quality of freshwater flows and ecosystem functioning is the domain of ecologists. Designing water infrastructure is engineering.

None of us will contradict the relevance of the various disciplines in water management, but why then do we let the market play a major role in governing our freshwater resources? We *know* that water is a common resource and we may *think* that governments take care, but reality is different. What governments in this world do to protect and wisely allocate water resources is hardly relevant when we realize that the major mechanism that changes the status of our freshwater resources is the economic mechanism of demand and supply of our daily commodities, like food, fibres, energy, minerals and so on. The market says: it's economically attractive to grow asparagus in the desert in Peru, so asparagus is grown in the desert in Peru and groundwater levels decline. The market says: import cheap stuff from China, so that is why the rivers in China are so polluted. Water is for free, so there is no way in which economies account for the scarcity of freshwater resources or the vulnerability of ecosystems to overexploitation or pollution. Other factors than water dictate economies. Economies develop certain spatial production patterns, which in turn determine where water will be used and polluted, irrespective the amount of water that can actually be sustainably abstracted or the assimilation capacity for pollutants. Cities grow where they grow, without any relation to whether there is water to sustain the cities. Agriculture and irrigation schemes are developed in places even though it's clear that there is not sufficient water to sustain crop production in the long run.

Governments may have programmes to combat pollution and promote efficient use of freshwater resources, but by facilitating economic growth that is based on the ignorance of freshwater, they effectively do more harm than good if it comes to sustainable water use. The USA may have good water laws and good ambient water quality standards, but why then is the Ogallala aquifer beneath the Great Plains overexploited? Why is the Colorado River running dry and why do nutrient and pesticide levels in water bodies violate the standards in so many places? Nobody seems to care about making freshwater scarcity and pollution a factor in economic decisions. Setting boundary conditions to expanding agriculture, industrial growth or city development is not within the mandate of a water minister, so these developments will occur irrespective of the sustainability boundaries given by the locally available water resources.

The central thesis of this book is that all problems of overexploitation and pollution of freshwater resources in this world relate to what we consume. Putting it this way is unusual. There is the assumption that it is relevant and even important to know whether or not the cotton in our pair of jeans comes from a place where rivers run dry as a result of cotton irrigation and whether or not the food we eat comes from places where groundwater aquifers are being depleted. Why would we need to care about water from the perspective of consumption and supply chains? The traditional view on issues of water overexploitation and pollution is that the farmers, industries and municipalities are to be held accountable, because in all those places where aquifers are depleted, rivers run dry or water bodies are polluted, it is because farmers, industries or municipalities abstract too much water, put too many chemicals on the field or discharge polluted effluents. Obviously, if this has to change, who else other than the farmers, industries and municipalities should act? Usually, state or national governments are recognized as key players as well. Governments must regulate it all properly – through water abstraction licences, effluent standards and permits, proper water pricing or whatsoever – so that water users receive proper incentives and clear boundary conditions.

The conventional view is thus: governments have to regulate and water users have to conform to the regulations. There are two reasons why this view is insufficient. First of all, all production is driven by or at least made possible by consumption. If producers and consumers are part of a system that is unsustainable, it should be the system as a whole that needs to be involved and evaluated. Consumers are as much a part of the system as producers. Second, theoretically, consumers could be left out of scope *if* governments would properly govern and *if* producers would produce in a sustainable way, but none of the two is the case. Governments fail at a large scale by not regulating water prices so that they reflect the actual value, by (indirectly) investing in water overexploitation rather than in conservation and efficiency, by setting water quality standards but not making sure that they are met, and so on. Producers fail by not caring either. Business strategies regarding sustainability do not often go beyond the factory gate, while unsustainable water use generally happens in the supply chain of companies.

If in all nations in the world, governments would set proper local standards, implement local regulations and make sure that enforcement takes place, there would be no room in this world to overexploit or pollute water resources. Production processes would operate within the boundaries of what is sustainable, so consumers could trust that whatever they buy must have been produced in a sustainable way, whatever the sources of the different product components. But reality shows that it does not work when all is left to governments and companies. There is no choice for consumers other than to engage, for their own interest, in their capacity as consumers, as well as in their capacity as voters, investors of savings and independent agents of change. Real changes in the world, changes in the rules on how we interact and manage good housekeeping, occur only if a broad public is interested and motivated. This book aims to inspire you to think critically about the way we manage freshwater in this world and about the roles that different players can have in moving towards a more sustainable, equitable and efficient use of our globe's limited freshwater resources.

In this first chapter, I will argue why freshwater is a special resource. Freshwater is a renewable resource but finite though. It is not a private good but a so-called common-pool resource. Water users typically externalize costs to others, either in their direct environment or downstream. Furthermore, freshwater availability varies strongly within the year and over the years and from place to place, so that scarcity fluctuates over time and space as well. Finally, water is generally priced far below its actual value, which misleads us in a way that does not benefit a wise use of the resource. There are thus numerous reasons why freshwater systems are so often and so easily overexploited, not only damaging ecosystems, but also at the cost of sustainable welfare. In the final section of this chapter, I will reflect on the question of what makes freshwater a local and a global resource and introduce the water footprint concept.

## Freshwater is a renewable but finite resource

Unlike oil, coal or gas, freshwater is a *renewable* resource. Other typical renewable resources are biomass, solar energy and wind. Renewable means that the resource is naturally replenished or formed in the course of time. The resource cannot be depleted in the sense of disappearing. Freshwater stocks on land, although they get depleted by evaporation and drainage to the oceans, will always be replenished by precipitation. Although freshwater is renewable, it is also a *finite* resource. Finite means that water availability is limited. This seems to contradict the renewability, because if water renews itself continuously, how can we say that its availability is limited? The reason is that we have to measure 'freshwater availability' in terms of water volume per unit of time. Over a certain period, precipitation is always limited to a certain amount. The same holds for the amount of water that recharges groundwater reserves or flows through a river. Rainwater can be used in agricultural production and water in rivers and aquifers can be used for irrigation or industrial or domestic purposes. But, over a certain period, one cannot consume more water than is available. One cannot take more from a river than what flows in it and, in the long term, one cannot take more water from lakes and groundwater reservoirs than the rate by which they are recharged. Deep aquifers are sometimes not even recharged at all, so that they cannot even be considered as renewable; water in such aquifers is therefore called fossil groundwater.

As a result of its finiteness and the various sorts of demand for freshwater, there is often competition over water, which makes it a *scarce* resource. It is impossible to 'produce' water; one can only deviate or temporarily store natural flows in order to have access to it at another location or point in time. There are, however, limitations to this, since water transfer and storage are due to different sorts of constraints. First of all, because water is bulky, transferring or storing water is quite costly, and requires large infrastructure. Second, taking water out of its natural flow and returning it elsewhere or at another point in time will affect ecosystems that are adapted to the natural flow. Significant changes to natural flows generally have undesired consequences for both downstream ecosystems and downstream users.

Freshwater is not only scarce, but also *non-reproducible*. I will go into the implications of that in a minute, but let me first reflect on the statement that freshwater cannot be 'produced'. One could argue that freshwater becomes an infinite resource as soon as we decide to produce freshwater by desalinating salt or brackish water from the oceans and coastal areas. This is true, but ignores the fact that the process of desalination costs a lot of energy, which is also bound to limitations, and that desalination can only be a solution on a small scale, in coastal areas, for high-value purposes, but not for supplying water to agriculture, the bulk water user.

The fact that water is essentially a non-reproducible good has great implications for our ability to manage supply. The distinction between reproducible and non-reproducible goods dates back to Ricardo (1821). Reproducible goods can be reproduced; their amount can increase. All manufactured goods are reproducible. Non-reproducible goods cannot be reproduced, so their supply is fixed. Most economic theory is about production, about demand and supply of reproducible goods. When we talk about non-reproducible goods, we should talk about 'protection' or 'conservation' rather than about 'production'. Every time we conserve valuable non-reproducible goods, we produce value, but for economists it does not count, because conservation is not considered part of production. At the scale of a catchment area, the supply of water is given by precipitation. People within the catchment get the water they get, whatever their demand. At a small scale, people can manipulate water supply, by temporary storage of water behind dams or by redirecting the water to other places with canals or pumps. But the potential for storing water in time and moving water in space is limited, so that at the larger scale there is little room for manipulation of the given supply.

When there is competition over a given supply, the best people can do is to preserve the resources as well as possible, so that the use of water for one purpose will not subtract from the possible use of the water for another purpose. This can be done by returning all abstracted water volumes after use and by not polluting the water. Unfortunately, protection of non-reproducible goods is only in a marginal way part of the economic discourse.

## Open access, competition and externalities

Freshwater is a so-called *common-pool resource*. Common-pool resources form a specific category of goods with two distinctive characteristics: they are 'open access', which means that they are not privately owned, and there is competition, which means that use of the resource by one subtracts from the possible use by another. People can own the land but not the freshwater that stays or flows on or underneath it. Freshwater is neither privately owned nor traded. When the term 'water privatization' is used, one generally refers to the privatization of water supply, which means that the services of collecting, purifying and distributing and/or the services of wastewater collection and treatment are privatized. The term does not mean that the water itself is privatized.

Common-pool resources are vulnerable to free-rider behaviour, which means that someone takes personal benefit from using the resource at the cost of the community as a whole. We can illustrate this with a simple example. Suppose that a farmer can obtain a benefit of one dollar for abstracting one additional cubic metre of water from an aquifer. Further suppose that, as a result of the additional water withdrawal, the groundwater level will slightly drop, so that all farmers pumping from the aquifer have to spend more energy in pumping. Suppose that the additional pumping cost for the community as a whole adds up to two dollars. From a macro-perspective, the benefit of the additional cubic metre (one dollar) does not outweigh the cost (two dollars). From the perspective of the individual farmer, however, it looks different. The cost of two dollars will be shared by all farmers depending on the aquifer. If there are 100 farmers, each one will bear two dollar cent. For the individual farmer it is thus profitable to pump the additional cubic metre of water, since it gives a benefit of one dollar whereas it costs only two dollar cent. Profit: 98 dollar cent.

Often, it is even worse. In the above example, the free rider pays at least its share in the cost (two dollar cent). It also happens that water users take the full profit without paying anything of the cost. This is related to the flowing character of water, which typically leads to costs created by upstream users but incurred by downstream users. The costs of emptying or polluting a river will not be felt by the upstream causers but by the downstream users of the river. In economics, such costs are called external costs, or externalities, of the upstream water use. In the world of freshwater it is not common that users pay for the externalities of their water use, which is an invitation to consume and pollute without accounting for downstream costs.

## Freshwater availability and demand strongly vary in space and time

The amount of freshwater varies strongly across regions. In this respect, freshwater is just like oil: some countries have a lot of it, while others don't. Given the vital role of water in many production processes, freshwater is thus a geopolitical resource in a similar way as oil (Hoekstra and Chapagain, 2008). Having abundant amounts of oil or water, while others have not, constitutes a form of political power (Allan, 2001). Upstream countries have power over downstream countries: Turkey exercises power over Syria and Iraq by exploiting the waters of the Euphrates and the Tigris; China exercises power over Cambodia and Vietnam by exploiting the Mekong. But political power over water is not restricted to upstream–downstream relations. Water-short countries in North Africa and the Middle East depend on the import of food from water-rich countries that lie far outside the region.

Confusingly, many regions in the world face both water scarcity and flooding. Scarcity happens in the dry period of the year, flooding in the wet period. The competition for and economic value of water resources fluctuate throughout the year accordingly. This is a very specific property of freshwater, a property that one cannot find for other resources or commodities.

Not only water availability, also water demand varies in time and space. The interesting thing about water is that typically demand is largest when supply is lowest. This is very much different as with other economic goods, where demand and supply dynamically interact in order to find the best match. It is very difficult to speak about 'water scarcity' in a way that somehow resembles how we speak about scarcity on the house market or scarcity on the market of electronic hardware. Water shortages can seriously affect harvests and industrial operations, but floods easily wipe away all memories of scarcity. It is tempting to dream of solving everything at once by storing the floodwaters in the wet period for use in the dry period, but there are limitations to finding suitable places for water storage. It is not uncommon that the building of a new dam forces thousands of people to move away from their home grounds that are to be inundated. For the Three Gorges Dam in the Yangtze River in China, over a million people had to move because their homes were in the area of the water reservoir behind the dam. Not only limited space puts a constraint on water storage, but also ecological considerations. A global overview of dam-based impacts on large river systems shows that over half of the systems are affected by dams, including the eight most biogeographically diverse (Nilsson *et al.*, 2005). Particularly river flow alteration and river fragmentation as a result of dams in the river can cause considerable ecological damage (Poff and Zimmerman, 2010).

## Freshwater is highly valuable but generally priced far below its value

Since water is naturally for free – rain comes as it comes and rivers flow as they flow – and since water is not owned or traded, there is no market mechanism that puts a price on water. Not only are rainwater, groundwater and river water for free, but more specific forms of freshwater supply are also generally grossly underpriced or for free. Most governments subsidize water supply on a huge scale by investing in infrastructure like dams, canals, water purification, distribution systems, desalination plants and wastewater treatment. These costs are often not charged directly to the water users. If water users pay for water supply at all, they pay for the service of the water supplier or for the costs they make themselves for pumping or purification, not for the water itself. It is unusual that water scarcity is reflected in the price of the water in the form of a scarcity rent. Furthermore, water users generally do not pay for the negative impacts that they cause on downstream people or ecosystems. Only in exceptional cases, governments make water users pay a price for the water itself, either as a water tax or by creating a market for water-use licences. In practice, however, if we consider the major part of water users, we see that water generally goes non-priced or grossly underpriced. As a result, there is insufficient economic incentive for water users to save water. Besides, water inputs do not form a substantial component of the total price of even the most water-intensive products. Consequently, the production of and trade in goods – even though various sorts of goods require a lot of scarce water inputs – is not or hardly governed by water scarcity. The only constraint on production is absolute water scarcity: when the river is dry there will be no further water use downstream. As Yang *et al.* (2003) have shown, absolute water scarcity indeed hampers production and necessitates imports of water-intensive goods like cereals in the most water-scarce regions of the world.

By focusing on the problem of improper water pricing, the attention may deviate a bit from the essence of the issue, which is that the scarcity of freshwater should be counted properly in economic decisions. Pricing water according to its real value can help in achieving wise allocation and use of freshwater, but it would be a misconception to consider proper pricing as 'the solution' to inefficient and unsustainable water use. It may be part of a solution, but will be insufficient. Additional regulation will remain essential. An even greater misconception is that 'water markets' are the logical instrument to achieve proper water pricing. A few countries – like Chile, Australia and the USA – have experimented with water markets, in which water use-rights (water entitlements) are traded (Bjornlund and McKay, 2002), but there is no evidence that water resources in these areas are actually better protected than elsewhere (Bauer, 1997; Dellapenna, 2000). In order to have prices better reflect the real value of water, governments are probably better setting tariffs for water than creating a water market. Getting water prices that reflect the actual value of water is important to provide proper price signals to water users and consumers of water-intensive commodities. In practice, setting proper prices for water appears to be difficult for governments for a variety of reasons, including the absence of water meters and a broad resistance from farmers and other large water users. But even if governments would succeed better, as a result of its public character, the allocation of water among users and the protection of water resources against contamination will remain subject to governmental regulation. It is a myth that proper pricing is sufficient to guarantee sustainable use of a resource. The reason is that economics is based on a discounted rate, so that a one-dollar benefit today counts more than a one-dollar cost tomorrow. Particularly in cases where immediate benefits can be obtained at a relatively low cost, as in the case of water use, discount rates work in the advantage of overexploitation in the long term.

## Why freshwater is easily 'overexploited'

We have come to a stage now in which it can be easily understood why freshwater is so easily spoiled. There are many spots in the world where water depletion or pollution is quite serious. We can observe rivers running dry (e.g. Colorado), dropping lake levels (Lake Chad), declining groundwater levels (Yemen) and endangered species because of contaminated water (Indus river dolphin). There is a number of reasons for this, all connected to the unusual characteristics of water as discussed above. One reason for the vulnerability of freshwater systems is their common-pool resource character. As already pointed out a few decades ago by Hardin (1968), for the case of cattle grazing in communal lands, common-pool resources are vulnerable to overexploitation. In the case of a freshwater lake or aquifer, shared by many users, water consumption and pollution can be at the direct benefit of the water user or polluter, while the negative effects are shared with the whole community. The costs of overexploitation are born by others than the water users, sometimes even by next generations, as in the case of disappearing lakes or polluted sediments. A second reason for the easy overexploitation of freshwater is caused by the flow-character of water. The negative effects of water consumption and pollution are often felt only downstream. A third reason is that different water users compete over freshwater supplies whereby nature is usually the closing entry. If water users have effectively abstracted all water from a river, nothing is left to sustain the riverine and downstream coastal ecosystems that depended on the natural river flow. The fact that water is 'available' does not mean that it can be fully consumed without undesired consequences. A fourth reason is that the low price of water does not provide an incentive for saving and prevents water scarcity being factored into the price of commodities, thus giving a wrong price signal to consumers. Finally, probably the most important reason for the fact that water resources are so often spoiled has little to do with the special characteristics or vulnerability of water systems, but with the apparent inability of societies to devise institutional arrangements to adequately respond. It is not inevitable that common-pool resources are destroyed; local communities are often creative in finding ways to organize in such a way that a sustainable and fair sharing of a common-pool resource is achieved (Ostrom, 1990). However, safeguarding common-pool resources shared by large communities appears to be a lot more difficult (Ostrom et al., 1999). Sharing water among farmers within an irrigation scheme in a sustainable manner is one thing (Tang, 1992), but sharing water within a river basin is more difficult (Van Oel et al., 2009). Sharing freshwater in an open global economy is even more challenging. We bump into an issue here that is key in addressing problems of local water scarcity and pollution: wise water governance has a global dimension.

## Freshwater is a local but also a global resource

Water is a local resource because it naturally moves within the boundaries of river basins, without crossing these boundaries. From the traditional engineering point of view, water demands within the basin need to be met with the water available within the basin. Water will only leave a river basin by evaporation or by drainage to the ocean, flows that water engineers generally consider as 'lost'. From an ecological point of view it is difficult to speak about lost flows because they are part of a natural water cycle, essential for all life and the functioning of ecosystems. But from a water-user point of view, one can indeed view water as a local resource, where local is interpreted here as 'available only within the catchment or river basin'.

Water can hardly be moved or traded over long distances, due to its bulky character. There are three exceptions, however, in which water is moved over long distances, crossing river basin boundaries: international trade of bottled water and other beverages; shipping of water in containers; and inter-basin water transfers. In the case of bottled beverages, we talk about relatively small volumes. People drink no more than a few litres of liquids per day, while the total water use per capita – for producing all goods and services consumed – amounts to at least a few thousands litres per day. From an hydrological point of view, international trade in bottled water is irrelevant. This is not to say that there is no reason to put a question mark behind the increasing trade in bottled water, because local tap water is generally much cheaper and environmentally friendly than bottled water (Gleick, 2010). But, whatever we may think of bottled water, we are talking about small amounts relative to other sorts of water use. In the case of shipping of water in containers, we still talk about relatively small volumes, although they can form a big relief for those depending on the imported water. An example of shipping freshwater was in spring 2008 when the Spanish city of Barcelona had to ship in freshwater from France. Various islands, including Aruba, Nauru, Tonga and the Canary Islands have at times received freshwater by tanker from elsewhere (Gleick et al., 2002). In the case of inter-basin water transfers we speak about something bigger. Currently there are 155 inter-basin water transfer schemes in the world, spanning 26 countries and with a total capacity of transferring 490 billion $m^3$/yr (ICID, 2006). Plans exist for another 60 schemes with a total capacity of 1,150 billion $m^3$/yr. The large infrastructure projects that are needed for inter-basin water transfers are, however, increasingly debated because of the huge negative social and environmental impacts of such projects.

Despite the big local impacts of some of the existing inter-basin water transfer schemes, one can say that water transfers crossing river basin boundaries are very small on a global scale. It is most likely that this will remain so. This feeds the idea that water is indeed mostly a local resource, whereby water demands need to be met from local supplies. What happens, however, on a very substantial scale, is long-distance transfer of water in embedded form, that is in the form of goods. It is not that the amounts of water actually contained in goods are so large, but the water volumes virtually embedded in goods can be huge. When water is consumed in one country to produce a product that is traded to another, the water is virtually transferred to the importing country (Hoekstra and Chapagain, 2008; Allan, 2011). In this context we speak about 'virtual water trade', although 'transfer' would be a better term, because the goods are traded, not the water. About one-fifth of freshwater appropriation in the world is related to the production of export commodities (Hoekstra and Mekonnen, 2012a). The idea that water demand is something local and to be met locally is a misconception. Most of the water consumed in this world is for making agricultural and industrial goods that are traded regionally or internationally. The global demand for water that relates to the global demand for food and other commodities is not a-priori localized in specific river basins. Water demands and supplies need to match at a global scale. This happens through the mechanism of trade. From this perspective, water is no longer a local resource, but a global resource.

Until today, water is still mostly considered a local resource, to be managed preferably at catchment or river basin level. This approach obscures the fact that many water problems are related to remote consumption elsewhere. Water problems are an intrinsic part of the world's economic structure in which water scarcity is not translated into costs to either producers or consumers; as a result there are many places where water resources are depleted or polluted, with producers and consumers along the supply chain benefiting at the cost of local communities and ecosystems elsewhere.

## How all water problems relate to what we consume: the water footprint concept

In order to visualize the link between the consumption of goods in one place and the consumption and pollution of freshwater in others, I introduced the water footprint concept over a decade ago (Hoekstra, 2003). Visualizing the hidden water use behind products can assist in understanding the global character of freshwater and in quantifying and mapping the effects of consumption and trade on water resources use (Hoekstra and Hung, 2002, 2005; Hoekstra and Chapagain, 2007, 2008).

The basic building block of all water footprint calculations is the water footprint of one single process or activity (Hoekstra et al., 2011). The water footprint of a product is the aggregate of the water footprints of the various process steps relevant in the production of the product. The water footprint of a producer or company is equal to the sum of the water footprints of the products that the producer or company produces. The water footprint of a consumer is the sum of the water footprints of the various products consumed by the consumer. The water footprint of a community of consumers – for example the inhabitants of a country – is equal to the sum of the water footprints of the members of the community. The water footprint within a geographically delineated area – for example a country or a river basin – is equal to the sum of the water footprints of all processes taking place in that area.

The water footprint is a multi-dimensional indicator, showing water consumption volumes by source and polluted volumes by type of pollution; all components of a total water footprint are specified geographically and temporally. The 'blue' water footprint refers to consumption of blue water resources (surface and groundwater) along the supply chain of a product. 'Consumption' refers to loss of water from the available ground–surface water body in a catchment area. Losses occur when water evaporates, returns to another catchment area or the sea or is incorporated into a product. The 'green' water footprint refers to consumption of green water resources (rainwater insofar as it does not become runoff). The 'grey' water footprint refers to pollution and is defined as the volume of freshwater that is required to assimilate the load of pollutants given natural background concentrations and existing ambient water quality standards.

The water footprint concept integrates a number of insights that had grown prior to the introduction of the concept. First of all, the concept introduces supply-chain thinking in the field of water resources management. In the environmental sciences, thinking in terms of supply chains and 'embedded' resources in final commodities is quite common; in the field of water resources management this was completely unknown. Second, the traditional focus of water engineers on the exploitation of ground- and surface-water resources (blue water) had appeared to be insufficient. Rainwater (green water) plays a major role in agricultural production; a good picture of water consumption in agriculture can only be obtained if we look at both green and blue water consumption. Furthermore, water consumption is not the only form of freshwater appropriation; water pollution is another form that should be accounted for. Finally, the insight had grown that measuring blue water *abstractions* is not the right manner to get information about the pressure on the blue water resources within a catchment, because part of the abstractions are often simply returned again. From a catchment perspective it makes more sense to measure blue water *consumption*, that is the effective, not returned blue water abstraction.

Until recently, all water-use statistics showed blue water withdrawals only. Still, reporting on water footprints is not very common. The water footprint differs from the classical measure of 'water withdrawal' in a few respects. The most important is probably that the water footprint is an indicator of freshwater use that looks not only at direct water use of a consumer or producer, but also at the indirect water use. In addition, the water footprint includes three components; it does not only show blue water consumption (the blue water footprint), but also rainwater consumption (the green water footprint) and pollution (the grey water footprint). Finally, the blue water footprint excludes blue water use insofar as this water is returned to where it came from. The water footprint thus offers a better and wider perspective on how a consumer or producer relates to the use of freshwater systems. It is a volumetric measure of water consumption and pollution. Water footprint figures give spatiotemporally explicit information on how water is appropriated for various human purposes. They can feed the discussion about sustainable and equitable water use and allocation and also form a basis for a local assessment of environmental, social and economic impacts of water use.

In order to make sure that scientifically robust methods are applied and to ensure that a fair comparison can be made between different water footprint studies, the Water Footprint Network with its partners developed the Global Water Footprint Standard, which was launched in February 2011 (Hoekstra *et al.*, 2011). In the current book I follow the definitions as provided in this standard. Sometimes I get asked the funny question whether the water footprint will solve the world's water problems. Obviously it will not, it will be people that will have to solve the problems. I hope, however, that the water footprint concept may inspire you to dig deeper into the issues raised in this book and get engaged.

# 2

# DRINKING TEN BATHTUBS
# OF WATER A DAY

Consumers associate drinks with water, so it is logical that if one sector must be interested in the water footprint, it must be companies that produce and sell bottled water, soft drinks, juices, beer, wine or other beverages. And indeed, the beverage sector shows a lot of interest in the water footprint (BIER, 2011). The first company to show interest in the water footprint was The Coca-Cola Company. I remember well my first meeting with Greg Koch, Managing Director Global Water Stewardship at Coca-Cola, in a café-restaurant along one of the canals in Amsterdam, on the first day of summer in 2007. Greg explained to me that the company had focused on reducing water use within their bottling plants worldwide already for a couple of years and that they had become interested in the water use in their supply chain as well. Coca-Cola is one of the biggest buyers of sugar in the world and Greg had noticed that producing sugar can take a lot of water. He realized that the water footprint concept offered the possibility to better understand the complete water footprint of a beverage, because the concept refers to water consumption and pollution over the whole supply chain. This first meeting with Greg was the start of a consequent number of efforts by The Coca-Cola Company to better understand the water footprint of their company. Initially they focused on their most famous product, Coca-Cola, but soon they started to look at other beverages within their product portfolio as well (TCCC and TNC, 2010).

PepsiCo soon followed the example of Coca-Cola and other companies also started to explore the water footprint of some of their products. Unilever already had some history in looking at the sustainability of their supply chain but had hardly looked at water use. At the occasion of the launch of the Global Water Footprint Standard in February 2011, Donna Jeffries, Sustainability Manager at Unilever, said that Unilever aims 'to halve the environmental footprint of its product portfolio across the life cycle'. She continued saying that 'water is one of our key metrics and we support efforts to standardize methodology and improve access to scientifically robust and standardized data'. As one of the first efforts, Unilever started to explore the water footprint of tea, which made sense given the fact that Unilever is the largest buyer of tea in the world, purchasing approximately 12 per cent of the world's supply of black tea.

Among the beer companies, the first company to explore the water footprint of their product was SABMiller. They started in 2009 by comparing the water footprints of beer bottled in South Africa and beer from the Czech Republic (SABMiller and WWF-UK, 2009). Differences could be explained mostly from differences in the water consumed for producing the barley and hops in the two countries. A year later SABMiller published a second report on the water footprint of their beer, with case studies from Tanzania, Peru, the Ukraine and again South Africa (SABMiller et al., 2010). Other beer companies also started to carry out water footprint studies, including Heineken, for example. In Chile, a couple of wine companies started to look into the water footprint of their products.

The major lesson for all those companies that recently started to explore the water footprint of their beverages was that the largest part of the total water footprint of a beverage is in the process of producing the ingredients, not in bottling. As a result, if companies want to make their beverages more sustainable, they will have to actively consider their supply chain. Most beverage companies know how many litres of water they use in their own operations and have often set targets in time to reduce this operational water use. Reduction of the water footprint in the bottling plants, however, will have only a minor effect on the total water footprint of the beverage. There have been no companies yet ready to adopt water footprint reduction targets for their supply chain, but this will inevitably happen. Consumers are increasingly aware of environmental issues in the supply chain of products; it is unlikely that future consumers will accept beverages that are labelled 'sustainable' based on efforts done in the bottling stage alone.

## The case of cola

This chapter will show how we can assess the water footprint of a beverage. We will consider cola contained in a 0.5 litre bottle made of PET (polyethylene terephthalate). The ingredients of a cola drink will be assumed based on public sources on what cola typically contains. Obviously, the numbers presented here cannot be used to refer to the cola drinks from specific brands, because each brand has its own (secret) recipe. Besides, even if a brand applies a specific recipe worldwide, the ingredients are sourced from different locations, so that the water footprint of a cola from one brand will vary across its bottling plants.

Our hypothetical beverage is produced in a hypothetical factory that takes its sugar alternatively from sugar beet, sugar cane and maize sourced from different countries. Sugar beet and sugar cane give sucrose, while maize is used to derive a mixture of glucose and fructose, in the form of high fructose maize syrup (HFMS). The latter is particularly used in the USA, where it is called high fructose corn syrup. Our hypothetical factory is assumed to be in the Netherlands, but many of the inputs come from other countries. The composition of the beverage and the characteristics of the factory are hypothetical but realistic. We take the point of view of the bottling plant that produces our 0.5 litre PET-bottle of cola. The water footprint of our product includes both an operational and a supply-chain component. The operational (or direct) water footprint is the volume of fresh-water consumed or polluted in the operations of the bottling plant itself. The supply-chain (or indirect) water footprint is the volume of freshwater consumed or polluted to produce all the inputs of production. In both cases, we distinguish between a green, blue and grey water footprint.

## The operational water footprint of bottling cola

The operational water footprint includes three components. First of all, there is the water incorporated into the product as an ingredient. Second, we have to con-sider the water consumed (i.e. not returned to the water system from where it was withdrawn) during the various production processes in the bottling plant and the water polluted when water is returned from the plant to the catchment. Finally, we have to consider the 'overhead water footprint' of the bottling plant. We have to think about the water consumed or polluted as a result of water consumption by employees (drinking water), water use in toilets and the kitchen, washing of the working clothes of the employees, cleaning activities in the factory or gardening on the premises around the bottling plant.

The water used as ingredient is 470 ml per bottle, let us round it off here to 0.5 litre per bottle. The production of our beverage includes the following process steps: bottle making (from PET resins to PET-bottles), bottle cleaning (by air), syrup preparation, mixing, filling, labelling and packing. Insofar as water is used in these processes, all water is returned to the catchment from which the water is taken. There is thus no water consumption in the bottling plant other than the water used for fill-ing the bottles. The little wastewater produced is treated at a municipal wastewater treatment plant. The concentrations of chemicals in the effluent of the wastewater treatment plant are equal and in some instances even lower than the natural concen-trations in the receiving water body. The grey water footprint is therefore zero.

Still, we need to look at the overhead operational water footprint of the bottling plant. We assume that the volume of drinking water consumed by employees is negligible and that there is no gardening. It is further assumed that all water used during the other activities specified above returns to the public sewerage system and is treated in a municipal wastewater treatment plant such that the effluent causes no grey water footprint. As a result, the overhead operational water foot-print of the bottling plant is estimated as zero.

The overall operational water footprint per bottle of cola is thus no more than the half a litre of water used as an ingredient. This is a *blue* water footprint; the green and grey water footprints are zero. The blue water footprint of the operations is smaller than the water withdrawal of the factory, because all water withdrawn by our hypothetical factory is returned (except for the water used as ingredient for the beverage) and purified before disposal. The return flows can be reused, so they do not impact on the available water resources.

## The supply chain

The three main ingredients of cola other than water are: sugar, carbon dioxide and syrup for flavouring. The syrup of our hypothetical cola drink contains phosphoric acid, caffeine from coffee beans, vanilla extract, lemon oil and orange oil. Other main inputs of production are the PET-bottle, cap, label, glue and packing materials. Table 2.1 specifies the precise amounts applied per 0.5-litre bottle. It also shows which raw material underlies each input and the country of origin of the raw material. In the case of sugar, the study considers three alternative sources: sugar beet,

**TABLE 2.1** Ingredients and other inputs used for our 0.5-litre PET-bottle of cola

| Input | Amount (g) | Raw material | Origin of raw material |
|---|---|---|---|
| Sugar | 50 | Sugar beet | Iran, Russia, USA, Italy, Spain, France, Netherlands |
| | | Sugar cane | Cuba, Pakistan, Brazil, India, Peru, USA |
| | | Maize | India, USA, France, China |
| $CO_2$ | 4 | Ammonia byproduct | Netherlands |
| Caffeine | 0.05 | Coffee beans | Colombia |
| Phosphoric acid | 0.2 | Phosphate rock | USA |
| Vanilla extract | 0.01 | Vanilla beans | Madagascar |
| Lemon oil | 0.007 | Lemon | World market |
| Orange oil | 0.004 | Orange | World market |
| Bottle – PET | 19.5 | Oil | World market |
| Closure – HDPE | 3 | Oil | World market |
| Label – PP | 0.3 | Oil | World market |
| Label glue | 0.18 | Glue | World market |
| Tray glue | 0.015 | Glue | World market |
| Tray cartoon – paperboard | 2.8 | Wood | World market |
| Tray shrink film – PE | 1.6 | Oil | World market |
| Pallet stretch wrap – PE | 0.24 | Oil | World market |
| Pallet label – coated paper | 0.003 | Wood | World market |
| Pallet – painted wood | 0.09 | Wood | World market |

Source: Ercin *et al.* (2011)

sugar cane and maize (which is used to make HFMs). The figures for the amounts used are based on realistic values, similar to the ones on the commercial market. During bottle production, 25 per cent of the material consists of recycled material. This ratio is taken into account in the calculations by using a fraction of 0.75 to calculate the amount of new material used. A similar approach has been used for pallets, which have a lifespan of ten years (fraction 0.1 applied to the total used).

In addition to the inputs that can be directly associated with our beverage, there are other inputs into the bottling plant that can be considered as a sort of overhead. Overhead inputs include all construction materials and machineries used in the factory, office equipment, cleaning equipment, kitchen equipment, working clothes used by employees, transportation, and energy for heating and power. This list can be extended further, but we will have to limit ourselves to the inputs that are probably most relevant from a water footprint point of view. In this study we considered the following overhead inputs: the concrete and steel used in the factory and machineries, the paper, gas and electricity used within the plant and the vehicles and fuel used for transport. These inputs cannot be solely attributed to the production of our cola beverage, because the bottling plant also produces other beverages. The overhead inputs of the bottling plant are distributed over the various products produced in the plant based on the relative value per product. The amounts of the overhead inputs are specified in Table 2.2. For paper and energy use in the factory and transportation fuels, annual amounts are given. For construction materials and vehicles, total amounts are given with a specification of the lifespan of the totals. The lifespan can be used to calculate annual figures from the totals. For the vehicles, it is assumed that the average lifespan of a truck is ten years. The value of the 0.5-litre PET-bottles of cola is 10 per cent of the total value of products produced in the factory. Therefore, 10 per cent of the total overhead water footprint of the factory

**TABLE 2.2** List of selected goods for assessing the overhead supply-chain water footprint

| Overhead item | Amount used | Unit | Raw material | Amount of raw material | Unit of raw material | Lifespan of material | Yearly amount |
|---|---|---|---|---|---|---|---|
| Concrete | 30,000 | tonne | Cement | 30,000 | tonne | 40 | 750 |
| Steel | 5,000 | tonne | Steel | 5,000 | tonne | 20 | 250 |
| Paper | 1 | tonne/year | Wood | 1 | tonne/year | – | 1 |
| Natural gas | 65,000 | GJ/year | Gas | 65,000 | GJ/year | – | 65,000 |
| Electricity | 85,000 | GJ/year | Several | 85,000 | GJ/year | – | 85,000 |
| Vehicles | 40 | numbers | Steel | 11.6 | tonnes/vehicle | 10 | 46.4 |
| Fuel | 150,000 | litres/year | Diesel | 15,0000 | litres/year | – | 150,000 |

Source: Ercin *et al.* (2011)

will be allocated to our product. The annual production is 30 million bottles per year, so the overhead water footprint per bottle is found by dividing the overhead water footprint, insofar as it is allocated to our product, by 30 million.

## The water footprint of a 0.5-litre PET-bottle of cola

Based on all the data, we calculated that the total water footprint of our cola drink is 168 to 309 litres, depending on the source of the sugar. When the sugar is sourced from sugar beet from the Netherlands, the water footprint of our cola will be smallest (Table 2.3). The effect of the type and origin of sugar used is shown in Figure 2.1. In calculating the total water footprint of the product, the amounts of all ingredients and other inputs are kept constant; only the type and origin of

**TABLE 2.3** The total water footprint of our 0.5 litre PET-bottle of cola when sugar is sourced from sugar beet grown in the Netherlands

| Component | Water footprint (litre) | | | |
| --- | --- | --- | --- | --- |
| | Green | Blue | Grey | Total |
| *Water footprint in production* | | | | |
| Water used as ingredient | 0 | 0.5 | 0 | 0.5 |
| Water consumption or pollution related to manufacturing processes in the bottling factory | 0 | 0 | 0 | 0 |
| *Overhead* | | | | |
| Water consumption or pollution related to overhead activities in the bottling factory (toilets, kitchen, etc.) | 0 | 0 | 0 | 0 |
| Operational water footprint | 0 | 0.5 | 0 | 0.5 |
| *Ingredients* | | | | |
| Sugar | 13.6 | 7.0 | 5.4 | 26 |
| $CO_2$ | 0 | 0.3 | 0 | 0.3 |
| Phosphoric acid or citric acid (e338) | 0 | 0 | 0 | 0 |
| Caffeine | 52.8 | 0 | 0 | 52.8 |
| Vanilla extract | 79.8 | 0 | 0 | 79.8 |
| Lemon oil | 0.01 | 0 | 0 | 0.01 |
| Orange oil | 0.9 | 0 | 0 | 0.9 |
| *Other inputs* | | | | |
| Bottle – PET | 0 | 0.2 | 4.4 | 4.6 |
| Closure – HDPE | 0 | 0.03 | 0.68 | 0.7 |
| Label – PP | 0 | 0.003 | 0.068 | 0.07 |

| Component | Water footprint (litre) | | | |
| --- | --- | --- | --- | --- |
| | Green | Blue | Grey | Total |
| Tray cartoon – paperboard | 1 | 0 | 0.5 | 1.5 |
| Tray shrink film – PE | 0 | 0.02 | 0.36 | 0.38 |
| Pallet stretch wrap – PE | 0 | 0.003 | 0.054 | 0.057 |
| Pallet label (2×) – coated paper | 0.001 | 0 | 0.0004 | 0.0014 |
| Pallet – painted wood | 0.033 | 0 | 0.007 | 0.04 |
| *Overhead components* | | | | |
| Concrete | 0 | 0 | 0.005 | 0.005 |
| Steel | 0 | 0.004 | 0.05 | 0.054 |
| Paper | 0.0012 | 0 | 0.0004 | 0.0016 |
| Natural gas | 0 | 0 | 0.024 | 0.024 |
| Electricity | 0 | 0 | 0.13 | 0.13 |
| Vehicles | 0 | 0.001 | 0.009 | 0.01 |
| Fuel | 0 | 0 | 0.5 | 0.5 |
| Supply-chain water footprint | 148.1 | 7.6 | 12.2 | 167.9 |
| Total water footprint | 148.1 | 8.1 | 12.2 | 168.4 |

Source: Ercin *et al.* (2011)

the sugar is changed in order to understand the effect of sugar type and production location on the total water footprint of the beverage.

The total water footprint of the beverage is largest (309 litres) when the sugar originates from sugar cane from Cuba or maize from India. When we compare the colas based on beet sugar, the water footprint of our product varies between 168 litres (Netherlands) and 241 litres (Iran). For colas made with cane sugar, we find values between 186 litres (Peru) and 309 litres (Cuba). When we use HFMS as a sweetener, the smallest water footprint is 172 litres (France) and the largest is 309 litres (India). The colour composition of the total water footprint of the product can differ substantially across countries. The water footprint of our beverage has the largest blue fraction (44 per cent) in Pakistan and the largest green water fraction (88 per cent) in the Netherlands.

Almost the entire water footprint of the product is stemming from the supply chain water footprint (99.7–99.8 per cent). This shows the importance of a detailed supply chain assessment. Common practice in business water accounting, however, is to focus on operational water consumption. The results imply that compared to the traditional water-use indicator (water withdrawal for own operations), the water footprint provides much more information.

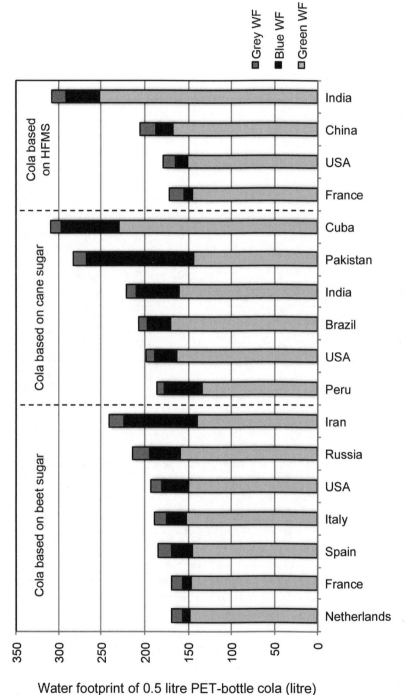

**FIGURE 2.1** The total water footprint of our 0.5-litre PET-bottle of cola depending on the type and origin of the sugar

Source: Ercin *et al.* (2011)

In our hypothetical cola drink, the amounts of vanilla extract (0.01 g) and caffeine from coffee beans (0.05 g) are very small in the total amount of the beverage. But although their physical content in the beverage is small, their contribution to the total water footprint of the product is very large. This illustrates that, without prior knowledge about the relevance of different inputs, a detailed and comprehensive supply-chain analysis is essential for the calculation of the water footprint of a product. Even small ingredients can significantly affect the total water footprint of a product.

## Sugar beet, sugar cane or maize?

Sugar is one of the main water-consuming ingredients in our beverage. Therefore, the type and origin of the sugar used immediately affects the total water footprint of the beverage. When we choose to use sugar beet as a sugar source, the water footprint of the sugar input can vary from 26 litres/0.5-litre bottle (when the sugar beet is grown in the Netherlands) to 99 litres (Iran). If our source is sugar cane, the water footprint of the sugar input can vary from 44 litres/bottle (Peru) to 167 litres (Cuba). If we use HFMS as a sweetener, the water footprint of the sugar input will range from 29 litres/bottle (when the maize comes from France) to 166 litres (India). It is important to identify and analyse the colours of the water footprint of the product as well. The smallest *blue* water footprint related to the sugar input alone is 7 litres (when the sugar is derived from sugar beet from the Netherlands); the biggest value is 124 litres (for sugar cane from Pakistan). The *grey* water footprint of the sugar input is smallest when the sugar intake is cane sugar from Brazil (2.4 litres) and largest with HFMS from China (12 litres). This analysis shows that the sugar type and production location affect the total water footprint of the product and the ratios of green/blue/grey water significantly. Including the spatial dimension in water footprint assessment is thus important. The differences can be even larger as shown in the above figures, because these represent national averages, which hide the differences that exist within the countries.

## Local impacts

The next step after quantifying, localizing and describing the colour of the water footprint is to identify the vulnerability of the local water systems where the footprint is located, the actual competition over the water in these local systems and the negative externalities associated with the use of the water. Understanding the water resources implications of growing sugar beet, sugar cane and maize are particularly important as there are different countries where they can be grown, and also because there is a growing interest in their potential as a source for biofuel (Gerbens-Leenes and Hoekstra, 2012).

Let's start with looking at the impact of sugar beet from Iran, where the water footprint of sugar beet is relatively large and mostly blue. With a population of more than 65 million people, Iran is one of the most water-scarce countries in the world. It is estimated that the average annual supply of renewable freshwater per person will fall from 1,750 (2005) to 1,300 m³ (2020). According to the 'Falkenmark thresholds', a country will experience periodic water stress when freshwater availability is below 1,700 m³/person per year (Falkenmark and Rockström, 2004). More than 94 per cent of the total annual water consumption in Iran is used for agriculture, so agriculture plays a significant role in water stress in the country. In addition, the productivity of water (yield per unit of water) is very low (Gerbens-Leenes and Hoekstra, 2012). The Iranian sugar beet usage in our product leads to 99 litres of water consumption per bottle, 84 per cent of which are from blue water sources. This leads to serious water problems in the sugar beet cultivation regions, especially where the production rate is high. One-third of the country's sugar factories are in the three provinces of Razavi Khorasan, North Khorasan and South Khorasan, which experience mostly arid conditions and face great water shortages (Larijani, 2005).

Another country with a relatively large water footprint of sugar beet is Russia. Cola from Russia has a sugar-related water footprint of 63 litres/bottle. Also here, the fraction of the blue water footprint in the total water footprint of sugar beet is high (53 per cent). The most important problems due to sugar beet cultivation in Russia occur in the area north of the Black Sea. Pollution in the rivers Dnieper and Don, which flow to the Black Sea, is causing serious environmental damage to the Black Sea ecosystem. In 1992, the Russian Federation's Committee on Fishing reported several cases of water bodies that were completely contaminated by agricultural runoff. Apart from pollution by excessive use of fertilizers, irrigation has resulted in water scarcity in some areas (Gerbens–Leenes and Hoekstra, 2012).

The region of Andalucía in Spain is a clear hotspot since it is a water-scarce region with a large water footprint in relation to sugar beet production. Sugar beet irrigation in this region has contributed to lowering water levels in the Guadalquivir River and drying of important wetlands during summer time (WWF, 2004).

A widespread problem related to sugar beet cultivation is eutrophication of water bodies due to the overuse of fertilizers (WWF, 2004). The nutrients in the fertilizers are not entirely taken up by the crop but partly leach to groundwater and flow into streams. The runoff of nitrate and phosphate into lakes and streams can contribute to a eutrophic status and the proliferation of toxic microalgae. In the Seine-Normandy Basin in France, irrigation has little quantitative impact on the resource, but does, however, have an indirect impact on its quality because it favours intensive farming techniques and spring crops, which leave the soil bare for long periods of the year and increase the chemical load in the rivers by leaching and draining (UNESCO, 2003). This has a harmful effect on both the environment and other water uses. Improving water quality is still a major concern for the basin, where non-point source pollution from farming and urban areas is still a major problem as nitrate, pesticide and heavy metal concentrations continue to increase.

While the impacts of maize are often similar to those of sugar beet – whereby differences mainly depend on local climate, water availability and agricultural practice – the impacts of sugar cane on water are often worse. Let's consider sugar cane from Cuba. Sugar cane is the most important plant on the island and it was the most important foreign exchange earner for decades. Cuba has been facing several environmental problems for the last decades in relation to sugar cane production. Cuba has high-quality resources of karst water, but the quality of this water is highly susceptible to pollution. Pollution resulting from sugar cane factories is one of the main reasons that the quality of karst aquifers has deteriorated (León and Parise, 2008). In addition, the untreated wastewater from sugar factories in Cuba has led to oxygen deficiency in rivers and the dominance of aquatic macrophytes, which results in thick mats of weeds. This situation partially blocks the water delivery capacity of canals, which has negative effects on fishing and tourism (WWF, 2004). Due to sugar cane cultivation, deforestation in Cuba has become a major environmental problem (Monzote, 2008). Cuba's forest area has also been drastically decreased as a result of demand for lumber; the sugar cane industry alone annually consumes 1 million $m^3$ of firewood (Cepero, 2000).

Another country with a large water footprint of sugar cane is Pakistan. If we choose Pakistani sugar cane for our product, the water footprint of the sugar per bottle will be 140 litres. The sugar cane in Pakistan heavily depends on irrigation; the blue water footprint constitutes 88 per cent of the total water footprint. Water abstractions for irrigation cause water shortage in the production regions and serious environmental problems. The Indus River is the major water resource of Pakistan. The freshwater reaching the Indus Delta has significantly decreased as a result of over-usage of water sources in the Indus Basin. Sugar cane is one of the main water-consuming agricultural products in the basin. The decrease in freshwater flow to the Indus Delta has negative impacts on the biodiversity of the Delta (decrease of mangrove forestlands and danger of extinction of the blind river dolphin). Additionally, excessive water use in sugar cane cultivation areas also leads to salinity problems (WWF, 2004). Moreover, untreated wastewater from sugar mills causes depletion of available oxygen in water sources, which results in endangering fish and other aquatic life (Akbar and Khwaja, 2006).

Brazil, the largest sugar cane producer in the world, has faced several negative impacts of sugar cane production as well. Much of the sugar cane produced is used as raw material for ethanol production. The extensive sugar cane production has contributed to the deforestation of rainforests. Moreover, sugar cane fields in the state of São Paulo are reported to cause air pollution due to pre-harvest burning (WWF, 2004). Water pollution due to sugar cane industries and the application of fertilizers and pesticides in the growing of sugar cane is another major environmental problem in Brazil (Gunkel et al., 2006).

India is also facing environmental problems due to sugar cane cultivation. In the Indian state of Maharashtra, sugar cane irrigation uses 60 per cent of the total irrigation supply, which causes substantial groundwater withdrawals (WWF, 2004). India's largest river, the Ganges, experiences severe water stress. Sugar cane is one of the major crops cultivated in the area and increases water scarcity

(Gerbens-Leenes and Hoekstra, 2012). Another problem resulting from sugar cane cultivation and sugar processing activity in India is the pollution of surface and groundwater resources (Solomon, 2005).

Water consumption and pollution related to sugar production are not the only concern with respect to our cola drink. Vanilla, which is part of the natural flavour of our beverage, contributes largely to the overall water footprint (from 27 per cent to 50 per cent). The source of the vanilla is Madagascar, which is the main vanilla producing country in the world. Cultivation of vanilla is one of the most labour-intensive agricultural crops and it takes up to three years before the crop can be harvested. Harvested flowers need a process called curing in order to take its aroma. This process needs heating of the vanilla beans in hot water (65 °C) for three minutes. Thermal pollution occurs as a result of hot water discharged into freshwater systems, causing sudden increases in the temperature of the ambient water systems above ecologically acceptable limits. In addition to water contamination by means of temperature changes, the necessity of obtaining wood, the main energy source of heating, causes deforestation of rainforests (Alwahti, 2003).

Another small ingredient of our hypothetical beverage is caffeine. Although the amount of caffeine used in the product is small, the water footprint is very large (53 litres/bottle). The caffeine is sourced from coffee beans produced in Colombia, which is one of the biggest coffee producers in the world. Among the problems in Colombia due to coffee cultivation are loss of bird species and soil erosion. Additionally, pollution of surface and groundwater resources resulting from the usage of fertilizers is a major environmental concern (Miura, 2001).

The oil-based materials used for the bottle of our beverage (PET-bottle, cap, stretch films and labels) have particularly a grey water footprint. In PET production, large amounts of water are used for cooling. Cooling water is considered as grey water as it increases the temperature of the receiving freshwater bodies more than what is acceptable from an ecological point of view. Water quality criteria for aquatic ecosystems indicate that water temperature may not increase by more than a few degrees Celsius compared to natural conditions (CEC, 1988). Additional freshwater sources are required to dilute hot water stemming from cooling water (to decrease the temperature of discharged cooling water in order to meet standards with respect to maximum increase of water temperature).

Summarizing, the main impacts of the beverage relate to the grey and blue water footprints of the product. Ingredients like sugar, vanilla and caffeine (coffee) cause contamination of natural freshwater sources (grey water footprint) because of the use of fertilizers and pesticides. The biggest water impact of the beverage is related to the sugar ingredient. Many sugar-producing countries are water-rich countries where the water footprint does not relate to water stress. There are, however, several localized hotspots, such as the sugar beet production in the Andalucía region in the south of Spain, sugar cane production in Pakistan (Indus River) and India (Ganges River), and sugar beet from Iran. With regard to water quality, pollution by nitrates is an issue in several regions, such as the case of the Netherlands, northern France, Russia (Black Sea), India, Pakistan, Cuba, Brazil, Iran and China. Careful nitrogen fertilization is important to reduce the environmental impact and to increase profitability in crop production. Better management practices to reduce the environmental impacts in the sugar industry do not necessarily imply reduced productivity and profits; on the contrary, measures to address environmental impacts can provide economic benefits for farmers or mills through cost savings from more efficient resource use. In addition, mostly sugar cane production relates to deforestation like in Cuba and Brazil. Other negative effects of sugar cane production are impacts on biodiversity (decrease of mangrove forestlands, and danger of extinction of the blind river dolphin in the Indus Delta).

## What the cola example teaches us

The total water footprint of our beverage is calculated as minimum 168 litres (using sugar beet from the Netherlands) and maximum 309 litres (using sugar cane from Cuba or maize from India). The operational water footprint of the product is 0.5 litres, which forms 0.2–0.3 per cent of the total water footprint. The supply-chain water footprint constitutes 99.7–99.8 per cent of the total water footprint of the product. Most of the supply-chain water footprint comes from its ingredients (95–97 per cent). A smaller fraction (2–4 per cent) comes from the other inputs, mainly from the PET-bottle. The overhead water footprint constitutes a minor fraction of the supply-chain water footprint (0.2–0.3 per cent).

The cola example shows the importance of a detailed supply-chain assessment. Companies usually restrict themselves to the accounting of operational water use. We have seen, however, that compared to the supply-chain water footprint, the operational side is almost negligible. The study further shows that the water footprint of a beverage product is very sensitive to the production locations of the agricultural inputs. Even though the amount of sugar is kept constant, the water footprint of our product significantly changes according to the type of sugar input and production location of the sugar. Additionally, the type of water footprint (green, blue and grey) changes according to location, mainly driven by regional differences in climatic conditions and agricultural practice. These results reveal the importance of the spatial dimension of water footprint accounting.

The general findings with respect to the ratio of operational to supply-chain water footprint and the relative importance of ingredients, other inputs and overheads can be extended to other beverages similar to our hypothetical beverage. The major part of the water footprint of most beverages will be stemming from the supply chain. This shows the importance of focusing corperate water policy towards supply chain rather than operational water use. It would make sense if companies change their key performance indicator (KPI) on water. Currently, beverage companies use the water withdrawal for their operations as their KPI, which inevitably leads to inefficient investments if it comes to the reduction of the water footprint of the product as a whole. Much bigger steps in making beverages more sustainable would be made if companies consider investments in their supply chain as well. Companies can for instance include sustainability criteria on water use in supply agreements with farmers and actively help them to meet those criteria. Great water footprint reductions can generally be achieved, even in the case of growing sugar beet in the Netherlands, where overuse and leaching of nutrients is still common practice. In countries where irrigation gives a substantial contribution to the overall water footprint, implementing better irrigation techniques can generally make large water savings.

## The water footprint of our daily drinks

How much water do we drink per day? Typical reported figures range between 2 and 5 litres. However, when we also take into account the indirect water use of what we drink, we will arrive at a much larger volume of water. Table 2.4 shows

**TABLE 2.4** The global average water footprint of some drinks, 1996–2005

| | Drink | Amount | Water footprint (litre) | | | |
|---|---|---|---|---|---|---|
| | | | *Green* | *Blue* | *Grey* | *Total* |
| Juice | Tomato juice | 1 glass (200 ml) | 27 | 16 | 11 | 54 |
| | Grapefruit juice | 1 glass (200 ml) | 98 | 23 | 14 | 135 |
| | Orange juice | 1 glass (200 ml) | 146 | 40 | 18 | 204 |
| | Apple juice | 1 glass (200 ml) | 156 | 37 | 35 | 228 |
| | Pineapple juice | 1 glass (200 ml) | 215 | 9 | 31 | 255 |
| Soft drinks | Cola | 1 glass (200 ml) | 59 | 3 | 5 | 67 |
| Milk | Cow's milk | 1 glass (200 ml) | 173 | 17 | 14 | 204 |
| | Soyamilk | 1 glass (200 ml) | 55 | 2 | 2 | 59 |
| Alcohol | Beer | 1 glass (200 ml) | 51 | 3 | 5 | 59 |
| | Wine | 1 glass (125 ml) | 76 | 17 | 16 | 109 |
| Hot drinks | Tea | 1 cup (3 g black tea) | 22 | 3 | 2 | 27 |
| | Coffee | 1 cup (7 g roasted coffee) | 127 | 1 | 4 | 132 |
| | Hot chocolate | 1 glass (10 g cocoa powder, 20 g beet sugar, 200 ml milk) | 333 | 20 | 19 | 372 |

Sources: Ercin *et al.* (2011) for cola based on sugar beet from the Netherlands; Ercin *et al.* (2012) for soyamilk; Mekonnen and Hoekstra (2012a) for cow milk; Mekonnen and Hoekstra (2011a) for the other drinks.

the water footprint of a number of common drinks. Let us assume a moderate Western drink pattern. Suppose someone drinks one glass of milk at breakfast (water footprint of 200 litres), one black coffee in the morning (130 litres), orange juice at lunch (200 litres), a black tea in the afternoon (30 litres), another coffee after dinner (130 litres) and a glass of wine in the evening (200 litres). In this case, the overall water footprint related to the drinks of the day will be approximately 900 litres. A typical bathtub contains 90 litres of water (although they come in much bigger sizes). This means that we drink about ten bathtubs a day.

# 3

# WATER FOR BREAD AND PASTA

A lot of water is needed to make our drinks, but much more water is used to produce our food. Wheat is the crop with the largest global water footprint. Fifteen per cent of the total water footprint of crop production in the world relates to growing wheat. Rice is a close second, accounting for 13 per cent of the water footprint of global crop production, and maize a good third with 10 per cent. When we focus on the blue water footprint alone, we find that wheat and rice put more or less the same claim on the world's blue water resources, together responsible for 45 per cent of the global blue water footprint of crop production (Mekonnen and Hoekstra, 2011a). Rice, wheat and maize are the three most popular staple foods in the world. In this chapter, we will focus on one of them: wheat. We will consider two of the most important appearances of wheat in our diets: bread and pasta.

Wheat is believed to originate in Southwest Asia and the most likely site of its first domestication is near Diyarbakir in Turkey (Dubcovsky and Dvorak, 2007). Nowadays, wheat is grown all over the world. Over 90 per cent of the global wheat production is common wheat or bread wheat (*Triticum aestivum aestivum*), while durum wheat (*Triticum turgidum durum*) accounts for an estimated 5 per cent (Dixon *et al.*, 2009). Bread wheat is mainly used for bread, noodles, cookies, cakes and breakfast cereals. Durum wheat has a very hard grain and is unsuitable for making bread; it is used mostly to produce semolina, pasta, gnocchi and cracked wheat products such as couscous or bulgur. Based on the growing period, wheat can be subdivided into spring and winter wheat.

As a starter, I will present the global water footprint of wheat production. We will see in which places the water footprint of wheat is relatively small and where relatively large, in terms of litres/kg. In addition, we will see in which regions the water footprint of wheat is largest in total terms, which depends on the water footprint per unit of production, but also on how much wheat is being produced.

I will zoom in on a few particular production regions: the Midwest of the USA and the Ganges and Indus Basins. After this, we will consider international virtual water flows related to trade in wheat products. The analysis of trade enables us to take the consumer perspective and trace the spatial spreading of the water footprint of wheat consumption per country. In many countries, the water footprint of wheat consumption lies substantially outside the country, which means that consumers rely on water resources elsewhere. In the long run, unsustainable water use in the export regions may thus impact on the supply of wheat in the importing countries. In the last part of this chapter, I will home in on wheat consumption in Italy, one of the main wheat consuming countries in the world, with a focus on the water footprint of pasta. The chapter is concluded with a reflection on the idea of setting a benchmark for the water footprint of wheat to provide an incentive for improvement in the areas where the water footprint of wheat production exceeds the benchmark.

## The water footprint of wheat production

In a recent study, we have quantified the green, blue and grey water footprint of wheat production by using a grid-based dynamic water balance model that takes into account local climate and soil conditions and nitrogen fertilizer application rates and calculates the crop water requirements, actual crop water use and yields and finally the green, blue and grey water footprint at grid level (Mekonnen and Hoekstra, 2010). The model has been applied at a spatial resolution of five arc minutes by five arc minutes, which at the equator implies grid cells of about $10\times10\,\text{km}^2$.

We found that the global water footprint of wheat production in the period 1996–2005 was 1,088 billion $\text{m}^3/\text{yr}$. In order to get an impression of the size of this volume: it is about the same, even a bit more, than the annual precipitation in France, Germany and Spain together. About 70 per cent of the water footprint of global wheat production was green, about 19 per cent blue, and 11 per cent grey. Data per country are shown in Table 3.1 for the largest producers. The global green water footprint related to wheat production was 760 billion $\text{m}^3/\text{yr}$. At a country level, large green water footprints can be found in the USA, China, Russia, Australia and India. About 49 per cent of the global green water footprint related to wheat production is in these five countries. At sub-national level (state or province level), the largest green water footprints can be found in Kansas in the USA (21 billion $\text{m}^3/\text{yr}$), Saskatchewan in Canada (18 billion $\text{m}^3/\text{yr}$), western Australia (15 billion $\text{m}^3/\text{yr}$) and North Dakota in the USA (15 billion $\text{m}^3/\text{yr}$). The global blue water footprint was estimated to be 204 billion $\text{m}^3/\text{yr}$. The largest blue water footprints were calculated for India, China, Pakistan, Iran, Egypt and the USA. These six countries together account for 88 per cent of the total blue water footprint related to wheat production. At sub-national level, the largest blue water footprints can be found in Uttar Pradesh (24 billion $\text{m}^3/\text{yr}$) and Madhya Pradesh (21 billion $\text{m}^3/\text{yr}$) in India and Punjab in Pakistan (20 billion $\text{m}^3/\text{yr}$). These three states in the two countries alone account for about 32 per cent of the global blue water footprint related to wheat production. The grey water footprint related to

**TABLE 3.1** The water footprint of wheat production for the major wheat-producing countries, 1996–2005

| Country | Contribution to global wheat production (%) | Total water footprint of production (million m³/yr) | | | | Water footprint of wheat per unit of weight (litre/kg) | | | |
|---|---|---|---|---|---|---|---|---|---|
| | | Green | Blue | Grey | Total | Green | Blue | Grey | Total |
| Argentina | 2.5 | 25,905 | 162 | 1,601 | 27,668 | 1,777 | 11 | 110 | 1,898 |
| Australia | 3.6 | 44,057 | 363 | 2,246 | 46,666 | 2,130 | 18 | 109 | 2,257 |
| Canada | 3.9 | 32,320 | 114 | 4,852 | 37,286 | 1,358 | 5 | 204 | 1,567 |
| China | 17.4 | 83,459 | 47,370 | 31,626 | 162,455 | 820 | 466 | 311 | 1,597 |
| Czech Republic | 0.6 | 2,834 | 0 | 900 | 3,734 | 726 | 0 | 231 | 957 |
| Denmark | 0.8 | 2,486 | 30 | 533 | 3,049 | 530 | 6 | 114 | 650 |
| Egypt | 1.1 | 1,410 | 5,930 | 2,695 | 10,035 | 216 | 907 | 412 | 1,535 |
| France | 6.0 | 21,014 | 48 | 199 | 21,261 | 584 | 1 | 6 | 591 |
| Germany | 3.5 | 12,717 | 0 | 3,914 | 16,631 | 602 | 0 | 185 | 787 |
| Hungary | 0.7 | 4,078 | 8 | 1,389 | 5,475 | 973 | 2 | 331 | 1,306 |
| India | 11.9 | 44,025 | 81,335 | 20,491 | 145,851 | 635 | 1,173 | 296 | 2,104 |
| Iran | 1.8 | 26,699 | 10,940 | 3,208 | 40,847 | 2,412 | 988 | 290 | 3,690 |
| Italy | 1.2 | 8,890 | 120 | 1,399 | 10,409 | 1,200 | 16 | 189 | 1,405 |
| Kazakhstan | 1.7 | 33,724 | 241 | 1 | 33,966 | 3,604 | 26 | 0 | 3,630 |
| Morocco | 0.5 | 10,081 | 894 | 387 | 11,362 | 3,291 | 292 | 126 | 3,709 |
| Pakistan | 3.2 | 12,083 | 27,733 | 8,000 | 47,816 | 644 | 1,478 | 426 | 2,548 |
| Poland | 1.5 | 9,922 | 4 | 4,591 | 14,517 | 1,120 | 0 | 518 | 1,638 |

| Country | Contribution to global wheat production (%) | Total water footprint of production (million m³/yr) | | | | Water footprint of wheat per unit of weight (litre/kg) | | | |
|---|---|---|---|---|---|---|---|---|---|
| | | Green | Blue | Grey | Total | Green | Blue | Grey | Total |
| Romania | 0.9 | 9,066 | 247 | 428 | 9,741 | 1,799 | 49 | 85 | 1,933 |
| Russian Fed. | 6.5 | 91,117 | 1,207 | 3,430 | 95,754 | 2,359 | 31 | 89 | 2,479 |
| Spain | 1.0 | 8,053 | 275 | 1,615 | 9,943 | 1,441 | 49 | 289 | 1,779 |
| Syria | 0.7 | 5,913 | 1,790 | 842 | 8,545 | 1,511 | 457 | 215 | 2,183 |
| Turkey | 3.3 | 40,898 | 2,570 | 3,857 | 47,325 | 2,081 | 131 | 196 | 2,408 |
| UK | 2.5 | 6,188 | 2 | 2,292 | 8,482 | 413 | 0 | 153 | 566 |
| Ukraine | 2.5 | 26,288 | 287 | 1,149 | 27,724 | 1,884 | 21 | 82 | 1,987 |
| USA | 10.2 | 111,926 | 5,503 | 13,723 | 131,152 | 1,879 | 92 | 230 | 2,201 |
| Uzbekistan | 0.7 | 3,713 | 399 | 0 | 4,112 | 939 | 101 | 0 | 1,040 |
| World | | 760,301 | 203,744 | 123,533 | 1,087,578 | 1,279 | 343 | 208 | 1,830 |

Source: Mekonnen and Hoekstra (2010)

the use of nitrogen fertilizer in wheat cultivation was 124 billion m³/yr. The largest grey water footprints were observed for China, India, the USA and Pakistan.

The calculated global average water footprint of wheat per unit of weight was 1,830 litres/kg. The results show a great variation, however, both within a country and among countries. Among the major wheat producers, the largest total water footprint of wheat per unit of weight was found for Morocco, Iran and Kazakhstan. On the other side of the spectrum, there are countries like the UK and France with a wheat water footprint of around 560–600 litres/kg.

The global average blue water footprint of wheat amounts to 343 litres/kg. For a few countries, including Pakistan, India, Iran and Egypt, the blue water footprint is much larger, up to 1,478 litres/kg in Pakistan. In Pakistan, the blue water component in the total water footprint is nearly 58 per cent. The grey water footprint of wheat is 208 litres/kg as a global average, but in Poland it is 2.5 times larger than the global average.

Table 3.2 shows the water footprint related to production of wheat for some selected river basins. About 59 per cent of the global water footprint related to wheat production is located in this limited number of basins. Large blue water footprints can be found in the Ganges-Brahmaputra-Meghna, Indus, Yellow, Tigris-Euphrates, Amur and Yangtze River Basins. Together, the Ganges-Brahmaputra-Meghna and Indus River Basins account for about 47 per cent of the global blue and 21 per cent of the global grey water footprint.

## Rain-fed versus irrigated agriculture

The global average water footprint of rain-fed wheat production is 1,805 litres/kg, while in irrigated wheat production it is 1,868 litres/kg (Table 3.3). Obviously, the blue water footprint in rain-fed wheat production is zero. In irrigated wheat production, the blue water footprint constitutes 50 per cent of the total water footprint. Although, on average, wheat yields are 30 per cent higher in irrigated fields, the water footprint of wheat from irrigated lands is larger than in the case of rain-fed lands. When we consider consumptive water use (blue plus green water footprint) only, the water footprints of wheat from rain-fed and irrigated land are more or less equal, as a global average. The reason is that, although yields are higher under irrigation, water consumption (evapotranspiration) is higher as well. Under rain-fed conditions, the actual evapotranspiration over the growing period is lower than the potential evapotranspiration, while under irrigated conditions there is more water available to meet crop water requirements, leading to an actual evapotranspiration that will approach or equal potential evapotranspiration.

The green, blue and grey water footprints of global wheat production put pressure on the freshwater system in different ways. Green water generally has a low opportunity cost compared to blue water. There are many river basins in the world where blue water consumption contributes to severe water scarcity and associated environmental problems, like in the Indus and Ganges Basins as will be discussed below. Since wheat has relatively low economic water productivity (euro/m³)

**TABLE 3.2** The water footprint of wheat production for some selected river basins, 1996–2005

| River Basin | Total water footprint of production (million m³/yr) | | | | Water footprint of wheat per unit of weight (litre/kg) | | | |
|---|---|---|---|---|---|---|---|---|
| | Green | Blue | Grey | Total | Green | Blue | Grey | Total |
| Ganges–Brahmaputra–Meghna | 30,288 | 53,009 | 12,653 | 95,950 | 665 | 1,164 | 278 | 2,107 |
| Mississippi | 79,484 | 2,339 | 9,413 | 91,236 | 1,979 | 58 | 234 | 2,271 |
| Indus | 22,897 | 42,145 | 13,326 | 78,368 | 604 | 1,111 | 351 | 2,066 |
| Ob | 51,984 | 225 | 511 | 52,720 | 2,680 | 12 | 26 | 2,718 |
| Nelson–Saskatchewan | 38,486 | 118 | 5,691 | 44,295 | 1,275 | 4 | 189 | 1,468 |
| Tigris–Euphrates | 29,219 | 10,282 | 2,670 | 42,171 | 2,893 | 1,018 | 264 | 4,175 |
| Yellow | 17,012 | 13,127 | 7,592 | 37,731 | 695 | 536 | 310 | 1,541 |
| Danube | 27,884 | 273 | 3,579 | 31,736 | 1,298 | 13 | 167 | 1,478 |
| Volga | 25,078 | 272 | 955 | 26,305 | 2,315 | 25 | 88 | 2,428 |
| Don | 24,834 | 384 | 927 | 26,145 | 2,658 | 41 | 99 | 2,798 |
| Yangtze | 17,436 | 2,700 | 4,855 | 24,991 | 1,112 | 172 | 310 | 1,594 |
| Murray–Darling | 20,673 | 343 | 987 | 22,003 | 2,061 | 34 | 98 | 2,193 |
| La Plata | 17,127 | 73 | 1,070 | 18,270 | 2,039 | 9 | 127 | 2,175 |
| Amur | 8,726 | 3,136 | 2,355 | 14,217 | 985 | 354 | 266 | 1,605 |
| Dnieper | 13,219 | 68 | 813 | 14,100 | 1,732 | 9 | 107 | 1,848 |
| Columbia | 7,238 | 1,877 | 1,122 | 10,237 | 1,852 | 480 | 287 | 2,619 |
| Ural | 9,338 | 94 | 192 | 9,624 | 2,542 | 26 | 52 | 2,620 |
| World | 760,301 | 203,744 | 123,533 | 1,087,578 | 1,279 | 343 | 208 | 1,830 |

Source: Mekonnen and Hoekstra (2010)

**TABLE 3.3** The global water footprint of wheat production in rain-fed and irrigated lands, 1996–2005

| Farming system | Yield (tonne/ha) | Total water footprint of production (billion $m^3$/yr) | | | | Water footprint of wheat per unit of weight (litre/kg) | | | |
|---|---|---|---|---|---|---|---|---|---|
| | | Green | Blue | Grey | Total | Green | Blue | Grey | Total |
| Rain-fed | 2.5 | 611 | 0 | 66 | 677 | 1,629 | 0 | 175 | 1,804 |
| Irrigated | 3.3 | 150 | 204 | 58 | 412 | 679 | 926 | 263 | 1,868 |
| World average | 2.7 | 760 | 204 | 124 | 1,088 | 1,279 | 343 | 208 | 1,830 |

Source: Mekonnen and Hoekstra (2010)

compared to many other crops (Molden, 2007), one may question to which extent water should be allocated to wheat production in relatively water-scarce basins. The relatively low yields in rain-fed lands show that there is still plenty of room to raise green water productivity in most countries, i.e. lowering the green water footprint. This is particularly relevant in policy aimed at addressing the negative externalities of blue water footprints, because increasing green water productivity and increased production from rain-fed lands will reduce the need for production from irrigated lands in water-scarce areas, and thus reduce blue water use. The grey water footprint in wheat production can generally be lowered substantially by applying fertilizers in the right amounts at the right time using appropriate application technology (precision farming), so that less fertilizers leach to groundwater or run off to surface water (Jenkinson, 2001; Norse, 2005).

## The Great Plains of the US

The Ogallala Aquifer, also known as the High Plains Aquifer, is a regional aquifer system located beneath the Great Plains in the United States in portions of the eight states of South Dakota, Nebraska, Wyoming, Colorado, Kansas, Oklahoma, New Mexico and Texas. It covers an area of approximately 451,000 $km^2$, making it the largest area irrigation-sustained cropland in the world (Peterson and Bernardo, 2003). Most of the aquifer underlies parts of three states: Nebraska has 65 per cent of the aquifer's volume, Texas 12 per cent and Kansas 10 per cent (Peck, 2007). About 27 per cent of the irrigated land in the United States overlies this aquifer system, which yields about 30 per cent of the nation's groundwater used for irrigation (Dennehy, 2000).

Water from the Ogallala Aquifer is the principal source of supply for irrigated agriculture. In 1995, the Ogallala Aquifer contributed about 81 per cent of the water supply in the Ogallala area while the remainder was withdrawn from rivers and streams, most of it from the Platte River in Nebraska. Outside of the Platte River Valley, 92 per cent of water used in the Ogallala area is supplied by groundwater (Dennehy, 2000). Since the beginning of extensive irrigation using groundwater, the water level of the aquifer has dropped by 3–15 m in most part of the aquifer (McGuire, 2007).

Within the Ogallala area, Kansas takes the largest share in wheat production (51 per cent), followed by Texas and Nebraska (16 per cent and 15 per cent, respectively). In Kansas, 84 per cent of the wheat production comes from rain-fed areas. In Nebraska, this is 86 per cent and in Texas 47 per cent. The Ogallala area accounts for about 14 per cent of the total wheat production in the USA. Our study shows that 16 per cent of the total water footprint of wheat production in the country lies in the Ogallala area. About 19 per cent of the *blue* water footprint of wheat production in the USA is in the Ogallala area. The total water footprint in the Ogallala area was 21 billion m³/yr (Table 3.4).

Texas takes the largest share (39 per cent) in the blue water footprint of wheat production in the Ogallala area, followed by Kansas (35 per cent). There is a considerable variation in the blue water footprint per kg of wheat within the Ogallala area. Besides, the blue water footprint per kg of wheat in the Ogallala area is relatively large if compared to the average in the USA.

In the period 1996–2005, the virtual water export related to export of wheat products from the USA was 57 billion m³/yr. About 98 per cent of the virtual water export comes from domestic water resources and the remaining 2 per cent is from the re-export of imported virtual water related to the import of wheat products. Taking the per capita wheat consumption in the USA of about 88 kg/yr (FAO, 2012a) and a population in the Ogallala area of 2.4 million (CIESIN, 2005) we can find that only 2 per cent of the wheat produced is consumed within the Ogallala

**TABLE 3.4** The water footprint of wheat production and virtual water export from the Ogallala area, 1996–2005

| States in the Ogallala area | Water footprint related to wheat production (million m³/yr) | | | | Virtual water export related to export of wheat products (million m³/yr) | | | |
|---|---|---|---|---|---|---|---|---|
| | Green | Blue | Grey | Total | Green | Blue | Grey | Total |
| Kansas | 9,136 | 368 | 1,077 | 10,581 | 8,914 | 359 | 1,051 | 10,324 |
| Texas | 1,981 | 417 | 301 | 2,699 | 1,933 | 407 | 294 | 2,634 |
| Nebraska | 2,952 | 78 | 345 | 3,375 | 2,880 | 76 | 337 | 3,293 |
| Colorado | 2,108 | 67 | 281 | 2,456 | 2,057 | 66 | 274 | 2,397 |
| Oklahoma | 693 | 26 | 91 | 810 | 676 | 25 | 88 | 789 |
| New Mexico | 317 | 94 | 45 | 456 | 309 | 91 | 44 | 444 |
| South Dakota | 211 | 0 | 24 | 235 | 206 | 0 | 23 | 229 |
| Wyoming | 299 | 6 | 34 | 339 | 291 | 6 | 33 | 330 |
| Ogallala area total | 17,696 | 1,056 | 2,196 | 20,948 | 17,266 | 1,031 | 2,143 | 20,440 |

Source: Mekonnen and Hoekstra (2010). Figures refer to the parts of the states within the Ogallala area only.

area and the surplus (about 98 per cent) is exported out of the Ogallala area to other areas in the USA or exported to other countries. This surplus of wheat constitutes 33 per cent of the domestic wheat export from the USA (Table 3.4). Figure 3.1 shows the major foreign destinations of wheat-related virtual water exports from the area of the Ogallala Aquifer.

The water footprint related to wheat production for export is putting pressure on the water resources of the Ogallala Aquifer (McGuire, 2007). Visualizing the hidden link between the wheat consumer elsewhere and the impact of wheat production on the water resources of the Ogallala Aquifer is quite relevant in policy aimed at internalizing the negative externalities of wheat production and passing on those costs to consumers elsewhere.

## The Ganges and Indus River Basins

The Ganges River Basin, which is part of the composite Ganges-Brahmaputra-Meghna River Basin, is one of most densely populated river basins in the world (443 persons/km²). It covers about 1 million km² (Gleick, 1993). The Indus River Basin, which extends over four countries (China, India, Pakistan and Afghanistan), is also a highly populated river basin (186 persons/km²). The area of the Indus Basin is a bit smaller than the Ganges Basin but covers nearly 1 million km² as well (Gleick, 1993).

Together, the two river basins account for about 90 per cent of the wheat production in India and Pakistan in the period 1996–2005. Almost all wheat production (98 per cent) in Pakistan comes from the Indus River Basin. About 89 per cent of India's wheat is produced in the Ganges (62 per cent) and the Indus

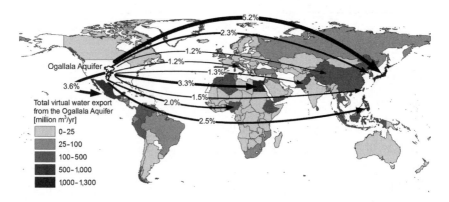

**FIGURE 3.1** Major destinations of wheat-related virtual water exports from the Ogallala area in the USA, 1996–2005. About 58 per cent of the total water footprint of wheat production in the area is for wheat consumption in the USA and 42 per cent is for export to other nations. Only the largest exports (> 1 per cent) are shown.

Source: Mekonnen and Hoekstra (2010)

Basin (27 per cent). About 87 per cent of the total water footprint related to wheat production in India and Pakistan lies in these two river basins. The total water footprint of wheat production in the Indian part of the Ganges Basin is 92 billion $m^3/yr$ (32 per cent green, 54 per cent blue, 14 per cent grey). The total water footprint of wheat production in the Pakistani part of the Indus Basin is 48 billion $m^3/yr$ (25 per cent green, 58 per cent blue, 17 per cent grey).

In the period 1996–2005, India and Pakistan together had a virtual water export related to wheat export of 5.1 billion $m^3/yr$ (29 per cent green, 56 per cent blue, 15 per cent grey), which is a small fraction (3 per cent) of the total water footprint of wheat production in these two countries. About 55 per cent of this total virtual water export comes from the Ganges Basin and 45 per cent from the Indus Basin. The blue water export to other countries from the Ganges and Indus River Basins was 1.3 and 1.1 billion $m^3/yr$, respectively.

Based on the annual water withdrawal-to-availability ratio, an often-used rough indicator of water stress (Cosgrove and Rijsberman, 2000), most parts of Pakistan and India can be characterized as highly water stressed (Alcamo *et al.*, 2003). In addition, when we look at water scarcity in more detail, by comparing monthly blue water footprint to monthly blue water availability, we find that both the Ganges and Indus River Basins face severe water scarcity (Hoekstra *et al.*, 2012). The Indus River Basin faces severe water scarcity almost three-quarters of the year (September to April). The basin receives around 70 per cent of its precipitation during the months of June to October (Thenkabail *et al.*, 2005). The low-water period in the Indus River Basin is from November through February. The high waters begin in June and continue through October as the snow and glaciers melt from the Tibetan plateau. Over 93 per cent of the blue water footprint related to crop production in Pakistan occurs in the two major agricultural provinces of Punjab and Sindh, which lie fully (Punjab) and mostly (Sindh) in the Indus Basin. Irrigation of wheat, rice and cotton crops account for 77 per cent of the blue water footprint in the basin. Groundwater abstraction, mainly for irrigation, goes beyond the natural recharge leading to depletion of the groundwater in the basin (Wada *et al.*, 2010). The Ganges River Basin faces severe water scarcity for five months of the year (January to May). The basin is fed by two main headwaters in the Himalayas – the Bhagirathi and Alaknanda – and many other tributaries that drain the Himalayas and the Vindhya and Satpura ranges. Most of the blue water footprint in the basin is due to evaporation of irrigation water in agriculture, mostly for wheat, rice and sugar cane. These three crops together are responsible for 85 per cent of the total blue water footprint in the basin. Also in the Ganges Basin, overexploitation of the aquifers for irrigation is leading to depletion of the groundwater (Wada *et al.*, 2010).

About 97 per cent of the water footprint related to wheat production in the two basins is for domestic consumption within the two countries. Since the two basins are the wheat baskets of the two countries, there are substantial virtual water transfers from the Ganges and Indus Basins to other areas within India and Pakistan. By looking at the virtual flows both within the country and to other countries, it is possible to link the impacts of wheat consumption in other places to the water stress in the Ganges and Indus Basins. For the case of India, Kampman *et al.* (2008) have shown that the states that lie within the Indus and Ganges River Basins, such as Punjab, Uttar Pradesh and Haryana, are the largest inter-state virtual water exporters within India. The highly subsidized irrigation water in these regions has led to an intensive exploitation of the available water resources in these areas compared to other, more water-abundant regions of India. In order to provide incentives for water protection, negative externalities such as water overexploitation and pollution, and also scarcity rents, should be included in the price of the crop. Both basins have a relatively high water productivity, which is shown by a smaller water footprint per kilogram of wheat, compared with other wheat producing areas in the two countries. However, since wheat is a low-value crop, one may question whether water allocation to wheat production for export in states such as Punjab, Uttar Pradesh and Haryana is worth the cost. A major destination of wheat exports from India's parts of the Indus and Ganges Basins is East India, to relatively water-abundant states like Bihar. Major foreign destinations of India's virtual water export related to export of wheat products are Bangladesh (22 per cent), Indonesia (11 per cent), Philippines (10 per cent) and Yemen (10 per cent). Pakistan's wheat export mainly goes to Afghanistan (56 per cent) and Kenya (11 per cent).

## International virtual water flows related to trade in wheat products

The total global virtual water flow related to international trade in wheat products averaged over the period 1996–2005 was 200 billion $m^3/yr$. This means that an estimated 18 per cent of the global water footprint of wheat production was related to production of wheat for export. About 87 per cent of this amount comes from green water and only 4 per cent from blue water and the remaining 9 per cent is grey water. Wheat exports in the world are thus basically from rain-fed agriculture. The world's largest 26 wheat producers, which account for about 90 per cent of global wheat production (Table 3.1), were responsible for about 94 per cent of the global virtual water export. The USA, Canada and Australia alone were responsible for about 55 per cent of the total virtual water export. China, which is the top wheat producer accounting for 17.4 per cent of the global wheat production, was a net virtual water importer. India and the USA were the largest exporters of blue water, accounting for about 62 per cent of the total blue water export. A very small fraction (4 per cent) of the total blue water consumption in wheat production was traded internationally. Surprisingly, some water-scarce regions in the world, relying on irrigation, show a net export of blue water virtually embedded in wheat. Saudi Arabia had a net blue virtual water export of 21 million $m^3/yr$ and Iraq exported a net volume of blue water of 6 million $m^3/yr$. The largest grey water exporters were the USA, Canada, Australia and Germany. Data per country are shown in Table 3.5 for the largest virtual water exporters and importers, respectively. The global water saving associated with the international trade in wheat products adds up to 65 billion $m^3/yr$ (39 per cent green, 48 per cent blue and 13 per cent grey).

**TABLE 3.5** Gross virtual water export and import related to the international trade of wheat products, 1996–2005

*Largest virtual water exporters (million m³/yr)*

|  | Green | Blue | Grey | Total |
|---|---|---|---|---|
| USA | 48,603 | 2,389 | 5,959 | 56,951 |
| Canada | 24,144 | 85 | 3,625 | 27,854 |
| Australia | 24,396 | 201 | 1,244 | 25,841 |
| Argentina | 15,973 | 100 | 987 | 17,060 |
| Kazakhstan | 16,490 | 118 | 0 | 16,608 |
| France | 9,347 | 21 | 89 | 9,457 |
| Russian Fed. | 7,569 | 100 | 285 | 7,954 |
| Ukraine | 4,587 | 50 | 200 | 4,837 |
| Germany | 3,537 | 0 | 1,090 | 4,627 |
| India | 1,266 | 2,338 | 589 | 4,193 |
| Turkey | 2,208 | 139 | 208 | 2,555 |
| UK | 1,189 | 0 | 441 | 1,630 |
| Spain | 1,242 | 42 | 249 | 1,533 |
| Hungary | 1,035 | 2 | 352 | 1,389 |
| Others | 13,107 | 2,202 | 2,488 | 17,797 |
| Global flow | 174,693 | 7,789 | 17,807 | 200,289 |

*Largest virtual water importers (million m³/yr)*

|  | Green | Blue | Grey | Total |
|---|---|---|---|---|
| Brazil | 11,415 | 88 | 801 | 12,304 |
| Japan | 10,393 | 320 | 1,147 | 11,860 |
| Italy | 7,345 | 174 | 760 | 8,279 |
| Egypt | 6,838 | 274 | 633 | 7,745 |
| Korea, Rep. | 6,511 | 398 | 685 | 7,594 |
| Indonesia | 6,512 | 364 | 577 | 7,453 |
| Iran | 6,105 | 60 | 504 | 6,669 |
| Malaysia | 5,616 | 185 | 636 | 6,437 |
| Algeria | 5,330 | 323 | 696 | 6,349 |
| Mexico | 5,155 | 205 | 660 | 6,020 |
| Russian Fed. | 5,334 | 69 | 92 | 5,495 |
| Philippines | 3,923 | 426 | 538 | 4,887 |
| Spain | 4,161 | 80 | 493 | 4,734 |
| China | 4,087 | 98 | 453 | 4,638 |
| Others | 85,967 | 4,725 | 9,131 | 99,823 |
| Global flow | 174,693 | 7,789 | 17,807 | 200,289 |

Source: Mekonnen and Hoekstra (2010)

Imports of wheat and wheat products by Algeria, Iran, Morocco and Venezuela from Canada, France, the USA and Australia resulted in the largest global water savings. Figure 3.2 illustrates the concept of global water saving through an example of the trade in durum wheat from France to Morocco.

## The water footprint of wheat from the consumption perspective

The global average water footprint of wheat is 1,830 litres/kg. Based on the relative economic value of the different elements of the whole grains of wheat, about 80 per cent of the water footprint of the whole grains is allocated to the flour that is derived from the whole grains; the rest is attributed to wheat pellets, the byproduct. One kilogram of wheat gives about 790 g of flour, so that the water footprint of wheat flour is about 1,850 litres/kg. One kg of flour gives about 1.15 kg of bread, so that the water footprint of bread is 1,608 litres/kg. This is a global average; the precise water footprint of bread depends on the origin of the wheat, on where and how it was grown. In western Europe, the water footprint of wheat is far below the global average. We calculated the water footprint of some typical European bread types. A French *baguette* of 300 g – when baked with French wheat – has a water footprint of 155 litres (517 litres/kg). A Dutch bread of 750 g – when baked with Dutch wheat – costs 460 litres (610 litres/kg). One slice of Dutch bread (30 g) has thus a water footprint of 18 litres of water. A German *Kaiser-Brötchen* of 60 g – when made with German wheat – has a water footprint of about 40 litres (690 litres/kg).

The consumption of wheat products in the world in the period 1996–2005 was equivalent to about 100 kg of wheat per person per year on average. The related water footprint was 177 m$^3$/yr per person. The people of Kazakhstan had the largest wheat-related water footprint, with 1,156 m$^3$/yr, followed by people from Australia and Iran, with 1,082 and 716 m$^3$/yr, respectively. Data per country are shown in Table 3.6 for the major wheat consuming countries. When the water footprint of wheat consumption per capita is relatively large in a country, this can be explained by either one or a combination of two factors: (i) the wheat consumption in the country is relatively high; (ii) the wheat consumed has a large water footprint per kilogram of wheat. As one can see in Table 3.6, in the case of Kazakhstan and Iran, both factors play a role. In the case of Australia, the relatively large water footprint related to wheat consumption can be mostly explained by the high wheat consumption per capita alone. Germany has a large consumption of wheat per capita – more than twice the world average – so that one would expect that the associated water footprint would be large as well, but this is not the case because, on average, the wheat consumed in Germany has a small water footprint per kilogram (43 per cent of the global average).

The wheat consumed in a country is not always grown in the country itself. About 82 per cent of the water footprint related to global wheat consumption was internal (within the country of consumption), while the remaining 18 per cent was external. The countries with the largest external water footprint related to wheat consumption

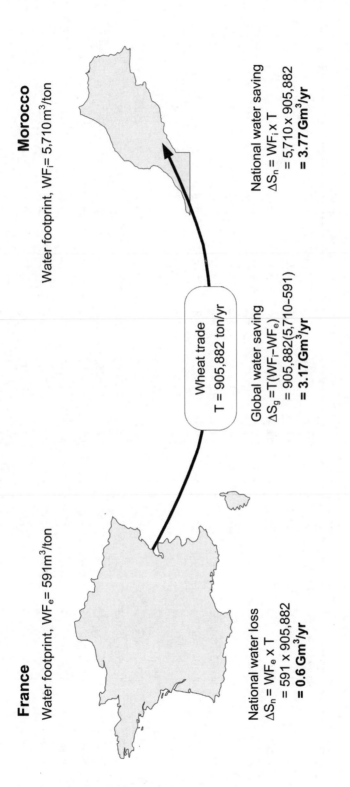

**France**

Water footprint, $WF_e = 591 m^3/ton$

National water loss
$\Delta S_n = WF_e \times T$
$= 591 \times 905,882$
$\textbf{= 0.6 Gm}^3\textbf{/yr}$

Wheat trade
$T = 905,882$ ton/yr

Global water saving
$\Delta S_g = T(WF_i - WF_e)$
$= 905,882(5,710-591)$
$\textbf{= 3.17 Gm}^3\textbf{/yr}$

**Morocco**

Water footprint, $WF_i = 5,710 m^3/ton$

National water saving
$\Delta S_n = WF_i \times T$
$= 5,710 \times 905,882$
$\textbf{= 3.77 Gm}^3\textbf{/yr}$

**FIGURE 3.2** Global water saving through the trade in durum wheat from France to Morocco, 1996–2005

Source: Mekonnen and Hoekstra (2010)

**TABLE 3.6** The water footprint of wheat consumption for the major wheat-consuming countries, 1996–2005

| Country | Internal water footprint (million m³/yr) | | | External water footprint (million m³/yr) | | | Water footprint | | WF per capita | Wheat consumption per capita | WF of wheat products |
|---|---|---|---|---|---|---|---|---|---|---|---|
| | Green | Blue | Grey | Green | Blue | Grey | Total (million m³/yr) | Per capita (m³/yr) | Fraction of world average | Fraction of world average | Fraction of world average |
| China | 82,990 | 47,091 | 31,442 | 4,064 | 97 | 450 | 166,134 | 133 | 0.75 | 0.86 | 0.88 |
| India | 42,786 | 78,997 | 19,903 | 931 | 17 | 64 | 142,698 | 135 | 0.76 | 0.66 | 1.15 |
| Russia | 83,967 | 1,112 | 3,152 | 4,915 | 63 | 85 | 93,294 | 635 | 3.59 | 2.67 | 1.33 |
| USA | 64,508 | 3,124 | 7,941 | 1,612 | 15 | 244 | 77,444 | 270 | 1.53 | 1.32 | 1.17 |
| Pakistan | 11,900 | 27,218 | 7,856 | 2,752 | 90 | 259 | 50,075 | 345 | 1.95 | 1.42 | 1.37 |
| Iran | 26,693 | 10,937 | 3,208 | 6,104 | 60 | 504 | 47,506 | 716 | 4.04 | 2.32 | 1.74 |
| Turkey | 38,810 | 2,434 | 3,659 | 2,238 | 54 | 181 | 47,376 | 691 | 3.90 | 2.98 | 1.30 |
| Ukraine | 21,905 | 239 | 955 | 1,021 | 12 | 30 | 24,162 | 496 | 2.80 | 2.78 | 1.01 |
| Australia | 19,671 | 162 | 1,005 | 8 | 1 | 3 | 20,850 | 1,082 | 6.11 | 5.47 | 1.16 |
| Brazil | 6,901 | 3 | 469 | 11,224 | 88 | 788 | 19,473 | 111 | 0.63 | 0.58 | 1.08 |
| Egypt | 1,409 | 5,924 | 2,692 | 6,837 | 274 | 633 | 17,769 | 264 | 1.49 | 1.62 | 0.92 |
| Kazakhstan | 17,312 | 124 | 1 | 83 | 1 | 7 | 17,528 | 1,156 | 6.53 | 3.92 | 1.85 |
| Italy | 8,274 | 114 | 1,284 | 6,837 | 165 | 697 | 17,371 | 300 | 1.69 | 2.35 | 0.70 |
| Poland | 9,687 | 4 | 4,478 | 572 | 7 | 94 | 14,842 | 386 | 2.18 | 2.48 | 0.87 |
| Morocco | 9,923 | 877 | 383 | 3,230 | 68 | 306 | 14,787 | 505 | 2.85 | 2.21 | 1.29 |
| Germany | 9,459 | 0 | 2,868 | 810 | 13 | 120 | 13,270 | 161 | 0.91 | 2.07 | 0.43 |
| World | 593,599 | 196,690 | 106,972 | 166,703 | 7,147 | 16,586 | 1,087,697 | 177 | | | |

Source: Mekonnen and Hoekstra (2010)

were Brazil, Japan, Egypt, Italy, the Republic of Korea and Iran. Together these countries account for about 28 per cent of the total external water footprint. Japan's water footprint related to wheat consumption lies outside the country for about 93 per cent. In Italy, with an average wheat consumption of 150 kg/yr per person, more than two times the world average, this was about 44 per cent. Most African, Southeast Asian, Caribbean and Central American countries strongly rely on external water resources for their wheat consumption as shown in Figure 3.3.

## The water footprint of Italian wheat consumption

Italy is an important wheat consuming country, particularly because of the various sorts of pasta that are a large part of the Italian diet. Wheat consumption in Italy amounts to 150 kg of wheat/year, which is about 400 g/day (FAO, 2012a). The country is the one of the biggest wheat importers of the world. Italy's water footprint related to the consumption of wheat products for the period 1996–2005 was 17.4 billion m³/yr. Nearly half (44 per cent) of the water footprint of Italian wheat consumption lies in other countries, mainly the USA (20 per cent), France (19 per cent), Canada (11 per cent) and Russia (10 per cent). The water footprint of Italy's wheat consumers in the USA lies in different regions of that country, among others in the Ogallala area as earlier shown in Figure 3.1. Italy also imports virtual water from the water-scarce countries of the Middle East, such as Syria (58 million m³/yr) and Iraq (36 million m³/yr). Still, more than half of the water footprint of Italian wheat consumption lies within the country itself. Growing wheat in Italy contributes 20 per cent to the total water footprint of crop production in the country (Mekonnen and Hoekstra, 2011b). A lot of the wheat grown in Italy is durum wheat, used for making pasta.

## The water footprint of Italian pasta

Durum wheat is an annual grass very similar to bread wheat but with larger, harder grains, a higher protein content and a different chromosome number (Van Wyk, 2005). It is cultivated in relatively dry regions and harvested in the same way as wheat and other cereals. Italian durum wheat is cultivated mainly in southern Italy (ISTAT, 2008). The national average green water footprint of durum wheat is 748 litres/kg; the blue water footprint is 525 litres/kg. Regional differences in both total water consumption and the green–blue ratios, however, are substantial. Most durum wheat is grown in Puglia and Sicily; the blue water footprint in these regions constitutes nearly half of the total consumptive water footprint. In northern Italy, in regions like Toscana and Marche, about a quarter of the consumptive water use is blue water. The total water footprint per kilogram is much larger in southern Italy compared to northern Italy.

In wheat growing, generally large amounts of fertilizers and pesticides are used. One of the key nutrients applied is nitrogen. Nitrate is essential for plant growth but excessive and careless application results in substantial amounts leaching to

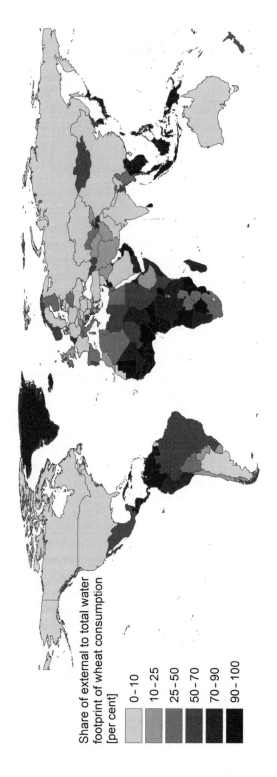

Share of external to total water
footprint of wheat consumption
[per cent]

0–10

10–25

25–50

50–70

70–90

90–100

**FIGURE 3.3** The extent to which countries rely on external water resources for their wheat consumption, 1996–2005

Source: Mekonnen and Hoekstra (2010)

groundwater or running off over the surface to streams, thus leading to the deterioration of water quality. The grey water footprint shows the volume of water required to assimilate chemicals that reach the water system. Based on the average nitrogen fertilizer application rate, an assumed leaching percentage of 10 per cent and a nitrogen water quality standard of 10 mg/litre, the grey water footprint of durum wheat in Italy has been estimated to be about 300 litres/kg (Table 3.7). This is a conservative estimate in two respects. First, the assimilation capacity of water bodies has been overestimated by assuming the natural background concentration of nitrate to be zero. Second, the effect of the use of other nutrients, pesticides and herbicides has not been analysed.

Summing up the green, blue and grey water footprint of durum wheat, we arrive at an estimated total of 1,574 litres/kg (Table 3.8). For pasta, the durum wheat grains need to be processed into flour. The wheat is milled in such a way that the grain is separated into bran, germ and semolina (flour). About 72 per cent of the original durum wheat weight becomes semolina. The semolina constitutes 88 per cent of the total value of the two separate products. Given a total water footprint of durum wheat of 1,574 litres/kg, we can calculate that the water footprint of semolina is $(1,574 \times 0.88/0.72 =)$ 1,924 litres/kg. The green component in this total figure is 48 per cent, the blue component 33 per cent and the grey component 19 per cent.

Authentic pasta is durum semolina to which various liquids (water, milk or eggs) are added. Pasta can be found in dried and fresh varieties depending on what the recipes call for. Pasta is dried in a process at specific temperature and time. Traditional pasta is allowed to dry slower, up to 50 hours at a much lower temperature than mass-produced pasta, which is dried at very high temperatures for a

**TABLE 3.7** Nitrogen application and the associated grey water footprint for the production of wheat in Italy

| Type of wheat | N fertilizer application rate | Area | Total N fertilizer applied | Nitrogen reaching water bodies | N standard | Volume of dilution water required | Production | Grey water footprint |
|---|---|---|---|---|---|---|---|---|
| | kg/ha | ha | tonne/yr | tonne/yr | mg/l | $10^6 \ m^3/yr$ | tonne/yr | litre/kg |
| Bread wheat | 82 | 629,778 | 51,642 | 5,164 | 10 | 516 | 3,111,352 | 166 |
| Durum wheat | 82 | 1,612,706 | 132,242 | 13,224 | 10 | 1,322 | 4,387,863 | 301 |

Source: Aldaya and Hoekstra (2010). Harvest area and production from ISTAT (2008) for the period 1999–2007. Fertilizer application rate from FAO (2012c) for the period 1999–2000. The N standard is the standard for $NO_3^-$ measured as mg N per litre from EPA (2009), which is more or less equivalent to the standard of 50 mg $NO_3^-$ per litre as in the European Union.

**TABLE 3.8** The water footprint of wheat and wheat flour made in Italy

| Type of wheat | Water footprint (litre/kg) | | | |
| --- | --- | --- | --- | --- |
| | Green | Blue | Grey | Total |
| Bread wheat | 495 | 125 | 166 | 786 |
| Bread wheat flour | 605 | 154 | 202 | 961 |
| Durum wheat | 748 | 525 | 301 | 1,574 |
| Durum wheat flour (semolina) | 914 | 642 | 368 | 1,924 |

Source: Aldaya and Hoekstra (2010)

short time. Let us consider a pasta made from semolina (1 kg), water (0.5 litres) and salt. The water is removed later again when drying the pasta. The water volume used in the pasta processing is very small if compared to the water quantity used in the durum wheat production. The water footprint of dry pasta is therefore about equal to that of the semolina it is made from, which is 1,924 litres/kg.

Taking into account that Italians eat on average 28 kg of pasta every year, the water footprint of pasta consumption by an Italian inhabitant is 54,000 litres/yr (Aldaya and Hoekstra, 2010). In relative terms, this is about 2 per cent of the average Italian water footprint (2,300 m³/yr per person). Given an Italian population of almost 60 million people, the water footprint of Italian pasta consumption amounts to about 3,200 million m³/yr. This quantity is equivalent to the volume of water required to fill more than 1 million Olympic-size swimming pools (one pool contains 2,500 m³ of water).

## Bread wheat versus durum wheat

Bread wheat, applied for making bread but also for the base of pizzas, is quite different from durum wheat when it comes to its water use. Compared to durum wheat, bread wheat consumes half of the amount of water per kilogram. This is mainly due to differences in yields and production conditions. Bread wheat is an annual crop adapted to a wet winter and rain-free summer (Van Wyk, 2005) and is mainly produced in the northern part of Italy (with the largest part in Emilia Romagna), whereas durum wheat is mostly produced in the (drier) southern regions. In general, crop yields in the north of Italy are higher than in the south, while evaporation is less.

Adding the green, blue and grey component of the water footprint gives a total water footprint of Italian bread wheat of 786 litres/kg (Table 3.8). When the grains are ground into flour, 72 per cent of the original wheat weight becomes flour; the remaining 18 per cent are the wheat pellets. The wheat flour constitutes 88 per cent of the total value of the two different products. Given a total water footprint of bread wheat of 786 litres/kg, we can calculate that the water footprint of bread wheat flour is $(786 \times 0.88/0.72 =)$ 961 litres/kg. Since 1 kg of flour gives 1.15 kg of bread, the water footprint of Italian bread is 836 litres kg (larger than for bread from France, the Netherlands or Germany, but smaller than the global average).

We also looked into the water footprint of pizza, the base of which is made from bread wheat flour. The basic ingredients for cooking a *pizza margherita* are bread wheat flour, tomato puree and mozzarella from cow's milk. Based on the average figures for its ingredients, we estimated that the water footprint of a *pizza margherita* is 1,216 litres (Aldaya and Hoekstra, 2010). About a quarter of this total refers to the water footprint of the pizza base made from bread wheat flour.

## Concerns over water use for Italian wheat production

In Italy, the availability of water varies a lot across regions. Like in all Mediterranean countries, the seasonal and regional variability of rainfall is extremely high. In the north of Italy, water is relatively abundant, whilst the south faces a considerably lower availability of water and an extremely high seasonal variability of runoff. Considering water quality, the situation is again differentiated throughout the country. In general, the biological and chemical quality of the largest rivers is poor, and the number of polluted sites has increased, spreading even outside highly urbanized areas. Pollution in the north and the centre is mostly due to industrial and agricultural activities (Goria and Lugaresi, 2002). Nitrate concentrations over the acceptable threshold established by the European Directive (50 mg/litre) are recorded in several cases, mainly in the coastal plains of the Tiber and Po Rivers. In other regions, particularly in the southern part of Puglia, and in the coastal plains of Campania, Calabria and the island of Sardinia, the main problem is salt intrusion, caused by over-abstraction of groundwater. Most of these problems have been exacerbated by a lack of attention and awareness (Goria and Lugaresi, 2002). Water has been perceived as an infinite, non-exhaustible resource, to be made available at a very low price. Wasteful behaviour has therefore been common and accepted.

The water footprint of durum wheat is concentrated in Puglia and Sicily, which face severe water scarcity. Groundwater abstraction is widespread in both regions. In Puglia, about two-thirds of the water supply comes from groundwater. In Sicily, this is about 40 per cent (ISTAT, 2008). In both Puglia and the coastal plains of Sicily, pervasive aquifer overdraft and water quality problems exist (OECD, 2006). Several aquifers in Sicily are overexploited, such as the case of the Catania plain in eastern Sicily (Ferrara and Pappalardo, 2004). Many of the groundwater extractions relate to private users, who are largely outside the control of the water administration (OECD, 2006). In Italy, there are an estimated 1.5 million illegal wells. In eight regions (Abruzzo, Molise, Puglia, Campania, Basilicata, Calabria, Sicilia and Sardegna) about 830,000 ha are irrigated legally while the total irrigated area reaches about 1.6 million ha. In the Puglia region alone, there are an estimated 300,000 illegal wells, which provide for one-third of the total irrigated area in that region (WWF, 2006). However, aqueducts are also common in these regions. The aqueduct serving Puglia, however, is riddled with so many holes that it leaks more water than it delivers according to a study by the Italian investment bank Mediobanca. The 102-year-old Acquedotto Pugliese, Europe's largest aqueduct with about 16,000 km of conduits, loses 50 per cent of the water it carries. In the south of Italy, the water footprint of durum wheat per unit of production is larger than in the north of the country, due to the high evapotranspiration and lower yields in the south. The large differences in average yield among the regions are mainly due to the different soil and climatic conditions (Bianchi, 1995). The northern parts of Italy are more adequate for the cultivation of durum wheat from the perspective of soil fertility but also because of the larger availability of water.

The story for bread wheat is quite different from that for durum wheat. Bread wheat production is concentrated in the north of Italy, where water is not so scarce as in the south. Besides, bread wheat production mainly relies on green water, not blue water, and production per cubic metre of water is much higher. In summary, the water footprint of wheat production is most severe in southern Italy, in Puglia and Sicily, where groundwater overexploitation for durum wheat irrigation is common. Bread wheat production mainly occurs in northern Italy, where water is used more efficiently and at the same time not so scarce as in the south.

## Lack of appropriate water policy

Water demand in Italy has been stimulated by a number of factors, such as inadequate pricing systems, lack of compliance with water-related legislation, as well as a lack of control by the competent River Basin Authorities, mainly in relation to illegal groundwater withdrawal (WWF, 2006; Bartolini et al., 2007). Regional prices of water in Italy do not reflect the scarcity value of water. Users also do not pay for the negative externalities and opportunity cost of water use (Goria and Lugaresi, 2002). Furthermore, subsidies hinder the move towards new technologies. Raising water tariffs and levying effluent or pollution charges can play significant roles in improving economic efficiency and environmental sustainability of water use (Rogers et al., 1998). Improving Italian irrigation schemes and water collection technology is crucial in limiting the use – and waste – of water. Concerning the lack of compliance with water-related legislation, Italy has been found to not comply with the EU Water Framework Directive, by inadequate or lack of reporting of water pollution, inadequate or lack of wastewater treatment, insufficient designation of sensitive areas and nitrogen surpluses in some regions of Italy in the order of 100–150 kg N/ha per year (EC, 2010). In Italy (northeast) a significant proportion of measured concentrations in ambient water bodies were between 10 and 25 mg $NO_3^-$/litre, which points at a serious risk of eutrophication (EC, 2010).

There are agricultural subsidies that support production and/or the development of irrigation systems, regardless of water availability. The Common Agricultural Policy of the European Union has led to increased water consumption through production-related subsidies which provoked a shift from traditional rain-fed crops to irrigated cultivation in Italy and other southern EU member states (Brouwer *et al.*, 2003). Although the Common Agricultural Policy reforms in the past few years have introduced some regulations towards new approaches for EU agricultural funding (decoupling subsidies and production volume, compliance), in practice national implementations are weakening these changes. It is still to be seen how member states will implement the regulations over the long run.

Food companies can play a role in reducing the water footprint of wheat, not only by reducing the water consumption and pollution in their own operations but, more important, through influencing and engaging with wheat suppliers, to increase the sustainability of water use in wheat production. This can be done for example by promoting rain-fed and organic agriculture, and by shifting to better irrigation techniques and water-saving modes of application where irrigation is required. In Italy, the awareness of the water footprint of pasta can help address the water scarcity problem. Companies should disclose their operational and supply-chain water footprint and their strategy towards reducing their water footprint. Priorities for water footprint reduction should be set based on where water productivities are still relatively low, where pollution is relatively high and where water footprints have the largest local impact. Since the late 1990s, the Italian producers of pasta have been striving to improve the environmental performance of their own operations and, nowadays, this effort is naturally to be extended to the whole supply chain (Bevilacqua *et al.*, 2007).

## Benchmarking the water footprint of wheat

Product transparency is a precondition for consumers to be able to make well-informed decisions on what to buy. Information on the water footprint can increase awareness about the huge volume of water appropriated for the production of different food items and about related environmental impacts. Informed consumers can reduce the impacts of their consumption through selecting the commodities that have a relatively small water footprint or that have a footprint in an area that does not have high water scarcity. Since adequate product information is generally not available in today's world, an important thing consumers can do now is ask product transparency from businesses and regulation from governments. Product transparency, however, is not just to create awareness and enable consumers to take informed consumer decisions. It is also relevant for investors interested in the sustainability of businesses they invest in. Companies relying on unsustainable water use in their supply chain run different sorts of business risks, which is unattractive for investors. Companies that take their social responsibility seriously should aim for good water stewardship, which includes transparency.

In order to understand when water footprints are unnecessarily large, it is important that water footprint benchmarks will be developed, for both final products like pasta and basic ingredients like wheat. Such benchmarks can be inspired by best-available technologies or by current variations in water footprints

(Zwart *et al.*, 2010). Let me give an example of how knowledge about the current variability of water footprints can be used to set benchmarks. The water footprint of wheat in litres per kg is not equal throughout the world. The world average green plus blue water footprint of wheat is 1,620 litres/kg, but we also find values below 600 litres/kg, for instance in large parts of western Europe (Mekonnen and Hoekstra, 2011a). We found that about 10 per cent of the global wheat production is produced with less than 600 litres of green plus blue water per kilogram. About 20 per cent of the global wheat production occurs at green plus blue water footprints of less than 1,000 litres/kg. Depending on the ambition of a food company, it can thus strive for getting wheat supplies with water footprints that fall in either the best tenth or the twentieth percentile of production. It does not mean that supplies are necessarily obtained from regions where this productivity is already achieved. Companies can help farmers anywhere to improve water productivity and thus lower the water footprint per unit of production, based on best-practice examples either nearby or elsewhere.

# 4

# THE MEAT EATER, A BIG WATER USER

Livestock puts a large claim on the planet's natural resources. In *Livestock's Long Shadow*, an influential report from the Food and Agriculture Organization (FAO) of the United Nations, it is figured out that the livestock sector is by far the single largest anthropogenic user of land (Steinfeld *et al.*, 2006). The total area occupied by grazing is equivalent to 26 per cent of the ice-free terrestrial surface of the planet. In addition, feed crop production requires 33 per cent of total arable land. In all, livestock production accounts for 70 per cent of all agricultural land and 30 per cent of the land surface of the planet. In the same report, it is argued that livestock may well be the leading factor in the reduction of global biodiversity. Livestock accounts for 20 per cent of the total terrestrial animal biomass, and the 30 per cent of the Earth's land surface now claimed by farm animals was once habitat for wildlife. Furthermore, the report calculates that the livestock sector is responsible for 18 per cent of anthropogenic greenhouse gas emissions, measured in $CO_2$ equivalents. The latter figure is still subject to debate, due to difficulties in quantification, methodological differences and discussion about what to attribute to the livestock sector (O'Mara, 2011). Estimates actually range from only 3 per cent (Pitesky *et al.*, 2009) to 51 per cent (Goodland and Anhang, 2009) but, after all, it seems that FAO's estimate isn't a bad one (Herrero *et al.*, 2011). Finally, the livestock sector is also very energy intensive. Pimentel and Pimentel (2008) estimate that an average of 25 kcal of fossil energy is required to produce 1 kcal of animal protein, which is ten times greater than the 2.5 kcal of fossil energy required per kcal of plant protein.

The livestock sector puts substantial claims on the world's land and energy resources, contributes significantly to climate change and plays an important role in reducing the world's biodiversity. How about the water needs of farm animals? In our most recent research, we have shown that nearly 30 per cent of the water footprint of humanity is related to the production of animal products (Mekonnen and Hoekstra, 2012a). The global water footprint of animal production amounts to 2,422 billion m$^3$/yr. One-third of this total is related to beef cattle, another 19 per cent to dairy cattle. Surprisingly, there is little attention among scientists or policy makers to the relation between meat and dairy consumption and water use. It becomes increasingly relevant, though, to study the implications of farm animals on water resources use, not only because the global meat production has almost doubled in the period 1980–2004 (FAO, 2005), but also because of the projected doubling of meat production in the period 2000–2050 (Steinfeld *et al.*, 2006).

In this chapter we will examine the hidden water resources use behind meat and dairy. We will consider the supply chain of meat and dairy and, then, because the water footprint of animal feed is by far the most significant component in the water footprint of animals, we will review the importance of feed composition and the so-called 'feed conversion efficiency'. Next, we will compare the water footprint of meat and dairy with the water footprint of crops, in terms of litres per kg, but also in terms of litres per unit of nutritional content. Subsequently, we will compare the water footprint of a meat-based diet with the water footprint of a vegetarian diet. Finally, we will highlight the international character of the livestock-water issue and argue for putting the issue higher on the agenda of consumers, governments and the meat and dairy sector itself.

## The supply chain

The supply chain of meat and dairy starts with feed crop cultivation and ends with the consumer (Figure 4.1). In each step of the chain there is a direct water footprint, which refers to the water consumption in that step, but also an indirect water footprint, which refers to the water consumption in the previous steps. The water footprint of meat and dairy as you buy it in the shop should be understood as the sum of the various sorts of water consumption and pollution along the supply chain. It includes water use at the retailer and the food processor, but the water use in these stages is very small compared to the water use in the agricultural stage. Besides, one should keep in mind that the water use of retailers and food processors is to be distributed over all products being sold, so that the relative small water footprints of those players become even smaller per unit of product. Most water consumption and pollution is thus in the agricultural stage.

The water footprint of an animal at the end of its lifetime can be calculated based on the water footprint of all feed consumed during its lifetime and the volumes of water consumed for drinking and for example cleaning the stables. One will have to know the age of the animal when slaughtered and the diet of the animal during its various stages of life. The water footprint of the animal as a whole is allocated to the different products that are derived from the animal. This allocation is done on the basis of the relative values of the various animal products, as can be calculated from the market prices of the different products. The allocation is done such that there is no double counting and that the largest shares of the total water input are assigned to the high-value products and smaller shares to the low-value products.

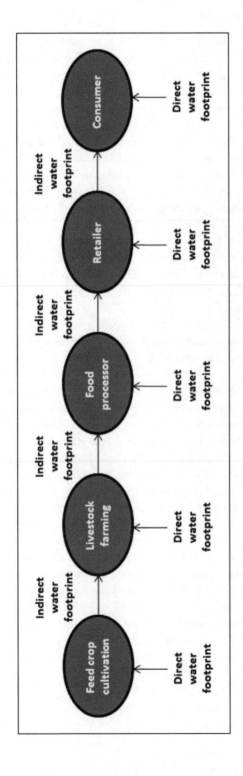

**FIGURE 4.1** The direct and indirect water footprint in each stage of the supply chain of an animal product

## The relevance of feed

By far the biggest contribution to the total water footprint of all final animal products comes from the first step in the production chain: growing the feed. The water footprint of feed contributes 98 per cent to the water footprint of meat and dairy as you buy it in the shop. Drinking water for the animals, service water and feed mixing water account for 1.1, 0.8 and 0.03 per cent, respectively (Mekonnen and Hoekstra, 2012a). The step of feed production is most far removed from the consumer, which explains why consumers generally have little notion about the fact that animal products require a lot of land and water (Naylor *et al.*, 2005). Besides, the feed will often be grown in areas completely different from where the consumption of the final product takes place. Much of the grains cultivated in the world are not for human consumption but for animals. In the period 2001–2007, on average 37 per cent of the cereals produced in the world were used for animal feed (FAO, 2012a).

There are two major determining factors for the water footprint of animal products (Mekonnen and Hoekstra, 2012a; Hoekstra, 2012). The first factor is the feed conversion efficiency, which measures the amount of feed to produce a given amount of meat, eggs or milk. As animals are generally able to move more and take longer to reach slaughter weight in grazing systems, they consume a greater proportion of food to convert to meat. Due to this, the feed conversion efficiency improves from grazing systems through mixed systems to industrial systems and leads to a smaller water footprint in industrial systems. The second factor works precisely in the other direction, that is in favour of grazing systems. This second factor is the composition of the feed eaten by the animals in each system. When the amount of feed concentrates increases, the water footprint will increase as well, because feed concentrates have a relatively large water footprint, while roughages (grass, crop residues and fodder crops) have a relatively small water footprint. The increasing fraction of animal feed concentrates and decreasing fraction of roughages from grazing through mixed to industrial systems (Hendy *et al.*, 1995) results in a smaller water footprint in grazing and mixed systems compared to industrial systems. In general, the water footprint of concentrates is five times larger than the water footprint of roughages. While the total mixture of roughages has a water footprint of around 200 litres/kg (global average), this is about 1,000 litres/kg for the package of ingredients contained in concentrates. As roughages are mainly rain-fed and crops for concentrates are often irrigated and fertilized, the blue and grey water footprint of concentrates are even 43 and 61 times that of roughages, respectively.

If we take beef as an example, it is clear from the above that the water footprint will strongly vary depending on the feed composition and origin of the feed ingredients. The water footprint of beef from an industrial system may partly refer to irrigation water (blue water) to grow feed in an area remote from where the cow is raised. This can be an area where water is abundantly available, but it may also be an area where water is scarce and where minimum environmental flow requirements are not met due to overdraft. The water footprint of beef from a grazing system will mostly refer to rainwater (green water) used in nearby pastures. If the pastures used are either drylands or wetlands that cannot be used for crop cultivation, the green water flow turned into meat could not have been used to produce food crops instead. If, however, the pastures can be substituted by cropland, the green water allocated to meat production is no longer available for food-crop production. This explains why the water footprint is to be seen as a multi-dimensional indicator. One should not only look at the total water footprint as a volumetric value, but also consider the green, blue and grey components separately and look at where each of the water footprint components are located. The social and ecological impacts of water use at a certain location depend on the scarcity and alternative uses of water at that location.

## The water footprint of animal products versus crop products

As we have recently quantified, the water footprint of any animal product is larger than the water footprint of a wisely chosen crop product with equivalent nutritional value (Mekonnen and Hoekstra, 2012a). This can be illustrated for example by comparing the water footprint of two soya products with two equivalent animal products (Ercin *et al.*, 2012). We calculated that 1 litre of soyamilk produced in Belgium has a water footprint of about 300 litres, whereas the water footprint of 1 litre of cow's milk is more than three times bigger. The water footprint of a 150 g soya burger produced in the Netherlands appears to be about 160 litres, while the water footprint of an average 150 g beef burger is nearly 15 times bigger. Table 4.1 shows the global average water footprint of a number of crop and animal products. The numbers show that the average water footprint per calorie for beef is 20 times larger than for cereals and starchy roots. The water footprint per gram of protein for milk, eggs and chicken meat is about 1.5 times larger than for pulses. For beef, the water footprint per gram of protein is six times larger than for pulses. Butter has a relatively small water footprint per gram of fat, even lower than for oil crops, but all other animal products have larger water footprints per gram of fat when compared to oil crops.

## The water footprint of a meat versus vegetarian diet

Dietary habits greatly influence the overall water footprint of people. In industrialized countries, the average calorie consumption is about 3,400 kcal/day (FAO, 2012a); roughly 30 per cent of that comes from animal products. When we assume that the average daily portion of animal products is a reasonable mix of beef, pork, poultry, fish, eggs and dairy products, we can estimate that 1 kcal of animal product requires roughly 2.5 litres of water on average. Products from vegetable origin, on the other hand, require roughly 0.5 litres of water per kcal, this time assuming a reasonable mix of cereals, pulses, roots, fruit and vegetables. Under these circumstances, producing the food for one day costs 3,600 litres of water (Table 4.2). For the vegetarian diet we assume that a smaller fraction is of animal origin (not

**TABLE 4.1** The global average water footprint of crop and animal products

| Food item | Water footprint per unit of weight (litre/kg) | | | | Nutritional content | | | Water footprint per unit of nutritional value | | |
|---|---|---|---|---|---|---|---|---|---|---|
| | Green | Blue | Grey | Total | Calorie (kcal/kg) | Protein (g/kg) | Fat (g/kg) | Calorie (litre/kcal) | Protein (litre/g protein) | Fat (litre/g fat) |
| Sugar crops | 130 | 52 | 15 | 197 | 285 | 0 | 0 | 0.69 | 0 | 0 |
| Vegetables | 194 | 43 | 85 | 322 | 240 | 12 | 2.1 | 1.34 | 26 | 154 |
| Starchy roots | 327 | 16 | 43 | 386 | 827 | 13 | 1.7 | 0.47 | 31 | 226 |
| Fruits | 726 | 147 | 89 | 962 | 460 | 5.3 | 2.8 | 2.09 | 180 | 348 |
| Cereals | 1,232 | 228 | 184 | 1,644 | 3,208 | 80 | 15 | 0.51 | 21 | 112 |
| Oil crops | 2,023 | 220 | 121 | 2,364 | 2,908 | 146 | 209 | 0.81 | 16 | 11 |
| Pulses | 3,180 | 141 | 734 | 4,055 | 3,412 | 215 | 23 | 1.19 | 19 | 180 |
| Nuts | 7,016 | 1,367 | 680 | 9,063 | 2,500 | 65 | 193 | 3.63 | 139 | 47 |
| Milk | 863 | 86 | 72 | 1,021 | 560 | 33 | 31 | 1.82 | 31 | 33 |
| Eggs | 2,592 | 244 | 429 | 3,265 | 1,425 | 111 | 100 | 2.29 | 29 | 33 |
| Chicken meat | 3,545 | 313 | 467 | 4,325 | 1,440 | 127 | 100 | 3.00 | 34 | 43 |
| Butter | 4,695 | 465 | 393 | 5,553 | 7692 | 0 | 872 | 0.72 | 0 | 6.4 |
| Pig meat | 4,907 | 459 | 622 | 5,988 | 2,786 | 105 | 259 | 2.15 | 57 | 23 |
| Sheep/goat meat | 8,253 | 457 | 53 | 8,763 | 2,059 | 139 | 163 | 4.25 | 63 | 54 |
| Bovine meat | 14,414 | 550 | 451 | 15,415 | 1,513 | 138 | 101 | 10.19 | 112 | 153 |

Source: Mekonnen and Hoekstra (2012a)

**TABLE 4.2** The water footprint of two different diets in industrialized countries

|  | Meat diet | | | Vegetarian diet | | |
|---|---|---|---|---|---|---|
|  | kcal/day | litre/kcal | litre/day | kcal/day | litre/kcal | litre/day |
| Animal origin | 950 | 2.5 | 2,375 | 300 | 2.5 | 750 |
| Vegetable origin | 2,450 | 0.5 | 1,225 | 3,100 | 0.5 | 1,550 |
| Total | 3,400 | | 3,600 | 3,400 | | 2,300 |

Source: Hoekstra (2010a)

zero, because of dairy products still consumed), but keep all other factors equal. This reduces the food-related water footprint to 2,300 litres/day, which means a reduction of 36 per cent. Keeping in mind that for the 'meat eater' we had taken the average diet of a whole population and that meat consumption varies within a population, larger water savings can be achieved by individuals that eat more meat than the average person.

From the above figures it is obvious that consumers can reduce their water footprint through reducing the volume of their meat consumption. Alternatively, however, or in addition, consumers can reduce their water footprint by being more selective in the choice of which piece of meat they pick. Chickens are less water-intensive than cows, and beef from one production system cannot be compared in terms of associated water impacts to beef from another production system.

## The international character of meat, dairy and water

Due to the international trade in feed, live animals and animal products, the consumption of meat or dairy in a certain place is often related to water use elsewhere. Regarding live animals, for example, Australia exports millions of sheep to the Middle East each year. The USA imports millions of cattle and pigs each year, mainly from Canada and Mexico. Within Europe, millions of different sorts of farm animals are taken on long journeys throughout the continent (Millstone and Lang, 2003). But the trade in processed animal products is even more intensive. We calculated that the total international virtual water flows related to global trade in live animals and animal products together add up to 272 billion $m^3$/yr, a volume equivalent to about half the annual Mississippi runoff (Mekonnen and Hoekstra, 2011b). About 16 per cent of this relates to trade in live animals; 84 per cent relates to trade in animal products. Not only livestock and livestock products are internationally traded, also feed crops are traded (Galloway et al., 2007). In trade statistics, however, it is difficult to distinguish between food and feed crops, because they are mostly the same crops, only the application is different. Worldwide, trade in crops and crop products results in international virtual water flows that add up to 1,766 billion $m^3$/yr (Mekonnen and Hoekstra, 2011b), a substantial amount of which must relate to feed.

Animals are often fed with a variety of feed ingredients and feed supply chains are difficult to trace. So unless we have milk, cheese, eggs or meat from an animal that was raised locally and that grazed locally or was otherwise fed with locally grown stuff, it is hard to quantify and localize precisely the water footprint of such products. The increasing complexity of our food system, and the animal product system in particular, hides the existing links between the food we buy and the resource use and associated impacts that underlie it. Therefore, more transparency about feed composition and feed origin is a precondition for a better understanding of how animal products from different production systems and different locations put pressure on scarce freshwater resources.

## Meat and dairy: the blind spot in the water sector

Water managers never talk about meat or dairy. The reason is obvious: livestock farmers are not big water users. It is the feed that takes so much water. Although meat and dairy together contribute more than a quarter to the global water footprint of humanity, it is hardly visible, because most of it is accounted under crop farming. The fact that 37 per cent of the cereals produced in the world are used for animal feed remains under the surface, known by professionals in the agricultural sector, but not by professionals in the water sector. Water managers don't see the difference between water use for growing food and water use for growing feed. The crops are often the same and the essential question for water managers is how to make sure there is sufficient water for crops; they don't address the question why crops are grown. If water managers were smart enough to look a bit further, they would recognize that addressing the issue of increasing scarcity of freshwater resources should include a careful examination of the water needs for meat and dairy. It may well be that good water policy means good policy regarding the growth of the meat and dairy sector. The current state of play is that there does not exist a national water plan in the world addressing the issue that meat and dairy are among the most water-intensive consumer products, let alone that national water policies somehow involve consumers or the meat and dairy industry in this respect. Water policies are often focused on 'sustainable production' but they seldom address 'sustainable consumption'. They address the issue of water-use efficiency within agriculture (more crop per drop), but hardly ever the issue of water-use efficiency in the food system as a whole (more kcal per drop).

While governments are blind regarding the claim of meat and dairy on the world's freshwater resources, the meat and dairy sectors have the same blindness. The interest in the water footprint in the food sector is growing rapidly, but most interest thus far comes from the beverage sector. Obviously, it is not in the immediate interest of an economic sector to be recognized as the number-one contributor to the water footprint of humanity but, in the end, things can better be faced as they are. For a sustainable development of the meat and dairy sector it is crucial that it recognizes its critical role in helping to solve the overexploitation and pollution of freshwater resources. For global society at large it is further key to acknowledge that increasing 'efficiency' cannot be the only road to improvement. The production of meat and dairy on an industrial scale, seemingly more efficient than the more conventional grazing and mixed systems, but based on the increased use of concentrates, leads to a greater demand for irrigation and to more water pollution due to the increased use of fertilizers rather than to less water consumption and pollution. It is a challenge to see how the meat and dairy sectors can be restructured such that they will put lower claims on freshwater but, because of the obvious constraints in making animals 'more efficient', it is probably more important to re-examine the place meat and dairy have in the diet of modern man. The debate on the topic of farm animal products and water can thus not be restricted to governments and the meat and dairy sector, but should involve consumers as well, which means us all.

# 5

# HOW OUR COTTON CLOTHES
# LINK TO A DISAPPEARING SEA

The global average water footprint of cotton fabric is 10,000 litres/kg. That means that one cotton shirt of 250 g costs about 2,500 litres. A pair of jeans of 800 g will cost 8,000 litres. These figures are global averages. The water footprint of cotton fabric varies from place to place. The water footprint of cotton fabric made with cotton from China is 6,000 litres/kg. For cotton from the USA this is 8,100 litres/kg, for Uzbekistan 9,200 litres/kg, Pakistan 9,600 litres/kg and India 22,500 litres/kg (Mekonnen and Hoekstra, 2011a). The proportion of blue water in the water footprint of cotton is relatively large, because cotton is often irrigated. On average, one-third of the water footprint of cotton is blue water. For some countries, the blue water proportion is much larger, like, for example, in Uzbekistan (about 90 per cent) and Pakistan (55 per cent). The blue water use in cotton growing often has great local impacts. The case that we will study in this chapter in some more detail is Central Asia, where excessive abstractions of water from the two main rivers, the Amu Darya and Syr Darya, mainly for cotton irrigation, have resulted in the near-disappearance of the Aral Sea.

Cotton is the most important natural fibre used in textile industries worldwide, contributing 36 per cent of apparel fibres in 2008 (synthetic fibres are the largest category, contributing 56 per cent). The consumption of a cotton product is connected to a chain of impacts on the water resources in the countries where cotton is grown and processed. Growing happens mainly in dry regions, thus requiring substantial irrigation volumes. Many cotton-processing industries are located in developing countries with poor conditions, resulting in great water quality problems, particularly related to the dyes used for colouring. The impacts of cotton production on the environment are easily visible and have different faces: rivers running dry, lake and groundwater levels dropping as a result of overabstractions for irrigation and water quality deterioration as a result of fertilizer and pesticide use in cotton farming and from the use of chemicals in the processing industries.

In 2011, the five leading exporters of cotton were the United States, India, Brazil, Australia and Uzbekistan (NCC, 2012). In the period 1996–2005, global cotton production contributed 3 per cent to the total water footprint of crop production in the world (Mekonnen and Hoekstra, 2011a). Global production of cotton products required 233 billion $m^3$ of water per year, out of which about 57 per cent was consumption of green water, 32 per cent consumption of blue water and 11 per cent water to assimilate nitrogen fertilizer. This estimate still excludes the grey water footprint from the textile industries.

For most consumers, the impacts of their cotton are not nearby, because cotton is often imported from other countries. In the European Union, for example, where little cotton is grown, most of the water footprint of cotton consumption is located outside Europe, with major impacts particularly in India and Uzbekistan, but also in Pakistan, Turkey, China, Syria, Turkmenistan and Egypt (Chapagain et al., 2006b). In most of the European countries, there is no cotton farming at all, so that 100 per cent of the cotton comes from elsewhere. Take for instance the United Kingdom, where all cotton is imported. Figure 5.1 shows how the blue water footprint of cotton consumed in the UK can be localized in different regions of the world. The most important growing regions of irrigated cotton consumed in the UK are Turkey and India.

If there is one single crop to be elected for its most disastrous effects on natural water flows and water quality in river basins, cotton has a good chance of winning. The blame is of course not on cotton, but on the people that have decided to grow it at too large a scale in unsuitable regions. When it comes to the question *who* precisely is to be blamed, it becomes a bit difficult. Farmers are the ones who actually use the water and apply fertilizers and pesticides, but governments have been promoting intensive farming practices at unsuitable locations, enabling it by developing irrigation infrastructure and providing subsidies. Furthermore, the apparel industry and consumers have contributed to the race to the bottom, whereby prices of cotton clothing are often extremely low, making it hard for farmers and small manufacturers to adopt better technologies. The interest in sustainable consumption and production has been marginal, but is fortunately growing. The awareness among cotton consumers about remote impacts is still low. A major problem is the complexity of the world cotton market, whereby it is hardly possible to trace the origin of the cotton for an individual shirt or pair of jeans (Rivoli, 2005). Most retailers and brands have no idea where the cotton with which they work was grown. Sometimes they know the source country or region, but in order to know the sustainability of a specific batch of cotton, one would need to know more, because there can be large differences in the performance of individual farmers from a certain region, caused for instance by the technique, amount and mode of irrigation and the practice of applying chemicals. Good examples of cotton growing do exist, but are not mainstream. Not all cotton is grown in areas with too little rain and too large irrigation demand. Not all cotton is grown with an overkill of artificial fertilizer and pesticides, witness for example the efforts in organic farming.

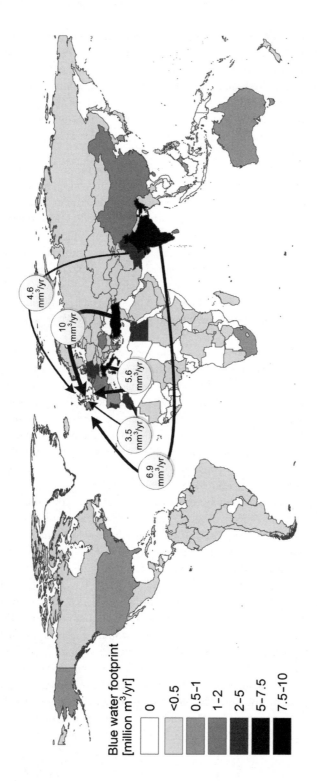

**FIGURE 5.1** The global blue water footprint of UK's cotton consumption, 1996–2005. The arrows represent the biggest virtual water flows to the UK related to cotton imports

Source: Mekonnen and Hoekstra (2011a)

## The disappearing Aral Sea

If there is one case of water overexploitation in the world to be elected as the worst example, the honour will probably go to the disappearing Aral Sea in Central Asia, a problem that is closely connected to cotton growing. The shrinking of the Aral Sea is mainly due to the increase in irrigation to produce cotton for export. As part of the central planning in the former Soviet Union, it was decided to have the desert bloom and made profitable. Since the 1960s, the irrigated area has grown to eight million hectares, using practically the entire available flow of the two main rivers, the Amu Darya and Syr Darya (UNESCO, 1998). The diminishing Aral Sea is the most visible sign of the environmental disaster of the Aral Sea Basin, even visible from space (Figure 5.2). The area of the sea in the Amu Darya Delta decreased from 400,000 ha in 1960 to 26,000 ha in 2001 (CAWater, 2012). The lacustrine ecosystem ceased to exist, the wetlands have disappeared or are heavily damaged, with serious consequences on economic activity and health (Nandalal and Hipel, 2007). The loss of soil productivity is of immediate concern. The polluted water in the rivers and the sand storms from the contaminated soil constitute health risks, particularly as good-quality drinking water is lacking in large areas of the basin (UNESCO, 1998). The five arid and semi-arid states of the Aral Sea Basin now

 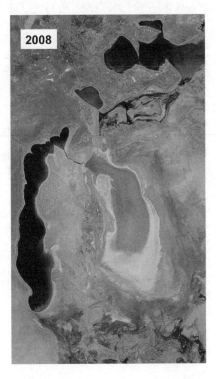

**FIGURE 5.2** The disappearance of the Aral Sea as visible from space

Source: NASA

have to rehabilitate the environment, at the same time caring for the subsistence and progress of the increasing population. Sustainable water management is thus an imperative, to be supported by coordinated political action of all the states involved (UNESCO, 2000).

Central Asia largely coincides with the geographical borders of the Aral Sea Basin, which completely includes the territories of Tajikistan, Uzbekistan, a large part of Turkmenistan, Kyrgyzstan and the south of Kazakhstan. In this arid to semi-arid region, agriculture is the main water-consuming sector. Wheat, cotton and fodder crops like alfalfa are the crops that take up most of the water. The five Central Asian countries are highly agrarian, with 60 per cent of the population living in rural areas and agriculture accounting for over 45 per cent of the total number of employed people (Lerman and Stanchin, 2006). In Kyrgyzstan, Tajikistan and Uzbekistan, agriculture contributes about 20 per cent to the GDP (in 2011). Kazakhstan, with its strong energy sector, has a less agrarian economy than the other Central Asian countries, with agriculture accounting for 5 per cent of GDP (in 2011), but still 26 per cent of total employment (CIA, 2012).

Since independence, the area of irrigated land has not changed significantly in the Central Asian states. The only exception is Turkmenistan, where the area of irrigated land during 1995–1996 increased by about 400,000 ha. Conversely, in Uzbekistan, Kyrgyzstan and particularly Tajikistan, substantial amounts of land have been put out of irrigation due to infrastructure decay as a result of a lack of maintenance. There has been some change in the crop pattern in the region. Cotton still remains one of the most important crops, but its share of irrigated agriculture decreased. However, the area under cereals (wheat, rice, maize and others) increased (CAWater, 2012).

## The water footprint of agriculture in Central Asia

The agricultural sector in Central Asia is responsible for over 90 per cent of the total water footprint in the region (Table 5.1). Wheat and cotton together

**TABLE 5.1** The water footprint in Central Asia, 1996–2005 (billion m$^3$/yr)

| Country | Water footprint of domestic water supply | Water footprint of industrial production | Water footprint of agricultural production | Largest water consumer(s) |
|---------|---------|---------|---------|---------|
| Kazakhstan | 0.59 | 5.8 | 67.7 | Wheat, fodder |
| Kyrgyzstan | 0.29 | 0.23 | 10.3 | Wheat, fodder |
| Tajikistan | 0.44 | 0.56 | 9.2 | Cotton |
| Turkmenistan | 0.42 | 0.19 | 14.7 | Cotton |
| Uzbekistan | 2.77 | 1.2 | 38.3 | Cotton |

Source: Mekonnen and Hoekstra (2011b)

contribute 56 per cent to the crop-related water footprint in the five countries. In Kazakhstan and Kyrgyzstan, wheat and fodder are the most important water users, but in Tajikistan, Turkmenistan and Uzbekistan, cotton is the most important. In the latter three countries, cotton contributes 40 per cent to the total crop-related water footprint and more than half of the total crop-related *blue* water footprint (Mekonnen and Hoekstra, 2011a).

Out of the total land resources of about 155 million hectares, about 8 million hectares are irrigated (that is 5 per cent of total territory of the Aral Sea Basin) (CAWater, 2012). The non-irrigated areas (pastures, hay, meadows, long-term fallow land) occupy about 54 million hectares. This area includes some 2 million hectares of rain-fed arable land, but its productivity is on average no more than one-tenth of the productivity of irrigated land. At the moment, the rain-fed land does not play any significant role in the total agricultural production in the Aral Sea Basin, with the exception of extensive (semi-nomadic) livestock husbandry (cattle and sheep) (CAWater, 2012). Nonetheless, raising productivity of non-irrigated (rain-fed) lands is an important goal. Some crops, like wheat, which at the moment are being increasingly grown in the irrigated areas, could be moved to non-irrigated areas, thus reducing substantially the volume of irrigation water withdrawn in the basin.

## The importance of cotton

In earlier times, Uzbekistan, Turkmenistan, Tajikistan and Kyrgyzstan were considered the cotton zone of the Soviet Union, and cotton remains an important commodity in the region (Figure 5.3), but grain production has become increasingly important since the republics became independent in 1991 and set grain self-sufficiency as a national priority. The area sown to cotton has slightly decreased over the recent past, while that of wheat – the chief grain crop – has increased.

Cotton remains a strategically important commodity for the three largest producing countries (Uzbekistan, Turkmenistan and Tajikistan). Uzbekistan is still one of the largest cotton exporters in the world (NCC, 2012). Every year, the country produces around 3.5 million tons of raw cotton and sells some 1 million tons of cotton fibre, generating more than US$ 1 billion – equivalent to half of the national budget revenues. The price of cotton in Central Asia was on average 840 US$/tonne during the period 1997–2007. Prices of rice and wheat were 720 and 270 US$/tonne, respectively (FAO, 2012a). When looking at the economic blue water productivity per crop type, we see that cotton has the highest value per water unit (about 0.5 US$/m$^3$). Rice and wheat display an average productivity of less than 0.2 and 0.1 US$/m$^3$, respectively.

## Cotton's water footprint

Cotton is mainly produced in the southern region of the Aral Sea Basin, using primarily blue water resources. It is precisely in the southern part of the region where

Harvested area (million ha)

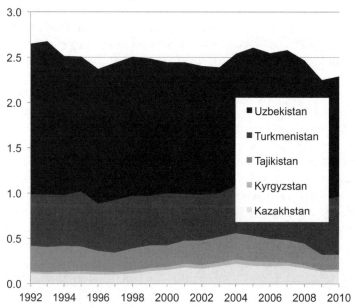

Production (million tonnes/yr)

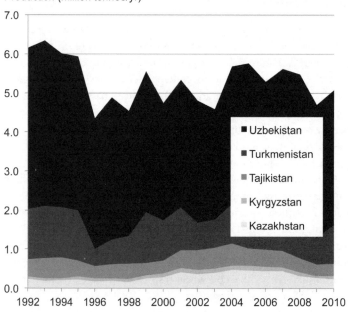

**FIGURE 5.3** Harvested area and production of cotton in the five Central Asian countries, 1992–2010

Source: FAO (2012a)

the water footprint of cotton is relatively large: largest in Turkmenistan, followed by Tajikistan and Uzbekistan. In Turkmenistan, the average blue water footprint over the period 1992–2007 was found to be 6,875 litres/kg of seed cotton, while the green water footprint was 191 litres/kg (Aldaya *et al.*, 2010b). Cotton's water footprint per kilogram was found to be smallest in Kazakhstan, where the blue water footprint is 1,461 litres/kg and the green water footprint 962 litres/kg (Table 5.2). This smaller footprint can be partly explained by the lower evapotranspiration in Kazakhstan.

Uzbekistan is the main water-consuming country in relation to cotton production, responsible for 60 per cent of the total water consumed for cotton in the region. From the total volume of water used for cotton production in Uzbekistan, a great amount is exported to various parts of the world (Figure 5.4). This means that non-water policies, like economic and trade policy, can have major impacts on overall water use (Abdullaev *et al.*, 2009). Wise water use will only result from tuning different sector policies – water, agricultural, economic and trade policies – in such a way that they all work in the same direction. The major challenge of agricultural developments in Central Asia is to preserve the environment in the long term without damaging the economy.

## Benchmarking the water footprint of seed cotton

Based on worldwide data on cotton production and associated water consumption and pollution, we can develop reasonable benchmarks for the water footprint of seed cotton. The global average green plus blue water footprint of seed cotton is 3,600 litres/kg. The best 10 per cent of the globally produced seed cotton, however, has a green–blue water footprint of 1,670 litres/kg or less. The best 20 per cent has a green–blue water footprint of 1,820 litres/kg or less. In Uzbekistan, the largest cotton producer in Central Asia, the green–blue water footprint is 4,426 litres/kg of seed cotton (Table 5.2). In Turkmenistan and Tajikistan, the next most important cotton producers, the situation is much worse. In other words, just from a water productivity point of view alone, cotton production in Central Asia does not belong to the better part of cotton production in the world. The worst 20 per cent of cotton production in the world has a green–blue water footprint of about 5,000 litres/kg, a value that is surpassed by producers in Turkmenistan and Tajikistan. This all shows that there is ample room for improvement in cotton production in Central Asia. There is nothing special in the region that justifies such low water productivities compared to other regions in the world. If the three most important cotton producing countries in the region – with, on average, a green–blue water footprint of about 5,000 litres/kg of seed cotton – would all manage to reduce the water footprint to the global 20-percentile benchmark of 1,820 litres/kg, the region would reduce cotton-related water use by nearly a factor of three. Cotton farmers, cotton traders, cotton industries and governments should work together to set water footprint reduction targets for cotton from this region, with a clear timeline and investment scheme, whereby funds will need to be generated not only by governments, but also

**TABLE 5.2** Evapotranspiration (ET), crop water use (CWU), yield (Y), production (Prod) and water footprint (WF) of cotton in the five Central Asian countries, 1992–2007

| | $ET_g$ | $ET_b$ | $CWU_g$ | $CWU_b$ | Y | $WF_g$ | $WF_b$ | WF | Prod | $WF_g$ | $WF_b$ | WF |
|---|---|---|---|---|---|---|---|---|---|---|---|---|
| | mm | mm | m³/ha | m³/ha | tonne/ha | litre/kg | litre/kg | litre/kg | mtonne/yr | mm³/yr | mm³/yr | mm³/yr |
| Kazakhstan | 193 | 293 | 1,925 | 2,925 | 2.0 | 962 | 1,461 | 2,423 | 0.3 | 297 | 451 | 749 |
| Kyrgyzstan | 166 | 594 | 1,657 | 5,941 | 2.5 | 665 | 2,384 | 3,049 | 0.1 | 57 | 206 | 263 |
| Tajikistan | 64 | 968 | 641 | 9,680 | 1.7 | 388 | 5,858 | 6,246 | 0.4 | 169 | 2,554 | 2,723 |
| Turkmenistan | 33 | 1,183 | 330 | 11,835 | 1.7 | 191 | 6,875 | 7,067 | 1.0 | 185 | 6,650 | 6,835 |
| Uzbekistan | 60 | 987 | 603 | 9,867 | 2.4 | 255 | 4,171 | 4,426 | 3.6 | 905 | 14,812 | 15,717 |

$ET_g$ = green water evapotranspiration; $ET_b$ = blue water evapotranspiration; ET = total evapotranspiration; $CWU_g$ = green crop water use; $CWU_b$ = blue crop water use; CWU = total crop water use; Y = yield; $WF_g$ = green water footprint; $WF_b$ = blue water footprint; WF = total water footprint; Prod = production.

Sources: yields and production from FAO (2012a); the rest of the data from Aldaya et al. (2010b). Note that production and water footprint figures refer to seed cotton

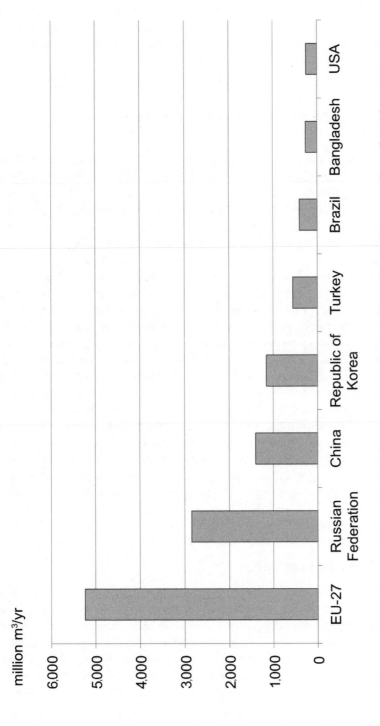

**FIGURE 5.4** The blue water footprint within Uzbekistan related to the production of cotton for export, shown by trade partner

Source: Mekonnen and Hoekstra (2011a)

by the cotton industries. Indirectly, consumers will have to pay the price of their cotton as well. We focused here on the growing stage of cotton. In the processing stages, water is being consumed and polluted as well. Water footprint benchmarks for each stage of the cotton supply chain can be combined into a water footprint benchmark for the final textile as we buy it in the shop. Consumers have the right to know the history of their cotton shirt or pair of jeans, including the extent to which certain production benchmarks along the production chain have been met or not.

## Setting a cap on the blue water footprint in the Aral Sea Basin

Cotton is not the only water-consuming crop in the Aral Sea Basin. The production of cereals and fodder crops takes a lot of water as well. It is the sum of all the water consumption that makes the Aral Sea gradually disappear. Achieving water savings through increased water productivities in crop production is very important, but likely insufficient for two reasons. First, increasing water productivities may not go as quickly as needed. Second, if farmers use less water to achieve a certain production volume, they will probably increase their production volume, thus nullifying the original water saving. Therefore, something else is needed, in addition to reducing the water footprint per kilogram of seed cotton. The governments that share the Aral Sea Basin will need to agree on a certain cap on the blue water footprint within the basin, and put regulations in place to ensure that the actual blue water footprint in the basin will remain below the cap. A 'water footprint cap' is to be understood as a maximum water footprint not to be exceeded, something comparable to a 'carbon footprint cap' or shortly 'carbon cap', although a cap on greenhouse gas emissions is something to be defined at a global level, while a water footprint cap is to be defined at river basin level. In order to increase the feasibility of successful implementation, the blue water footprint cap for the Aral Sea Basin will have to be initially defined at a level substantially below the current blue water footprint in the basin, but not too much below. In order to ensure long-term sustainability, the cap will need to gradually move down to a certain final sustainable level, at which an acceptable Aral Sea water level is maintained over the long term. From this analysis, one thing becomes clear: regional cooperation will be a precondition for sustainability of the region.

## Other fibres than cotton?

The water footprint of cotton fibres is substantially larger than for most other plant fibres. In order to honestly compare, we will compare cotton lint, which is the cotton fibre separated from the cotton seed, with other plant fibres. The global average water footprint of seed cotton is 4,030 litres/kg (the sum of green, blue and grey). The seed cotton is split into cotton seed (63 per cent of the weight, 21 per cent of the economic value) and cotton lint (35 per cent of the weight, 79 per cent of the economic value). The water footprint of the cotton lint can thus be calculated as $(0.79/0.35) \times 4{,}030 = 9{,}100$ litres/kg. In the process from cotton lint to final cotton fabric, there are again some weight losses and byproducts, so that the water footprint of cotton fabric is again a bit larger. In this way we arrive at the 10,000 litres/kg mentioned in the beginning of the chapter when referring to the water footprint of a shirt or pair of jeans. For the purpose of a fair appraisal, we can either compare water footprints per kilogram at the level of the fibres or at the level of the final textile. For the outcome it will make little difference, because the big differences in water use are in the growth of the plants, not in the water use of processing of fibres into final textile. Here, we will compare the water footprint of cotton lint with the water footprint of the fibres of other plants. An overview is given in Table 5.3. From this overview, it is clear that, on average, the water footprint of cotton fibres is a bit larger than the water footprint of sisal and agave fibres, much larger than that of ramie and flax fibres, and much much larger than the water footprints of hemp and jute fibres. We should be careful to jump immediately to the conclusion that we better replace cotton fibres by for example hemp fibres, because fibres are different and textiles made from different fibres have different characteristics. But on the other hand, it shows that it is worth investigating how cotton compares to hemp and other fibres in other respects and to which extent and in which applications cotton can be substituted by other plant fibres. It would also make sense to compare the performance of plant fibres with animal fibres (like different sorts of wool) and synthetic fibres (often made from petroleum), whereby, again, the claim on water resources of a fibre can be just one of a more extended set of criteria.

In summary, in many places in the world, much more water is consumed and polluted in cotton production than necessary. The shrinking of the Aral Sea is a sad example of what can happen when water productivities are poor while, at the same

**TABLE 5.3** The global average water footprint of different plant fibres, 1996–2005

| Product | Global average water footprint (litre/kg) | | | |
|---|---|---|---|---|
| | Green | Blue | Grey | Total |
| Abaca fibre | 21,529 | 273 | 851 | 22,653 |
| Cotton lint | 5,163 | 2,955 | 996 | 9,114 |
| Sisal fibre | 6,791 | 787 | 246 | 7,824 |
| Agave fibre | 6,434 | 9 | 106 | 6,549 |
| Ramie fibre | 3,712 | 201 | 595 | 4,508 |
| Flax fibre | 2,866 | 481 | 436 | 3,783 |
| Hemp fibre | 2,026 | 0 | 693 | 2,719 |
| Jute fibre | 2,356 | 33 | 217 | 2,606 |

Source: Mekonnen and Hoekstra (2011a)

time, cotton production volumes and associated water demands exceed by far the carrying capacity of the basin. Cotton-related overexploitation of water resources is not unique for Central Asia, but can be found all over the world. Together with other irrigated crops, cotton leads to severe water scarcity also for example in the river basins of the Indus (Pakistan), the Tigris-Euphrates (Turkey to Iraq), the Colorado (USA) and the Murray (Australia). Since the nature of the cotton market is global, it is clear that the challenge of moving to a more sustainable system of cotton production and consumption is global as well, whereby consumers could be a constructive drive in the right direction if they would demand for sustainable cotton. Similarly, it would help if the apparel industry takes responsibility as well, by making the market more transparent and by actively engaging with cotton farmers to help them make their business more sustainable.

# 6

# BURNING WATER

## The water footprint of biofuels

The 'water–energy nexus' has recently become a hot topic at water seminars. There is a growing recognition that water policy and energy policy must somehow be related, because energy production requires water, and water supply costs energy. In the past, in fact until today, water and energy policies have most of the time been disconnected altogether. Whereas efforts have been undertaken to improve both water-use efficiency and energy efficiency, we can observe two interesting trends. First, the water sector is becoming more energy-intensive; think for example of the energy needed for pumping groundwater from deeper and deeper, for constructing and moving water through large inter-basin water transfer schemes and for desalination of salt or brackish water. Second, the energy sector is becoming more water-intensive – especially because of the increasing focus on biomass as a source of energy. All energy scenarios for the coming decades show a shift towards an increased percentage of bioenergy.

In this chapter, I will not address the full scope of the water–energy nexus and all the challenges that lie herein. I will focus on the question of how much water is involved in the production of biofuels and how much water it would take to drive our cars, trains and airplanes on bioenergy. I will also briefly consider the water footprint of hydroelectricity, another form of energy with a relatively large water footprint, and the water footprint of other energy carriers (fossil fuels, nuclear, solar and wind).

## Bioenergy

According to our latest research, the water footprint of the agricultural sector, which is mostly related to the production of biomass for food and fibre, contributes 92 per cent to the water footprint of humanity (Hoekstra and Mekonnen, 2012a). In many parts of the world, the use of water for agriculture competes with other uses such as urban supply and industrial activities, while the aquatic environment shows signs of degradation and decline (Postel *et al.*, 1996). An increase in the demand for food in combination with a shift from fossil energy towards bioenergy will put additional pressure on the world's freshwater resources. For the future, hardly any new land is available, so all production must come from the natural resource base currently available (Bruinsma, 2003), requiring a process of sustainable intensification by increasing the efficiency of land and water use.

Globally, many countries explore options to replace gasoline by biofuels (Hughes *et al.*, 2007). The EU, the USA, China and other countries have set targets for the replacement. When agriculture grows crops for bioenergy, however, it needs land and water that cannot be used for food anymore or will subtract from the amount of land and water available to sustain natural vegetation or from the amount of water that flows through our rivers and sustains river-dependent ecosystems and communities. Large-scale cultivation of biomass for the substitution of fossil fuels increases future water demand (Berndes, 2002). An important question is whether we should apply our freshwater resources for the production of bioenergy or food. The World Bank recognizes biofuels production as a major factor driving food prices. It estimates that 75 per cent of the increase of food prices in the period 2002–2008 was due to biofuels (Mitchell, 2008). Raising food prices may lead to decreasing food security of the poor.

The source of bioenergy can be crops specifically grown for that purpose, natural vegetation or organic wastes. Many of the crops used for bioenergy can also – alternatively, not at the same time – be used as food or feed. Biomass can be burnt to produce heat and electricity, but it can also be used for the production of bioethanol or biodiesel, biofuels that can displace fossil energy carriers in motor vehicles (Figure 6.1). Biofuels are often categorized into 'first-generation' and 'next-generation'. First-generation biofuels refer to biofuels made from food crops using conventional technology, which means fermentation of carbohydrates contained in the crop into ethanol or extracting and processing oil from oil crops into biodiesel. First-generation biofuels directly compete with food, because the crops used can also be used as food (or animal feed).

Next-generation biofuels are all those fuels that do not directly compete with food, because they are based on biomass that cannot be eaten. Biomass does not only contain sugar, starch and oil that can be processed into biofuels; it also contains large amounts of cellulosic biomass. This cellulosic fraction of biomass is unsuitable as food. So far, the cellulosic fraction could be used for energy by burning it, to provide heat and produce electricity. It is expected that these cellulosic fractions will form an attractive source for the production of next-generation biofuels, using techniques that are currently under development. Next-generation biofuels concern future available biofuels produced using new technology that aims to convert cellulosic fractions from crops into biofuels (Worldwatch Institute, 2007). In addition, biofuel from algae is considered a next-generation biofuel as well.

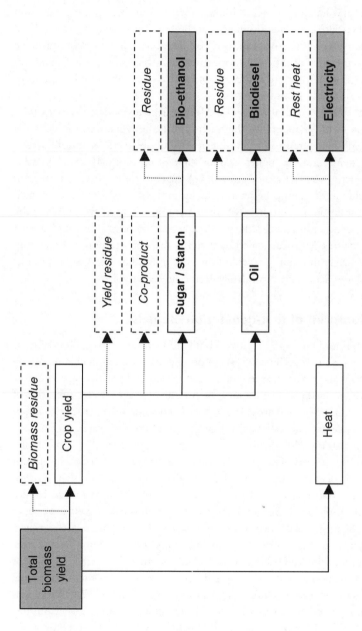

**FIGURE 6.1** The use of biomass for energy. Total biomass yield can be converted into heat and subsequently into electricity. Alternatively, the crop yield, which is part of the total biomass, can be used to produce bioethanol (in the case of starch and sugar crops) or biodiesel (in the case of oil crops). In every step in the production chain, residues or rest heat are generated

Source: Gerbens-Leenes et al. (2009b)

The composition of biomass determines the availability of energy from a specific biomass type, resulting in differences in combustion energy and options for biofuel production. First-generation biofuels are based on processing the sugar, starch or oil contained in crops into either bioethanol or biodiesel. Sugar crops (sugar beet and sugar cane) and starch crops (cereals like barley, maize, rice, rye, sorghum and wheat; and tubers like cassava and potato) can be used for producing ethanol; oil crops (for instance rapeseed, soyabean, palm oil, jatropha) can be used to produce biodiesel. The efficiency of different crops to produce biofuel mainly depends on the crop production per hectare and per cubic metre of water and the content of sugar, starch or oil in the plant biomass.

The ethanol-energy yield of a crop (in MJ/kg) depends on the dry mass fraction in the crop yield (gram/gram), the fraction of carbohydrates in the dry mass of the crop yield (gram/gram), the amount of ethanol obtained per unit of carbohydrate (gram/gram) and the higher heating value of ethanol (MJ/kg). Likewise, the biodiesel-energy yield of a crop (in MJ/kg) depends on the dry mass fraction in the crop yield (gram/gram), the fraction of fats in the dry mass of the crop yield (gram/gram), the amount of biodiesel obtained per unit of fat (gram/gram) and the higher heating value of biodiesel (MJ/kg). The water footprint of ethanol from a crop in terms of litres/MJ is calculated by dividing the water footprint of the crop in litres/kg by the ethanol-energy yield of the crop in MJ/kg. The water footprint of biodiesel-energy from a crop is calculated in a similar way.

## The water footprint of first-generation biofuels

The water footprint of biofuel varies across both crops and countries. The variation is due to differences in crop yields across countries and crops, differences in energy yields across crops and differences in climate and agricultural practices across countries. Table 6.1 shows the global average green, blue and grey water footprint of biofuel for a number of crops providing ethanol and some other crops providing biodiesel. The table presents estimates both in terms of litres of water/litre of biofuel and in terms of litres/MJ. Figure 6.2 ranks the total water footprint of biofuel derived from different sorts of crops. As a general picture, we see that ethanol from sugar crops (sugar beet and sugar cane) has a smaller water footprint than ethanol from starch crops (like maize) and that biodiesels from oil crops mostly have a larger water footprint than bioethanol. Among the crops providing ethanol, sugar beet has the smallest global average water footprint with 1,200 litres of water/litre of ethanol, equivalent to 50 litres/MJ. Bioethanol based on sorghum has the largest water footprint, with 7,000 litres of water/litre of ethanol, which is equivalent to 300 litres/MJ. Among the crops presented here, biodiesel from coconuts has the largest water footprint: 158,000 litres/litre, equivalent to 4,750 litres/MJ. Biodiesels from oil palm, rapeseed and groundnuts are more efficient, with water footprints in the range of 5,000–7,000 litres/litre (150–200 litres/MJ). The largest blue water footprint is observed for biodiesel from cotton: 177 litres/MJ (32 per cent of the total water footprint).

**TABLE 6.1** The global average water footprint of biofuel for ten crops providing ethanol and seven crops providing biodiesel, 1996–2005

| Crop | Water footprint per unit of energy | | | Water footprint per litre of biofuel | | |
|---|---|---|---|---|---|---|
| | Green | Blue | Grey | Green | Blue | Grey |
| *Crops for ethanol* | *litres water/MJ ethanol* | | | *litres water/litre ethanol* | | |
| Barley | 119 | 8 | 13 | 2,796 | 182 | 302 |
| Cassava | 106 | 0 | 3 | 2,477 | 1 | 60 |
| Maize | 94 | 8 | 19 | 2,212 | 190 | 453 |
| Potatoes | 62 | 11 | 21 | 1,458 | 251 | 483 |
| Rice, paddy | 113 | 34 | 18 | 2,640 | 785 | 430 |
| Rye | 140 | 2 | 10 | 3,271 | 58 | 229 |
| Sorghum | 281 | 10 | 9 | 6,585 | 237 | 201 |
| Sugar beet | 31 | 10 | 10 | 736 | 229 | 223 |
| Sugar cane | 60 | 25 | 6 | 1,400 | 575 | 132 |
| Wheat | 126 | 34 | 20 | 2,943 | 789 | 478 |
| *Crops for biodiesel* | *litres water/MJ biodiesel* | | | *litres water/litre biodiesel* | | |
| Coconuts | 4,720 | 3 | 28 | 156,585 | 97 | 935 |
| Groundnuts | 177 | 11 | 12 | 5,863 | 356 | 388 |
| Oil palm | 150 | 0 | 6 | 4,975 | 1 | 190 |
| Rapeseed | 145 | 20 | 29 | 4,823 | 655 | 951 |
| Seed cotton | 310 | 177 | 60 | 10,274 | 5,879 | 1,981 |
| Soyabeans | 326 | 11 | 6 | 10,825 | 374 | 198 |
| Sunflower | 428 | 21 | 28 | 14,200 | 696 | 945 |

Source: Mekonnen and Hoekstra (2011a)

Comparing data for the two main bioethanol producing countries – Brazil and the United States – we find that, in Brazil, ethanol from sugar cane is more efficient than ethanol from maize (1,380 versus 4,077 litres of water/litre of ethanol), while in the United States, maize is more attractive than sugar cane (1,780 versus 2,132 litres/litre). A large amount of different crops is being used as feedstock for biodiesel. Among the popular crops are oil palm (Indonesia and Malaysia), rapeseed (in Europe) and soyabean (in the USA). Biodiesel from soyabean is relatively inefficient, with a water footprint of 11,400 litres of water/ litre of biodiesel, on average. In the USA, where soyabean is the most impor- tant crop being used for biodiesel, the water footprint is a bit smaller than the

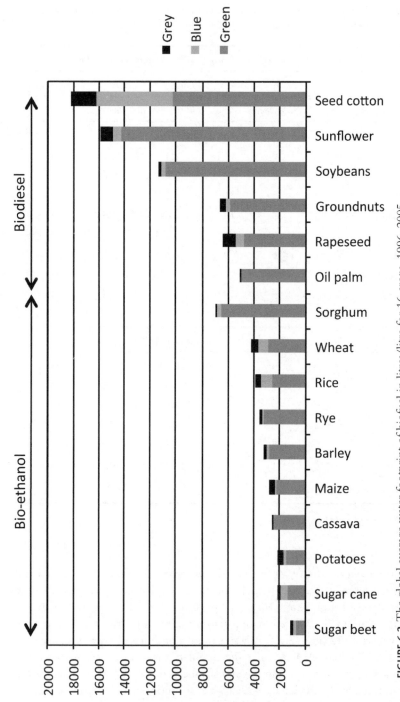

**FIGURE 6.2** The global average water footprint of biofuel in litres/litre for 16 crops, 1996–2005

Source: Mekonnen and Hoekstra (2011a)

Water footprint (litres of water per litre of biofuel)

global average, but still large at 8,800 litres/litre. Biodiesel from rapeseed, with a global average water footprint of 6,400 litres/litre, has a smaller water footprint than biodiesel from soyabean. In Germany, the largest rapeseed producer within Europe, the water footprint of rapeseed biodiesel is 3,500 litres/litre, which is substantially lower than the global average.

An important disclaimer to the water footprint figures presented here is that we looked at the *gross* production of energy, not the *net* production. Let me explain. In assessing the water footprint of biofuels, we looked at the water footprint of the gross energy output from crops. We did not study energy inputs in the production chain, like energy requirements in the agricultural system (e.g. energy use for the production of fertilizers and pesticides) or the energy use during the industrial production of the biofuel. This means that we underestimate the water footprint of biofuels, mostly in cases where agricultural systems have a relatively large energy input. As an example, in a case where the energy input equals 50 per cent of the energy output – a case common in bioenergy production systems (Pimentel and Patzek, 2005) – the water footprint of the net bioenergy production would be twice the water footprint of gross energy production. Another important remark is that we quantified only the water footprint in growing the crops. We neglected water use in the industrial links of the production chain. Although the water footprint in the agricultural stage of the biofuel supply chain is by far the most important, a complete picture can only be obtained when considering the water footprint in each section of the whole supply chain.

## Next-generation biofuels

First-generation biofuels are made using conventional technology. For the sake of simplicity, I will call all other sorts of biofuel 'next-generation'. I prevent the terms second and third generation, which are widely used but for which every author seems to use his own definition. Next-generation biofuels form a very broad category, for which different sorts of feedstock can be used: non-food crops like switchgrass or miscanthus, garden waste, stems and branches of plants, leaves, husks and other crop residues, pulp from fruit pressing, trees, wood chips, algae, skins, manure and all sorts of organic waste from industries and households, including organic residues from municipal sewage. The list of possible sorts of feedstock is endless. The resultant biofuel can be either biogas (like biomethane or syngas) or a liquid fuel (like bioethanol, biomethanol and biodiesel). Next-generation biofuels are still under development; not only are experiments being done with a large variety of feedstock types, also different techniques are being explored. One of the challenges is to efficiently turn the lignocellulose content of biomass into fuel. In a few cases, next-generation fuels are being produced already, but still on a small scale. Currently, hardly any study has been carried out yet regarding the water footprint of next-generation biofuels, which is hampered by the fact that most techniques are all still in a developmental stage, so that efficiencies quickly improve, and there is an absence of data on water consumption or pollution in the supply chain of the different sorts of feedstock used. The focus in the development is clearly on economic optimization, not on considering the intensity of natural resources use.

## The myth of 'no competition with food'

When we grow crops for bioenergy, it makes sense to look at the related claim on land and water resources. Instead, there is a tendency to ignore those claims and to focus the discussion on the question of whether we use food or non-food crops for biofuels. Since competition with food is generally considered a downside of biofuels, it is often regarded as attractive to focus on growing non-food crops for biofuels, or at least crops that the general public associates less with food (like rapeseed or oil palm). One of the non-food crops that has been embraced as an energy crop is jatropha. *Jatropha curcas* is a shrub-like tree species that can provide oil from the seeds, using conventional technology (Banerji *et al.*, 1985). Indeed, we cannot eat that shrub, but in many places where it is now grown commercially, one could have easily grown a food crop as well, so the claim that using non-food crops for biofuels does not compete with food is quite misleading. The same holds for switchgrass or miscanthus, plants that are often mentioned as suitable candidates for producing second-generation biofuels. The question is not whether it is wise or not to use food crops for energy. Formulated in this way, using food crops for energy is put in a bad light and using non-food crops in a good light. The right question to be posed is whether, or to what extent, we should apply scarce land and water resources for producing biomass for energy. If in the overall evaluation it is attractive to allocate certain amounts of land and water to biofuels, then one can go for the most efficient option rather than growing inefficient non-food crops just for keeping up the illusion that there is no competition with food. Jatropha seems to be such an inefficient choice.

## Biodiesel from jatropha

The case of jatropha is interesting because there has been a strong lobby promoting this plant for bioenergy based on two arguments: it can grow under dry conditions on poor soils and it does not compete with food. Under water-constrained circumstances, evapotranspiration from a jatropha field is relatively low, but yields are low accordingly. Worldwide, about half of jatropha is irrigated to boost yields (Renner *et al.*, 2008). With better conditions, yields increase, but evapotranspiration as well. Low water use does not go together with high oil yields (Jongschaap *et al.*, 2007). Investors are interested in high yields under optimal circumstances (often requiring irrigation). Based on a study of irrigated jatropha plantations under good growing conditions in four different countries, we concluded that the water footprint of jatropha oil ranges between 250 and 330 litres/MJ (Gerbens-Leenes *et al.*, 2009c). This shows that jatropha is not a particularly efficient biofuel crop when compared to other crops (Table 6.1). For a jatropha plantation in India with poor growing conditions we found a very large water footprint of 1,700 litres/MJ, but others found that water-stress does not necessarily result in a bigger water footprint per unit of energy. Jongschaap *et al.* (2009) give and example for South Africa, where annual evapotranspiration is $4,052 \, m^3/ha$ and the oil yield $450 \, kg/ha$ per year. With a higher heating value of $37.7 \, MJ/kg$, we can calculate an energy yield of $17 \, GJ/ha$ per year. This implies a water footprint of 240 litres/MJ. This finding is interesting, because it shows that a lower yield (production/ha) does not necessarily imply lower water productivity (production/$m^3$ of water). Jatropha is a drought-resistant crop that can survive under dry conditions and still provide a yield, although little. Under such conditions, growing jatropha can be a good option, since there will be few other options. Growing jatropha under good conditions is a questionable idea. Yields will be higher, but under good conditions also food crops can be grown, so that jatropha will compete with food. Besides, under good conditions, also other crops for bioenergy than jatropha can be grown, so the question becomes whether jatropha is still a good option. Data that have become available thus far show that jatropha has a lower energy yield per unit of water than some other oil crops, like oil palm and groundnuts, and a much lower energy yield than ethanol-yielding crops like sugar cane or cassava. It is therefore essential to differentiate between rain-fed jatropha cultivation under highly water-stressed conditions – whereby hardly anything else can grow – and jatropha cultivation with irrigation or under rainfall conditions that are sufficient to grow other crops (Hoekstra *et al.*, 2009).

## The water footprint of biofuel-based transport

Let us now switch to another question. What will happen if we replace, on a substantial scale, fossil fuels with biofuels? In Western societies, transport requires about one-third of total energy use and contributes substantially to greenhouse gas emissions. Energy for transport in transition countries, such as Romania and Bulgaria, and in developing countries, such as China and India, is still relatively small. Along with economic growth in these countries, transport will also grow, increasing transport fuel needs. Many countries have set targets for the introduction of renewable transport biofuels (biodiesel and bioethanol). For example, India aims to have replaced 20 per cent of petro diesel by biodiesel in 2017 (GoI, 2008). China aims for a 15 per cent biofuel share for transport in 2020 (Yang *et al.*, 2004). In the United States, the Energy Independence and Security Act of 2007 mandated to produce 36 billion gallons of biofuel from corn and cellulosic crops in 2022 (Pimentel *et al.*, 2009). The European Union aims to replace 10 per cent of its transport fuels by renewables in 2020, 7 per cent of which should be biofuels, the other 3 per cent electrification (EC, 2009).

Recently, in a study on the water footprint of bio-based transport in Europe (Gerbens-Leenes and Hoekstra, 2011), we considered bioethanol and biodiesel, but also electricity from biomass. For each form of bioenergy we considered the crop that currently provides energy at the lowest water cost (given current yield and efficiencies in Europe): sugar beet for bioethanol, rapeseed for biodiesel and maize for bioelectricity. The calculated water footprints for different transport modes in the EU, when fueled with bioenergy, are presented in Table 6.2. The figures are presented in litres/passenger kilometre. We considered the following transport modes: walking, bike, train, bus, car and airplane. By expressing the water footprint per passenger kilometre, we make sure that the footprints made by cars, buses, trains and airplanes are divided over the average number of passengers travelling in the different vehicles. For walking and biking we assumed sugar from sugar beet as the energy source. For the other modes of transport we considered different energy sources: bioethanol, biodiesel and, where possible, also bioelectricity. When biking and walking are excluded, the electric train and electric car are the most water-efficient transport modes, airplanes using biodiesel the most water-inefficient. The differences in water footprints shown in Table 6.2 are caused by differences in energy requirements per passenger kilometre among transport modes and differences in water footprints of the fuels used. For airplanes, the difference between smallest and largest water footprint per passenger kilometre is a factor of ten. For cars, the difference is even larger. This is caused by the large variability in energy use of cars. Although diesel cars are more efficient in terms of energy use than petrol cars, cars using biodiesel generally have a larger water footprint than cars using bioethanol, because biodiesel is less water-efficient than

**TABLE 6.2** The water footprint of passenger transport in the EU when based on first-generation bioenergy

| Transport mode | Energy source | Crop source | WF (litres/passenger km) | | |
| | | | Green | Blue | Total |
| --- | --- | --- | --- | --- | --- |
| Airplane | Biodiesel | Rapeseed | 142–403 | 0 | 142–403 |
| | Bioethanol | Sugar beet | 42–79 | 1–10 | 43–89 |
| Car (large) | Biodiesel | Rapeseed | 214–291 | 0 | 214–291 |
| | Bioethanol | Sugar beet | 136–257 | 2–32 | 138–289 |
| Car (small efficient) | Biodiesel | Rapeseed | 65–89 | 0 | 65–89 |
| | Bioethanol | Sugar beet | 23–44 | 0–5 | 23–49 |
| Bus | Biodiesel | Rapeseed | 67–126 | 0 | 67–126 |
| | Bioethanol | Sugar beet | 20–52 | 0–5 | 20–57 |
| Train | Biodiesel | Rapeseed | 15–40 | 0 | 15–40 |
| Electric train | Bioelectricity | Maize | 3–8 | 0–3 | 3–11 |
| Electric car | Bioelectricity | Maize | 4–5 | 1–2 | 5–7 |
| Walking | Sugar | Sugar beet | 3–5 | 0–1 | 3–6 |
| Bike | Sugar | Sugar beet | 1–2 | 0 | 1–2 |

Source: Gerbens-Leenes and Hoekstra (2011)

bioethanol. The water footprint of an electric car applying bioelectricity is much smaller than the water footprint of a biofuelled conventional car, the precise difference depending on which conventional car is used for comparison.

In the same study as mentioned above, we found that, if 10 per cent of the fuel used in the transport sector in Europe is replaced by first-generation bioethanol, biofuel-based transport will have a water footprint equal to 10 per cent of the European water footprint of food and cotton consumption. If the same biofuel target is applied in other regions as well, the additional water consumption in China would be equivalent to 5 per cent of the water footprint for food and cotton consumption, in the rest of Asia 3 per cent, in Africa 4 per cent, in Latin America 6 per cent, in the former USSR 9 per cent and both in North America and Australia 40 per cent. The global water consumption related to biofuel-based transport in this scenario would be 7 per cent of the current global water consumption for agriculture. The trend towards the increased use of biofuels is thus a significant factor for total agricultural water use and aggravates the competition for freshwater resources.

There are a number of caveats in the figures presented for future water needs of transport if more biofuels are used. For example, we assumed that the energy requirements of transport (in MJ/km) will remain constant when switching from fossil to biofuels. The truth, however, is that currently biofuels give the same energy efficiency (km/MJ) only when added in relatively marginal amounts to fossil fuels. Ethanol has solvent characteristics that, in high concentration blends, can cause metal corrosion or deterioration of rubber or plastics. The major automobile manufacturers warranty their cars to run on petrol ethanol blends with up to 10 per cent ethanol, while cars sold in Brazil have components that are resistant to the solvent characteristics of ethanol in blends up to 25 per cent of ethanol. Another caveat is that we considered current volumes of fuel needed for transport, whereas the expectation is that energy use will grow (IEA, 2006), with a corresponding growth in water needs for biofuels (Gerbens-Leenes et al., 2012). Further, we assumed that transport fuels will be produced in the most water-efficient way – using crops with the smallest water footprint per unit of energy obtained and using best technology – which means that the resulting water footprint figures are probably conservative. Whereas bioethanol from sugar beet is more efficient than biodiesel from rapeseed, Germany promotes rapeseed, thus not following our assumption. However, we assumed that agricultural water productivities remain constant. If yields could be increased without increasing water consumption per hectare, the water footprint per unit of energy could be lowered. Finally, for estimating the biofuel-related water footprint per country and region, we have taken the agricultural water productivities in the country or region considered, implicitly assuming that the biomass is grown domestically. Today, most countries are mostly self-sufficient in biofuels (IEA, 2006). When demand increases, this situation may change because countries with few opportunities will have to import biofuels. Many countries will thus start externalizing their biofuel-related water footprint.

## Water footprint of hydroelectricity

The discussion about the water implications of biofuels is relatively new. The debate about dams and hydropower is somewhat older. At the end of the last century, the debate about the pros and cons of dams had heated up so much, that in 1998 the World Commission on Dams was formed, in an attempt to have an independent commission study the environmental, social and economic impacts of the development of large dams. Two years later, the commission delivered a report that formed a milestone in the thinking about dams (WCD, 2000). The chair's preface sets the tone: "We dammed half our world's rivers at unprecedented rates of one per hour, and at unprecedented scales of over 45,000 dams more than four storeys high." The report led to the acknowledgement that dams can heavily impact on riparian ecosystems and societies and that any further damming of rivers should be subject to careful considerations. Relatively recently, a new element has entered the discussion about dams. Many of the large dams in the world are primarily built for the generation of hydroelectricity. Hydropower accounts for about 16 per cent of the world's electricity supply. The controversy that has risen recently is around the question whether hydroelectric generation is merely an in-stream water user or whether it is also to be considered a 'water consumer'. This is not just an academic question, because there is something at stake. There is an increasing call for charging a water price to water consumers, so the question who will be charged and how much becomes a relevant one. Traditionally, hydropower has always been categorized as an 'in-stream water user'. However, in a recent study we showed that hydroelectric generation is in most cases a significant water consumer as well (Mekonnen and Hoekstra, 2012b). We quantified the blue water footprint of hydroelectricity for 35 selected sites by looking at the water evaporated from the reservoir behind the dam. Without the dams and without the reservoirs, the evaporated water would have stayed within the river, so we can speak of true water consumptive use. The aggregated blue water footprint of the selected hydropower plants was estimated to be 90 billion m³/yr, which is equivalent to 10 per cent of the blue water footprint of global crop production in the year 2000. Hydroelectric generation is thus a significant water consumer. The average water footprint of the selected hydropower plants was 68 litres/MJ. Great differences in water footprint among hydropower plants exist (with values ranging from 0.3 litres/MJ for the San Carlos dam in Colombia to 846 litres/MJ for the Akosombo-Kpong dam in Ghana). The variation is due to differences in climate in the places where the plants are situated, but more importantly the result of large differences in the area flooded per unit of installed hydroelectric capacity. More detailed studies will undoubtedly revise our fist rough estimates, but it seems wise, at least, to include the assessment of the blue water footprint in evaluations of newly proposed hydropower plants. And, of course, if water consumers like farmers and industries will have to pay for water, why not also send a bill to hydroelectric power companies.

## The water footprint of fossil fuels

Now we have considered the water footprint of bioenergy and hydroelectricity, it would be interesting to know also the water footprint of fossil fuels – coal, oil and gas – and of nuclear, solar and wind energy. Let us start with the fossil fuels. Finding good data in this field is quite hard, because the coal mining and the oil and gas sectors are not very transparent if it comes to the question of water use and pollution in the extraction and processing stages of production. There are many scattered data and only a few wider inventories. General problems are that water use data often refer to blue water abstractions, not consumptive water use (in many cases it's not even clear what is being reported), and that volumes of water use for specific sites are generally given as totals, not in relation to the volume of energy generated. A complication is that water use probably varies greatly among sites, so that data for a few specific cases (or a specific country) may not be representative for the global sector as a whole. One thing is sure: water consumption for producing fossil fuels – when expressed in litres/MJ – is a few orders of magnitude smaller than water consumption for biofuels (Gleick, 1994; Gerbens-Leenes et al., 2009a). Estimates across the various types of fossil fuel range from the order of 0.001 to the order of 1 litre/MJ (Gleick, 1994; Maheu, 2009; Olsson, 2012). Sometimes, estimates refer to water consumption in extraction only, while other times they also include water consumption in different stages of processing. The estimates refer to the blue water footprint of the fuel. In the case of electricity generation, we should also count the water consumption related to wet cooling in the thermal power plant, which is in the range of 0.3–0.7 litres/MJ (Gleick, 1994).

The grey water footprint of fossil fuels is probably much larger than the blue water footprint (the consumptive water use), but reliable estimates do not exist, because industries in this sector do not report the loads of chemicals that enter ground or surface water bodies as a result of their operations. Measuring such loads can be difficult, because in the case of extraction we typically talk about diffuse forms of pollution. There are quite some concerns about the effects of coal mining and oil and gas exploration and extraction on water quality, increasingly now with the application of techniques like hydraulic fracturing to disclose shale gas (Cooley and Donnelly, 2012) and the development of tar sands (Schindler, 2010).

In tables that compare the water consumption for different sorts of energy, we can see that fossil fuels perform relatively well in terms of litres/MJ compared to biofuels. This may lead to the wrong conclusion that, regarding water use, fossil fuels win from biofuels. In a way, this is an unfair comparison. Strictly speaking, one should also account for the green water consumption over the millions of years that it took to form fossil fuels. I guess that most people would find that irrelevant for the issue of water allocation and scarcity today, but it makes sense to make the point at least. The essence of fossil fuels is that they are fossil: they were formed a long time ago and over very long periods of time. In a comparison between fossil fuels and biofuels, it does not make sense to argue that fossil fuels cost less water than biofuels. In the end, fossil fuels are based on biomass formed and preserved over millions of years, in a very inefficient process (because only a very small fraction of biomass turns into fossil fuel reserves), so that fresh biofuels are actually much more efficient in terms of resource use than fossil fuels. The point is of course that using fossil fuels is nothing else than using up reserves that have historically been built up. They are essentially unsustainable.

## Nuclear, solar and wind energy

The story for nuclear energy is roughly the same as for fossil fuels. Operational water use is in the same range and water quality problems do occur as well (Gleick, 1994). In the case of nuclear energy, there is the additional risk of radioactive pollution of water bodies related to the storage of nuclear waste or in the case of accidents with nuclear energy plants or with the transport of radioactive materials.

Regarding the water footprint of solar and wind energy, even less is known than in the case of fossil fuels. Operational water use in the generation of electricity through photovoltaic cells or wind is negligible (Gleick, 1994), so that the question remains what the water footprint is of the materials applied. When writing this, no studies are available in this respect, but they will undoubtedly be undertaken. My expectation is that the water footprint related to materials used in solar and wind energy will not be substantially larger than the water footprint related to materials applied in other forms of electricity generation.

Electricity generation through 'concentrating solar power' systems requires some water to make up for evaporation losses (in the case of wet cooling) and to clean the mirrors. Concentrating solar power plants use the same wet-cooling technologies as fossil and nuclear power plants. Water consumption for wet cooling in the case of concentrating solar power plants has been estimated to be around 3,000 litres/MWh (Carter and Campbell, 2009), which is equivalent to 0.8 litres/MJ. This can potentially be reduced by using other cooling techniques.

It goes far beyond the scope of this book to reflect on promising energy mixes. The only thing I have tried to do in this chapter is to reflect on energy supply from a water perspective. The overall conclusion is that from a water point of view, and taking into account the unsustainable character of fossil fuels and nuclear energy, solar and wind energy are the most attractive sources of energy. We should be careful with large-scale implementation of first-generation biofuels. Bioenergy can play a role insofar as it does not conflict with food production. Burning organic waste will not add to the overall water footprint. In addition, next-generation biofuels like algae may have a much lower water footprint than crops.

## Harmonizing water and energy policies

We are back where we started this chapter. If something is clear from the figures presented, it is that any concern on the sustainable use of our scarce freshwater resources should be reflected in a well-thought-out energy policy. Current policies towards the increase of using biofuels, without good consideration of the possible implications on the additional use of land and water resources, can impossibly be good policies. A shift away from fossil fuels is absolutely crucial and an increase in the use of biofuels is inevitable and necessary, but we should be careful to not aggravate the pressure on land and water resources. If we take into account the constraints in the availability of suitable lands and in freshwater availability to produce crops for bioenergy, it will become even more clear that reduction in energy demands is a challenge that is at least as big as making the shift from fossil to renewable energy.

# 7

# THE OVERSEAS WATER
# FOOTPRINT OF CUT FLOWERS

Often, the cut flowers that we buy as a gift are not grown in our home country, but imported. For example, in the Netherlands, known for its flowers, of all roses sold more come from abroad than from Dutch producers. For roses, the most important sources are Kenya, Ethiopia, Tanzania, Ecuador, Zambia and Uganda, not places next door. The Netherlands is a cut-flower hub in Europe, which means that a lot of the imported flowers are re-exported to other destinations.

In this chapter, we will follow the 'Dutch' flowers back to Kenya, the main supplier of cut flowers to the Netherlands. We will further zoom in to the area around Lake Naivasha, the main cut-flower producing area within Kenya. Lake Naivasha lies in the Rift Valley, about 80 km northwest of Nairobi. It is Kenya's second largest freshwater lake without surface outlet. The lake remains fresh due to a significant outflow of groundwater. The flower farmers around the lake consume substantial amounts of water, which they pump from the groundwater or take from the lake itself or from the rivers that feed the lake. At the same time, the lake is listed as a wetland of international importance under the Ramsar Convention, an intergovernmental treaty for the conservation and sustainable use of wetlands. In the last three decades, the area around Lake Naivasha has become the main site of Kenya's horticultural industry (mainly cut flowers), which is Kenya's third most important foreign exchange earner after tea and tourism. Since the late 1990s, the flower farms started to expand at a faster rate (Becht et al., 2005). The total irrigated commercial farm area around Lake Naivasha is now estimated to be about 4,450 ha. Cut flowers account for about 43 per cent of the irrigated area, followed by vegetables with 41 per cent and fodder with 15 per cent (Musota, 2008).

The major flower varieties grown and exported from Kenya are roses, carnations, alstroemeria, lisianthus, statice and cut foliage. Roses dominate the export market, accounting for over 70 per cent of the export volume (HCDA, 2007). The main flower growing regions are Lake Naivasha, Thika and Kiambu/Limuru (EPZA, 2005), with Lake Naivasha accounting for about 95 per cent of the cultivated area.

Lake Naivasha has attracted attention and concerns from both national and international organizations. The main stakeholders have shown concern about the health of the lake, mainly related to the decline of the lake level, deterioration of the water quality and reduction of biodiversity. Some of the main stakeholders active around the lake are the Lake Naivasha Riparian Association, the Lake Naivasha Growers Group and Kenya Wildlife Services. The concerns have led to the development of a Management Plan in 1996 by the main stakeholders (Becht et al., 2005). Around that time, the Lake Naivasha Management Implementation Committee was formed to execute the management plan. The plan was officially approved by the Government of Kenya in 1997.

In this chapter I will report on a study we carried out on the water footprint of horticulture within the Lake Naivasha Basin, with a focus on the flower farms (Mekonnen et al., 2012). We assessed the potential for mitigating this footprint by involving cut-flower traders, retailers and consumers overseas. More specific, we explored the idea of a voluntary sustainable-flower agreement between major agents along the flower supply chain, involving a water-sustainability premium to be paid by the consumers in the countries importing flowers from Kenya.

## Irrigation and fertilizer use around Lake Naivasha

The Lake Naivasha Basin can be schematized into two parts: the upper catchment with smallholder farms and the area around Lake Naivasha with big farms producing for export. About 62 per cent of the cut flowers around Lake Naivasha are grown in greenhouses (Musota, 2008). The evapotranspiration in greenhouse conditions is assumed to be 65 per cent of the outdoor condition as suggested by various authors (Baille et al., 1994; Orgaz et al., 2005; Mpusia, 2006). The average water footprint of cut flowers was estimated based on the weighted average of indoor and outdoor farm areas. The green, blue and grey components of the water footprint of the different crops were calculated following Hoekstra et al. (2011). Table 7.1 gives the irrigated area and fertilizer application rate for irrigated crops around Lake Naivasha. For the loss of nitrogen fertilizers to ground- and surface water, a leaching-runoff fraction of 10 per cent was assumed, following Hoekstra and Chapagain (2008).

## The water footprint within the Lake Naivasha Basin

We can distinguish two groups of crops: fully irrigated crops, grown by commercial farms mainly for export and concentrated around Lake Naivasha, and other crops that are cultivated by small farmers in the upper catchment. The total water footprint related to crop production in the Lake Naivasha Basin sums up to 102 million $m^3$/yr (Table 7.2). About 68.7 per cent of the water footprint is related to green water, 18.5 per cent blue water and 12.8 per cent grey water. The

**TABLE 7.1** Irrigated crops around Lake Naivasha, 2006

| Crop | Irrigated area | | Nitrogen application rate (kg/ha) |
|------|------|------|------|
| | Area (ha) | % | |
| Total flowers | 1,911 | 42.8 | 325 |
| Roses | 1,028 | 23.0 | 325 |
| Roses & carnations | 730 | 16.3 | 325 |
| Roses & hypercium | 21 | 0.5 | 325 |
| Other flowers | 132 | 3.0 | 325 |
| Total vegetables | 1,824 | 40.8 | 185 |
| Babycorn | 205 | 4.6 | 41 |
| Babycorn & beans | 143 | 3.2 | 252 |
| Babycorn, beans & cabbage | 169 | 3.8 | 235 |
| Babycorn, beans & onions | 906 | 20.3 | 244 |
| Beans/tomatoes | 21 | 0.5 | 235 |
| Cabbage | 374 | 8.4 | 68 |
| Cabbage & beans | 6 | 0.1 | 235 |
| Total fodder | 665 | 14.9 | 68 |
| Grass | 286 | 6.4 | 68 |
| Grass & lucerne | 40 | 0.9 | 68 |
| Lucerne | 163 | 3.7 | 68 |
| Lucerne, babycorn & beans | 176 | 3.9 | 68 |
| Macadamia | 50 | 1.1 | 68 |
| Eucalyptus | 17 | 0.4 | – |
| Total | 4,467 | 100 | |

Sources: irrigated areas from Musota (2008) and Becht (2007); nitrogen application rates from Tiruneh (2004), Xu (1999) and Ariga *et al.* (2006).

commercial crops contribute two-fifths to the total water footprint of crop production. About 98 per cent (18.4 million $m^3$/yr) of the blue water footprint and about 61 per cent of the grey water footprint in the catchment area can be attributed to the commercial farms around the lake.

In addition to the irrigated farms that are found around Lake Naivasha, the basin is used mainly for cattle and game rangeland. Smallholder farmers, growing mainly maize, vegetables and other crops, occupy areas that receive high rainfall. There are about 18,000 ha of farmland in the upper catchment of which only 2 per cent is irrigated. The average water footprint related to the production of these crops over the period 1996–2005 was about 60 million $m^3$/yr (90.7 per cent green water, 0.8 per cent blue water and 8.5 per cent grey water).

**TABLE 7.2** The water footprint of crops grown in the Lake Naivasha Basin, 1996–2005

| Land use | Area cultivated | | Water footprint (1,000 m³/yr) | | | |
|---|---|---|---|---|---|---|
| | Area (ha) | Irrigated (%) | Green | Blue | Grey | Total |
| *Commercial farms around the lake* | | | | | | |
| Total flower | 1,712 | 100 | 3,640 | 7,576 | 5,627 | 16,843 |
| Flowers open | 652 | 100 | 3,640 | 1,770 | 2,122 | 7,532 |
| Flowers greenhouse | 1,076 | 100 | 0 | 5,805 | 3,504 | 9,309 |
| Vegetables | 1,885 | 100 | 7,887 | 7,375 | 1,834 | 17,096 |
| Fodder | 665 | 100 | 3,716 | 3,194 | 452 | 7,362 |
| Macadamia | 50 | 100 | 278 | 303 | 34 | 615 |
| Total of commercial farms | 4,327 | 100 | 15,521 | 18,448 | 7,947 | 41,916 |
| *Farms in the upper catchment of the basin* | | | | | | |
| Cereals | 12,125 | 1 | 34,776 | 82 | 1,655 | 36,513 |
| Pulses | 2,199 | 0 | 3,958 | 0 | 2,673 | 6,631 |
| Others | 3,813 | 7 | 15,876 | 382 | 809 | 17,067 |
| Total of upper catchment farms | 18,137 | 2 | 54,609 | 465 | 5,137 | 60,211 |
| Grand total | 22,465 | 21 | 70,130 | 18,913 | 13,084 | 102,127 |

Sources: areas of the commercial farms based on 2006 data from Musota (2008) and Becht (2007), adjusted for 1996–2005; water footprint estimates from Mekonnen *et al.* (2012).

Cut flowers take a large share of the water footprint of crop production around Lake Naivasha, contributing about 98 per cent and 41 per cent to the blue and total water footprint, respectively. The water footprint of cut-flower production is about 16.8 million m³/yr (Table 7.2). Flowers grown in greenhouses are fully supplied with irrigation water, while flowers cultivated in the open field get both rainwater and irrigation water. When we consider the water footprint of cut flowers per unit of weight, we find that the footprint of cut flowers grown in greenhouses (326 litre/kg) is smaller than for flowers grown in the open field (435 litre/kg), but the *blue* water footprint in the case of greenhouses (203 litre/kg) is about double compared to the case of flowers from the open field (102 litre/kg). The average water footprint of cut flowers grown around Lake Naivasha is 367 litre/kg. About 45 per cent of this water footprint refers to blue water, 22 per cent to green water and 33 per cent to grey water, the volume of water needed to assimilate the nitrogen fertilizers that enter the water systems due to leaching or runoff.

It was interesting to find that the six biggest commercial farms – Logonot Horticulture, Delamere, Oserian, Gordon-Miller, Marula Estate and Sher Agencies – account for about 56 per cent of the total operational water footprint around Lake Naivasha and 60 per cent of the blue water footprint related to crop production. This means that working with a limited number of farms on reducing their water footprint can already yield substantial results.

## The water footprint related to cut-flower export

Depending on the yield and weight of a rose flower stem, the water footprint per stem varies from 7 to 13 litres/stem (Table 7.3). If we assume an average rose flower stem weights about 25 g, its green water footprint would be 2 litres/stem, its blue water footprint 4 litres/stem and its grey water footprint 3 litres/stem, resulting in a total water footprint of 9 litres/stem.

When we assume that about 95 per cent of Kenya's cut-flower export comes from the area around Lake Naivasha, the average virtual water export from the Lake Naivasha Basin related to export of cut flowers was 16 million m³/yr in the period 1996–2005 (Table 7.4). The European Union is Kenya's principal market for cut flowers, with the Netherlands, the UK and Germany together receiving more than 90 per cent of the cut-flower-related virtual water export from the basin. The Netherlands is the principal market, accounting for 69 per cent of the total export. The virtual water export in relation to export of cut flowers has shown a significant growth, with virtual water export almost doubling from 11 million m³ in 1996 to 21 million m³ in 2005.

In addition to cut flowers, vegetables such as beans, sweet corn, tomato, cabbage and onions are produced for both export and domestic consumption. About 50 per cent of the vegetables produced around Lake Naivasha is exported and the remaining is supplied to local markets, mainly to Nairobi. The virtual water export related to vegetable products was 8.5 million m³/yr. Most of the virtual water related to vegetable products was exported to the United Arab Emirates, France and the UK. For the period 1996–2005, the total virtual water export related to the export of cut flowers and vegetable products was 24.5 million m³/yr.

**TABLE 7.3** The water footprint of a rose flower, 1996–2005

| Weight of rose (gram/stem) | Cut flower production (stem/m²) | Water footprint (litre/stem) | | | |
|---|---|---|---|---|---|
| | | Green | Blue | Grey | Total |
| 20 | 134 | 1.6 | 3.3 | 2.5 | 7.4 |
| 25 | 107 | 2.0 | 4.1 | 3.1 | 9.2 |
| 35 | 77 | 2.8 | 5.8 | 4.3 | 12.9 |

Source: Mekonnen *et al.* (2012)

**TABLE 7.4** Virtual water export from the Lake Naivasha Basin related to cut-flower export, 1996–2005

| Importing country | Virtual water export from Lake Naivasha Basin (1,000 m³/yr) | | | |
| --- | --- | --- | --- | --- |
| | Green | Blue | Grey | Total |
| Netherlands | 2,399 | 4,993 | 3,708 | 11,100 |
| United Kingdom | 611 | 1,272 | 944 | 2,827 |
| Germany | 230 | 478 | 355 | 1,064 |
| Switzerland | 59 | 122 | 91 | 272 |
| South Africa | 37 | 77 | 57 | 171 |
| France | 33 | 68 | 51 | 152 |
| United Arab Emirates | 16 | 33 | 25 | 74 |
| Italy | 10 | 20 | 15 | 45 |
| Others | 64 | 133 | 98 | 295 |
| Total | 3,458 | 7,196 | 5,345 | 16,000 |

Source: Mekonnen *et al.* (2012)

The cut-flower industry is an important export sector, which contributed an annual average of US$ 141 million foreign exchange (7 per cent of Kenyan export value) over the period 1996–2005, and US$ 352 in 2005 alone. Hence, Kenya is generating foreign exchange of (141/16 =) 8.8 US$/m³.

## Sustainability of water use in the Lake Naivasha Basin

The horticulture sector in Naivasha employs some 25,000 people directly and the same number of people is indirectly dependent, both as dependents and service providers (Becht *et al.*, 2005). Most of the farms pay more than the legal minimum wage. The farms also provide housing, free medical services, schools for children of farm workers and social and sport facilities. Some of the larger farms also participate in the community development such as provision of clinic and ambulance services, water management and tree planting and watering of the community trees. A continued supply of freshwater to sustain the economy is a concern, however.

Lake Naivasha has been used for irrigation since the 1940s. Water is extracted directly from the lake, but also from groundwater and the rivers feeding the lake. Besides the irrigation water used for crop production, water from the basin is used for drinking water supply and since 1992 a pipeline became operational pumping 20,000 m³ per day from the Malewa sub-basin to Gilgil and Nakuru Town (Becht and Nyaoro, 2006; Musota, 2008). The total water use for domestic purposes in the basin is estimated as 1.2 million m³/yr. Altogether, the blue water footprint within the Lake Naivasha Basin is estimated to be 27 million m³/yr (Table 7.5).

**TABLE 7.5** The blue water footprint in the Lake Naivasha Basin

|  | Blue water footprint (million m³/yr) | Contribution to the total blue water footprint (%) |
|---|---|---|
| Cut flowers | 7.58 | 28 |
| Vegetables and macadamia | 7.68 | 28 |
| Grass and fodder | 3.19 | 12 |
| Upper catchment crops | 0.47 | 2 |
| Nakuru and Gilgil town[1] | 7.3 | 27 |
| Lake Naivasha Basin potable water[2] | 1.19 | 4 |
| Total | 27.4 | 100 |

Sources: data for Nakuru and Gilgil town from Becht and Nyaoro (2006) and Musota (2008); the potable water use in the basin is estimated based on a population of 650,000, a per capita daily consumption of 50 litres and assuming a 90 per cent return flow and 10 per cent of the abstraction actually consumed; other data from Mekonnen et al. (2012).

**TABLE 7.6** The long-term average annual water balance of the Lake Naivasha Basin

|  | Basin water balance (million m³/yr) | Fraction (%) |
|---|---|---|
| Rainfall | 2,790 | 100 |
| Evaporation of rainwater from land | 2,573 | 92.2 |
| Evaporation from the lake | 256 | 9.2 |
| Groundwater outflow | 56 | 2.0 |
| Blue water footprint | 27 | 1.0 |
| Closing error | −122 | −4.4 |

Sources: blue water footprint from Mekonnen et al. (2012); other data from Becht (2007)

The rainfall regime within the Lake Naivasha Basin is influenced by the rain shadow from the surrounding highlands of the Aberdare range to the east and the Mau Escarpment to the west. The long-term rainfall varies from about 600 mm at Naivasha town to some 1,700 mm on the slopes of the Nyandarua Mountains (Becht et al., 2005). Total basin rainfall and evapotranspiration are estimated at 2,790 million m³/yr and 2,573 million m³/yr, respectively (Becht, 2007). The annual runoff generated in the Lake Naivasha Basin is estimated at 217 million m³/yr (Becht and Harper, 2002). The long-term average annual water balance of the basin is presented in Table 7.6.

The sustainability of the water footprint in Lake Naivasha Basin can be assessed by comparing the blue water footprint with the available blue water resources. The available blue water for human use is the difference between the natural runoff and the environmental flow requirements, which is here assumed to be 80 per cent of natural runoff (Hoekstra et al., 2011; Richter et al., 2012). For the Lake Naivasha Basin the total blue water footprint is about 13 per cent of the annual average runoff, which leaves 87 per cent of the runoff for meeting environmental flow requirement. When we take the blue and grey water footprint together, they make 19 per cent of the annual average runoff.

Comparing the blue–grey water footprint with the blue water available for human use at annual basis, however, hides the seasonal variation, which is relevant particularly in basins with highly variable flow regimes. Therefore, it is quite important to make the comparison on a monthly basis. When we do that, we find that in the dry period, from January to March, the blue plus grey water footprint is double the usable runoff. This means that twice the usable runoff is appropriated for either consumptive water use or assimilation of pollution. In November and December, the blue plus grey water footprint slightly exceeds the environmental flow requirement. There is no violation of the environmental flow requirements in the period from April to October.

A fluctuating lake level is a natural phenomenon for Lake Naivasha and a necessity for the functioning of the ecosystem. The climate and geographic context have caused a natural fluctuation in the lake water level over the past 100 years of 12 m (Mavuti and Harper, 2006). However, the more recent decline in the lake level coincides with and can be explained by the commencement of horticulture crops in the area in 1982. Becht and Harper (2002) show that in late 1998, the lake was 3.5 m lower than it would have been had it followed the hydrological records. Though the current level of water abstraction has not yet led to a water level outside the range of water levels recorded in the past, and there is no evidence that lake level fluctuations themselves risk biodiversity losses (Harper and Mavuti, 2004). According to Becht (2007), if water abstraction rates remain constant from now on, it may result in a new dynamic equilibrium lake level. If the consumptive water use within the catchment will keep increasing, however, the lake level may reach below the lowest recorded water level in the past 100 years.

Although the recent reduction in the lake's water level can be attributed mainly to the commercial farms around the lake, the deterioration of the lake water quality as a result of the inflow of nutrients is due to both the commercial farms and the farm activities in the upper catchment. This finding is supported by Kitaka et al. (2002), who also showed that a large amount of the nutrient load to the lake originates from the upper catchments and municipal sewage through surface runoff. The nutrient transport from the upper catchments is mainly through surface runoff, while for the riparian agriculture nutrient transport is mainly through leaching to the groundwater.

The long-term protection of the lake ecosystem and the economic and social benefits that depend on the lake require a sustainable use of Lake Naivasha and its catchment. The most pressing issues are the increasing consumptive water use for growing horticulture crops, the growing domestic water use and the eutrophication of the lake due to an increase in agricultural nutrients inflow both from the

commercial farms and from the upper catchment. The increase in nutrients is probably the combined effect of the loss of riparian vegetation, which acts as a buffer to
trap sediments, an increase in the sediment flow from the catchment and an increase
in fertilizers leaching and running off to the water system. The situation has wors-
ened by the increase in subsistence farming even on steep slopes right down to the
river edge which has destroyed the riparian zone (Everard and Harper, 2002).

## Setting a cap to the blue and grey water footprint in the basin

Long-term gains from a sustainable use of water require coordinated action at
the catchment scale. There is a need to define the maximum allowable level of
consumptive water use at the basin scale. This would set a cap to the blue water
footprint in the basin. The total allocation of blue water among the various water
users in the basin should not exceed this cap. Decisions on the allocation of the
limited volume of available blue water should be based on considerations of equitability (big versus small farms, farmers versus other water users), but also take
into account differences in economic water productivity among crops. Cut flowers generate more economic return than the low-value fodder crops and grasses.
Indoor flowers are more efficient compared to outdoor flowers; therefore greenhouse cultivation coupled with rainwater harvesting should be encouraged. The
use of blue water for the production of water-intensive products such as beans and
low-value products such as grass and fodder should be discouraged. Wise use of
rainwater, in particular in the upper catchment, for growing fodder and grass needs
to be encouraged. Controlling of unlicensed and illegal water abstraction through
legal means and community involvement is quite essential.

The grey water footprint in the basin needs to be capped as well. There is a need
to reduce the flow of sediments and agricultural nutrients to the lake both from the
commercial farms around the lake and subsistence farmers in the upper catchment.
The sedimentation problem is aggravated due to the loss of riparian vegetation that
could have acted as a buffer in trapping sediments and increasing infiltration. An
urgent and coordinated action is needed to stop the destruction of vegetation along
the riverbanks and lake caused by cultivation and overgrazing. Therefore, prohibi-
tion of cultivation in the riparian areas is important.

## Current water regulations in the Lake Naivasha Basin

Kenya's water sector reform came a long way before the adoption of the Water
Act in 2002. The first water sector reform in Kenya was in 1974, when the first
National Water Master Plan was launched (Mangiti, 2007). The publication
of the 'Sessional Paper No. 1 of 1999 on National Policy on Water Resources
Management and Development' led to a new momentum (Owuor and Foeken,
2009). The Water Act 2002 has introduced comprehensive and, in many instances,
radical changes to the legal framework for the management of the water sector in

Kenya (Mumma, 2005). The National Water Resources Management Strategy document specifies ten 'specific objectives'. Among these are (Owuor and Foeken, 2009): (a) manage the water demand in a sustainable way, and (b) water pricing that recognizes water as an economic good.

The Kenyan government considers water as both a social and economic good, to be available for all Kenyans and at a price reflecting its market value. This principle is reflected in the different water sector strategies and water resources management rules. Among the strategies pursued are demand management, the re-allocation of water to where it has high return and efficient allocation of water through appropriate pricing.

As water is becoming an increasingly scarce resource, full-cost pricing of water is recognized as an effective tool for its management. The need to have full-cost pricing of water has received worldwide acknowledgement since the International Conference on Water and the Environment held in Dublin in 1992. Agenda 21 of the United Nations (UN, 1992) further supported the internalization of environmental costs and the use of economic instruments for rational use of water resources. The World Water Commission (2000) stated that 'the single most immediate and important measure that we can recommend is the systematic adoption of full-cost pricing for water services'. Hoekstra (2011a) and Rogers et al. (2002) argue that sustainable and efficient use of water requires full-cost pricing of water use, including all cost components: the operation and maintenance costs, capital costs, opportunity costs, scarcity rent and externality costs of water use.

However, there are few successful examples of implemented full-cost pricing of water (Dinar and Subramanian, 1998; Rosegrant and Cline, 2002; Cornish et al. 2004). In most OECD countries, let alone in developing countries, the implementation of water pricing policies has been slow and uneven (Rosegrant and Cline, 2002; Perry, 2003; Molle and Berkoff, 2007). The World Bank (2004) acknowledged the complexity of water pricing reform (both in theory and practice) for irrigation. It further advocates a 'pragmatic but principled' approach that respects principles of efficiency, equitability and sustainability while recognizing that water resources management is intensely political and that reform requires the articulation of prioritized, sequenced, practical and patient interventions.

Lack of funding is one of the main challenges in the Lake Naivasha Basin for implementing community-based basin rehabilitation and lake conservation (Becht et al. 2005). Under such conditions, raising enough funds would be an additional objective of water pricing, besides creation of an incentive for efficient and sustainable use of water. However, the implementation of full marginal-cost pricing under the existing conditions in Kenya and around Naivasha is highly unlikely. The flower farms feel that they are already overtaxed and burdened with a number of remittances and some even have threatened to relocate to Ethiopia if local authorities force them to pay more tax (Riungu, 2007). Attracted by a number of incentives including ten-year tax holidays, better security, duty-free import of capital goods and low land price, five major flower companies have already made the switch to Ethiopia with more to follow (ARB, 2007).

According to the 2007 Water Resource Management Rules, domestic water users have to pay 0.50 Kenyan Shilling/m³ and non-domestic water users have to pay 0.50–0.75 Kenyan Shilling/m³. Major water users need a licence to abstract water and need to install water meters. Implementation of the regulation is actually hampered, however, by a reluctance of many water users to follow the regulation and difficulties the government encounters in enforcing the regulation. The current water pricing policy has several weaknesses. One is that illegal water abstractions from both ground- and surface water are very common. In practice it is difficult for the government to check whether farmers, particularly in the upper catchment, have actually installed water meters as legally required, due to a lack of cars and fuel for the staff responsible for control. Despite the fact that farmers have indicated that the newly introduced water tariff is too high, the tariff actually does not by far cover the full economic cost of the water. As a result, the funds generated by the current water-pricing scheme are very small. The level of water price increase that would be required to have a significant impact on demand would be politically very difficult to enforce. Besides, a unilateral implementation of a stringent water pricing strategy by Kenya could affect the competitiveness of its local companies in the global market (Cornish *et al.* 2004).

## A sustainable-flower agreement between major agents along the cut-flower supply chain

Given the recent emergence of more environmentally conscious consumers, combined with an increased interest on the side of traders and retailers in providing environmentally sustainable consumer products, involving consumers and other stakeholders forms an opportunity to achieve sustainable water use in cut-flower production. Consumers are becoming more and more concerned with how their consumption behaviour is affecting the world around them. This is reflected in the growing consumption of fair-trade products and organic produce. Annual growth rates of 20 per cent or more in market volume have been observed for many years for both organic and fair-trade products (Krier, 2005; Poisot *et al.* 2007). Several studies show that consumers are willing to pay more for products that are environmentally and socially responsible (De Pelsmacker *et al.*, 2005; Arnot *et al.*, 2006; Aizaki and Sato, 2007; Didier and Lucie, 2008).

Here, I will describe the possible characteristics of a 'sustainable-flower agreement' between major agents along the flower supply chain focused on sustainable water use. The agreement should include two key ingredients: a fund-raising mechanism at the consumer end of the supply chain, which will raise the funds for making water use in flower production sustainable, and a labelling or certification scheme, which will provide the guarantee that the funds are properly spent and that the flower production actually moves in the direction of sustainable water use.

The premium collected when selling cut flowers from the Lake Naivasha Basin to consumers in Europe should be used to invest in better watershed management and, most in particular, in reducing the water footprint of the flower farmers. Clear criteria need to be formulated for how collected funds can or should be spent. The criteria could be formulated so that small farmers also belong to the beneficiaries of the funds, because particularly smallholder farmers generally have more difficulty than the large farmers to comply with environmental standards or raise funds to be able to comply.

There is a need to provide institutional infrastructure through which the funds could flow back to the basin and be used in environmental protection, watershed management, support to farmers to improve their water management and community development. Fair-trade organizations can be instrumental in making sure that funds raised at the consumer end flow back to the watershed for the support of local programmes for improved watershed management and support to farmers to reduce their water footprint.

The approach of collecting a water-sustainability premium at the end of the supply chain differs from the current approach of local water pricing by where the funds to invest in sustainable water use are generated (Figure 7.1). Local water pricing is a mechanism applied at the beginning of the chain: the farmers pay. A water-sustainability premium is raised at the end of the chain: the consumers pay. Due to the increase of the price per flower along the supply chain, generating substantial funds is easier at the end of the chain. Currently, the water abstraction fee in Kenya for commercial farmers is 0.50 Kenyan Shillings/m³ of water abstracted (€ 0.007/m³). The total water abstraction by the commercial farms around the lake is estimated at 40 million m³/yr and out of this the flower farms receive about 50 per cent (Becht, 2007). With a water abstraction fee of € 0.007/m³, this would raise € 0.13 million/year. Given an annual cut-flower export of 1.7 billion stems, they will thus pay, on average, € 0.000076/stem of cut flower for abstracting irrigation water. This is a very optimistic estimate because, as explained before, the conditions are not such that the government is actually able to enforce farmers to pay. On the other hand, if we assume a water-sustainability premium of € 0.01/stem of cut flower at the retailer, to be paid by the consumer, one would raise €17 million per year. When we look at the capability of generating funds for watershed management, we find that a water-sustainability premium raised at the consumer end of the supply chain will yield 100 to 200 times the amount of money potentially raised through local water pricing.

Collecting a water-sustainability premium at the lower end of the supply chain needs to go hand in hand with a mechanism for certification of the farmers that deliver the premium flowers and a mechanism for labelling the premium flowers. Labelling can be interpreted here in a physical sense – where indeed a consumer-oriented label is attached to a flower – but it can also get the shape of 'attached information' to whole batches of flowers. Customers can be encouraged to buy flowers from certified farms or labelled flowers and pay an agreed premium to contribute to the sustainability of production and consumption. Certification and labelling would help to segregate environmentally sustainable products from other products and provide consumers with the quality assurance. The success depends on a transparent, credible monitoring and certification system. Farmers would

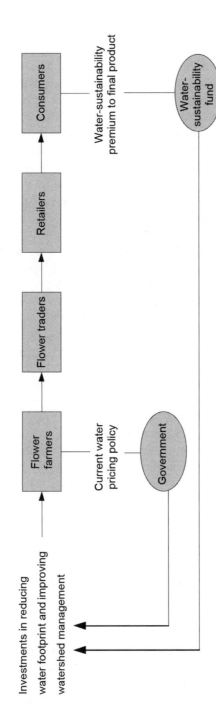

**FIGURE 7.1** A schematization of the flower supply chain

benefit by having an advantage on the market by achieving standards of production that are internationally recognized.

The certification of farmers and labelling of products could be carried out by the already existing institutional setup of the Global Good Agricultural Practices (GlobalGAP). The water-sustainability standards can possibly be integrated into the existing standards of GlobalGAP. GAP is already applied in many developed and developing countries, including Kenya. Farmers who have complied with the GlobalGAP have benefited in the form of increased access to market, increased productivity and reduced cost of production through careful application of pesticides and fertilizer.

The approach sketched here would encourage flower farmers to comply with criteria on sustainable use of water resources. The costs involved in certification and labelling should be covered by the funds raised, but should be small relative to the funds raised, since the funds are primarily meant to promote sustainable water use within the catchment. This is a serious concern when implementing a water-sustainability agreement, because when costs become too high the instrument loses its effectiveness.

In its most modest form, a water-sustainability agreement would involve one major retailer in the Netherlands (the most important destination country for Kenyan flowers), one trader and one of the major farmers. In a more ambitious setting, several retailers, traders and farmers could be involved. Retailers, traders or farmers could also be represented by their respective branch organizations. In the case of the flower farmers this could be the Lake Naivasha Growers Group or the Kenyan Flower Council. In the Netherlands, the flower market is organized by FloraHolland, which may take a central role in facilitating an agreement.

Apart from the funds raised to reduce the water footprint in the Lake Naivasha Basin, an additional advantage of a water-sustainability premium to the final consumer product at the retailer is that it helps to create awareness regarding the value of water along the supply chain down to the consumers. An advantage of raising funds at the consumer end over local full-cost water pricing is that the latter would reduce local competitiveness and diminish profitability. This may lead to a shift of flower farming out of Kenya to other countries, like Ethiopia, which is currently experiencing a growth in the horticulture sector.

## Integrating sustainability into economic development

Cut flowers are an important export sector in Kenya. Next to their contribution to the gross domestic product and foreign exchange earnings, the commercial farms provide employment, housing, schools and hospitals, free to employees and their families. Losing the cut-flower business would mean an economic and social tragedy for Kenya and the area around Lake Naivasha in particular. On the other hand, the treatment of Lake Naivasha as a free common-pool resource will be at the cost of the lake's sustainability and the corporate image of the commercial farms. Therefore, sustainable management of the water resources of the Lake Naivasha

Basin is needed. One will need to decide on the maximum allowable drop in the lake water level as a result of water abstractions and on the maximum allowable blue and grey water footprint in the basin.

Pricing water at its full marginal cost is important, but probably difficult to achieve under current and near-future conditions in Kenya. The alternative of a water-sustainability premium to flowers sold at the retailer may be more effective. It will generate a larger fund than can be achieved through local water pricing, a fund that can be used for financing improved watershed management and measures that reduce the blue and grey water footprint within the Lake Naivasha Basin. Besides, it would create awareness among consumers on the value of water. The mechanism of a water-sustainability premium will reduce the risk of Kenya losing its flower business in the long term. In addition it is fair to have consumers pay: in the current situation, the overseas consumers of cut flowers get the benefit but do not cover the environmental cost of the flowers. The water-sustainability premium can enhance the green image of the commercial farms that participate and increase chances in the market for sustainable products. Effective implementation of the idea depends on the commitment of all stakeholders: the Kenyan government, civil society organizations, farmers, traders, retailers and consumers. A prerequisite for success is also a clearly defined certification procedure and institutional arrangement for the flow of funds to ensure that the proper investments are made to make water use in the basin sustainable.

# 8

# THE SUPPLY-CHAIN WATER FOOTPRINT OF PAPER

Paper industries are known for their large water demand and for producing polluted effluents, which, if not properly treated, can cause significant ecological damage in the streams into which the effluents are disposed. The pulp and paper industry in the USA withdraws approximately 5,500 billion litres of water annually from surface and groundwater sources (Figure 8.1), which is 2.5 per cent of the total industrial water withdrawal in the USA and a bit over 1 per cent of the total water withdrawal from ground- and surface-water bodies in the country (FAO, 2012b). A major part of the water used in the pulp and paper industry, however, returns to the catchments from where the water has been taken, so that consumptive water use is much less than the total abstraction: an estimated volume of 507 billion litres of water annually evaporates from pulp and paper mills in the USA, and 10 billion litres of water per year leave the mills (and the catchments) incorporated in products.

Probably more important than the consumptive use of water in pulp and paper mills is the pollution that comes from those mills. Chemical pulps are made by cooking the raw materials and adding chemicals. The mixture of chemicals added depends on the process applied; we should distinguish between the kraft (sulfate) process, the sulfite process and the sodium process. Although mechanical pulping is applied as well, chemical pulping is the most commonly used pulping process, whereby the sulfate process is the most common technique applied. After pulping, the pulp is generally bleached to make it whiter. Different sorts of chemicals are used in this process, including for example chlorine, sodium hypochlorite and chlorine dioxide. Particularly the use of elemental chlorine or chlorine compounds result in high concentrations of undesired compounds in effluents. Water pollution from pulp and paper mills mostly stems from the organic matter contained in the effluents, which generally include a lot of chlorinated organic compounds like dioxins and other adsorbable organic halides (which go under the abbreviation

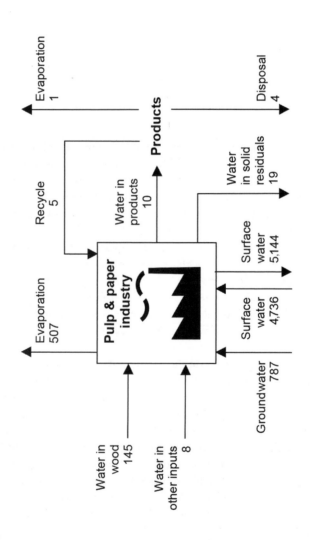

**FIGURE 8.1** The water balance of the US pulp and paper industry. Water flows in billion litres per year. Data from NCASI (2009). The 'water in wood' refers to the water physically embedded in wood inputs; the balance does not show the indirect water use for wood production.

AOX). The organic matter content in effluents from pulp and paper mills is meas-ured by the 'biochemical oxygen demand' (BOD) in the effluent; a large BOD in effluents can lead to oxygen depletion and fish kills in rivers. High concentrations of AOX can lead to toxicity and fish kills as well.

In addition to the water consumption and pollution in the pulp and paper industry, there is a huge indirect demand for water to grow the trees that form the raw material for pulp. Most of the time, this is rainwater transpired by the trees or otherwise evaporated from the tree plantations. This evapotranspiration in itself is quite natural and most of the time not causing great changes in the hydrology of the catchments where the plantations are located. From a resource allocation point of view, however, it is relevant to quantify the amount of water resources allocated to forestry products like paper, timber and firewood, because land and water resources reserved for producing forestry products cannot be applied for producing crops or for sustaining natural forests and biodiversity. According to the latest Global Forest Resources Assessment (FAO, 2010), 30 per cent of the 4,000 million ha of forest in the world is production forest. The area of planted forest is estimated at 7 per cent of the total forest area and is increasing. Water resources associated with lands that are primarily used as production forest are designated to the production of forestry products and not available for other pur-poses. When considering the water demand for paper, it is interesting to look at the water use in pulp and paper mills, but relevant to consider the water claims related to wood production as well. As we will see in this chapter, we are talking about vast amounts of water that are allocated to wood production and indirectly for paper products.

It is true that wood production primarily depends on rainwater (green water), while pulp and paper mills primarily consume ground and surface water (blue water) and that problems of water use are usually associated with blue and not green water use, but it is a misunderstanding that green water is not scarce. Indeed, discussions about freshwater scarcity are generally focused on the scarcity of blue water resources (rivers and groundwater), but there is as much reason to be concerned about the allocation of green water resources (rainwater). There is competition over green water resources as well as over blue water resources. Both green and blue water resources can be made productive for a large variety of pur-poses (food, feed, clothing fibres, biomass for biofuels, timber, firewood and paper) or left undisturbed (to sustain natural ecosystems). Forestry products put a large claim on the world's green water resources, which cannot therefore be designated for other purposes. A complete picture of the water footprint of paper can only be obtained when we look at all sorts of water claims in all stages of production.

## Estimating the water footprint of paper

The water footprint of a final paper product (expressed in litres/kg) is the sum of the water footprints in the forestry and the industrial stage. The first stage pro-duces wood; the second stage processes wood into pulp and paper. A pulp mill converts wood chips or other plant fibre sources into a thick fibre board which can be shipped to a paper mill for further processing into final paper products. The blue water footprint in the industrial stage can be estimated by summing up the evaporation flows from the pulp and paper mills, the amount of water incorporated in the products delivered by the mills and the volume of water contained in solid residuals. The grey water footprint depends on the loads of different chemicals contained in the mill effluents discharged into the environment. If effluents are treated before disposal, the loads are measured after treatment. In the industrial stage there is no green water footprint. The water footprint during the forestry stage contains both a green and blue component. These green and blue water footprint components cannot easily be determined separately because trees use rainfall water and tap from groundwater resources simultaneously. The grey water footprint component in wood production will generally be zero, assuming that no chemicals are applied in the plantations.

There has been quite some interest in the water footprint of paper from the pulp and paper industry. One of the early partners of the Water Footprint Network was the Confederation of European Paper Industries, joining as a partner in early 2009. Paper industries that started to explore the water footprint of their products include the UPM-Kymmene Corporation (based in Finland), Stora Enso (Sweden) and the Smurfit Kappa Group (Ireland). In 2010, a student from the University of Natural Resources and Applied Life Sciences in Austria carried out an explorative study on the water footprint of paper from three Austrian paper mills (Kellner, 2010). At the same time, my own group made a global estimate of the water footprint of paper (Van Oel and Hoekstra, 2010). Interest from the research community has also come from the Papiertechnische Stiftung (PTS), a research organization for the German paper industry.

## The UPM case

The UPM-Kymmene Corporation, a Finnish pulp, paper and timber manufacturer, was the first in its sector to publish a detailed study on the water footprint of paper. In a detailed case study, they assessed the operational and supply-chain water footprint of their Nordland paper mill in Germany (Rep, 2011). The majority of chemical pulp used at this paper mill comes from three pulp mills: the Kaukas and Pietarsaari pulp mills in Finland and the Fray Bentos pulp mill in Uruguay. In the Finnish pulp mills, three different types of tree are used: broadleaves, pine and spruce. In the pulp mill in Uruguay, eucalyptus trees are used as the raw resource. The Nordland paper mill in Germany produces two paper grades: wood-free coated paper ($150\,g/m^2$) and wood-free uncoated paper ($80\,g/m^2$). Wood-free paper is paper made from chemical pulp instead of mechanical pulp. Chemical pulp is made from pulpwood and is considered wood-free as most of the lignin is removed and separated from the cellulose fibres during processing, in contrast to mechanical pulp which retains most of its wood components and can therefore still be described as wood-containing. It was found that the total water footprint of one A4-sheet of paper leaving the Nordland paper mill is 13 litres for wood-free uncoated paper and 20 litres for wood-free coated paper. The colour composition of that total water footprint is 60 per cent green, 39 per cent grey and 1 per cent blue. Around 99 per cent of the total water footprint originates from the raw material supply chain (forestry stage and pulp mills in Finland and Uruguay) and the remaining 1 per cent from the production processes within the Nordland paper mill in Germany. The grey water footprint assessment showed that AOX was the most critical indicator from an environmental impact perspective, requiring the biggest volume of water to dilute to acceptable concentrations.

## The water footprint of paper related to wood production

Let's look now in a bit more detail at the water footprint of the first production stage, the stage of wood production. For estimating the water footprint of a unit of paper product in its forestry stage, we need a number of input variables (Van Oel and Hoekstra, 2012). First of all, we need to estimate the evapotranspiration from a forest or woodland (in $m^3$ of water per hectare per year). Second, we need to know the wood yield (in $m^3$ of wood per hectare per year) and the volumetric fraction of water in freshly harvested wood ($m^3/m^3$). Generally, this fraction is around $0.4\,m^3$ of water per cubic metre of freshly harvested wood (Gonzalez-Garcia *et al.*, 2009; NCASI, 2009). The total evapotranspiration plus the water incorporated in the harvested wood are divided by the wood yield to obtain an estimate of the water footprint of the harvested wood ($m^3$ of water/$m^3$ of wood). This needs to be multiplied by three different factors in order to arrive at an estimate of the water footprint of the final paper product.

The first factor is the wood-to-paper conversion factor, which represents the harvested wood volume in cubic metres needed to produce a metric ton of paper (Table 8.1). The second factor is the fraction of the total value of the forest that is associated with paper production. This factor is applied to make sure that the total

**TABLE 8.1** Average wood-to-paper conversion factors

| Product | Conversion factor ($m^3$/tonne) |
| --- | --- |
| Mechanical wood pulp | 2.50 |
| Semi-chemical wood pulp | 2.67 |
| Chemical wood pulp | 4.49 |
| Dissolving wood pulp | 5.65 |
| Newsprint | 2.87 |
| Printing & writing paper | 3.51 |
| Other paper & paperboard | 3.29 |

Source: based on UNECE and FAO (2010)

water consumption is fairly distributed over the various forest products (based on the relative value of the different forest products). Forests generally serve multiple functions, one of which may be the production of paper, but others may be the production of timber, firewood, biodiversity conservation and carbon storage. Therefore, not all evapotranspiration from a forest should necessarily be attributed to the production of paper. A fair way of accounting is to allocate the water consumption over the various forest functions according to their economic value (Hoekstra *et al.*, 2011). One would need estimates of the various values of forests, as for instance reported in Costanza *et al.* (1997). For estimating the water footprint figures that will be presented later on in this chapter, we assumed that paper is produced from forests that have wood pulp production as the primary function and for which annual harvest is equal to annual growth.

The final factor to be taken into account is the fraction of pulp used in paper production that is derived from wood and not from recycled paper. Paper recycling is an important factor for the water footprint, because fully recycled paper avoids the use of fresh wood and thus nullifies the water footprint in the forestry stage. When more recovered paper is used, the overall water footprint will decrease. On average, an estimated 41 per cent of all produced pulp is obtained from recycled paper (FAO and CEPI, 2007; UNECE and FAO, 2010), with large differences between producers using no recycled paper at all to producers that achieve relatively high percentages. The 'recovered paper utilization rates' for the main pulp-producing countries are shown in Table 8.2. This rate is defined as the amount of recovered paper used for paper and paperboard as a percentage of paper and paperboard production. Losses in repulping of recovered paper are estimated to be between 10 and 20 per cent (FAO and CEPI, 2007). For the water footprint estimates that will be shown later on in this chapter we assumed a loss of 15 per cent for all countries.

## Forest evapotranspiration

There are several factors that influence evapotranspiration from forest biomes, including meteorological conditions, tree type and forest management. Table 8.3 shows the average annual evapotranspiration for the main pulp-producing countries by forest type. Together, these countries produced 95 per cent of globally produced pulp in the period 1998–2007. For large countries covering several climatic zones, such as the USA, values of evapotranspiration may vary considerably. For the spatial distribution of different types of forest we could make use of The World's Forests 2000 (FAO, 2001), a dataset that gives the global distribution of forest biomes at a resolution of 1 km. Five different forest types are distinguished: boreal (typical trees include pine, fir and spruce), tropical (typical trees include eucalyptus), subtropical, temperate (typical trees include oak, beech and maple) and polar forest. Data on annual actual evapotranspiration could be obtained from FAO (2009), a dataset containing annual average values for the period 1961–1990 at a resolution of five arc minutes. Country averages for the annual evapotranspiration

**TABLE 8.2** Recovered paper utilization rates and fractions of pulp derived from recycled paper for the main pulp-producing countries

| Country | Recovered paper utilization rate | Fraction of pulp derived from recycled paper |
|---|---|---|
| USA | 0.37 | 0.31 |
| Canada | 0.24 | 0.20 |
| China | 0.42 | 0.36 |
| Finland | 0.05 | 0.04 |
| Sweden | 0.17 | 0.14 |
| Japan | 0.61 | 0.52 |
| Brazil | 0.40 | 0.34 |
| Russia | 0.42 | 0.36 |
| Indonesia | 0.42 | 0.36 |
| India | 0.42 | 0.36 |
| Chile | 0.42 | 0.36 |
| France | 0.60 | 0.51 |
| Germany | 0.67 | 0.57 |
| Norway | 0.22 | 0.19 |
| Portugal | 0.21 | 0.18 |
| Spain | 0.85 | 0.72 |
| South Africa | 0.42 | 0.36 |
| Austria | 0.46 | 0.39 |
| New Zealand | 0.25 | 0.21 |
| Australia | 0.64 | 0.54 |
| Poland | 0.36 | 0.31 |
| Thailand | 0.59 | 0.50 |
| Average | 0.42 | 0.36 |

Source: recovered paper utilization rates from FAO and CEPI (2007). When country data are missing, we assume the average as for the other countries (42 per cent). The fraction of pulp derived from recycled paper is assumed to be 85 per cent of the recovered paper utilization rate, due to losses in processing.

**TABLE 8.3** Contribution to global pulp production, share of chemical pulp and annual evapotranspiration by forest type in the main pulp-producing countries

| Pulp producing country | Contribution to global pulp production | Share of chemical pulp | Average evapotranspiration by forest type (mm/year) | | | |
|---|---|---|---|---|---|---|
| | | | Boreal | Temperate | Subtropical | Tropical |
| USA | 29.5% | 85% | 278 | 516 | 635 | 1,730 |
| Canada | 13.5% | 52% | 358 | 360 | – | – |
| China | 9.2% | 11% | 370 | 416 | 608 | 547 |
| Finland | 6.5% | 60% | 355 | 293 | – | – |
| Sweden | 6.3% | 69% | 345 | 318 | – | – |
| Japan | 5.9% | 87% | – | 637 | 725 | – |
| Brazil | 4.8% | 93% | – | – | 965 | 1,048 |
| Russia | 3.3% | 74% | 310 | 362 | – | – |
| Indonesia | 2.4% | 93% | – | – | – | 1,071 |
| India | 1.7% | 37% | – | – | 455 | 551 |
| Chile | 1.6% | 86% | – | 567 | 578 | – |
| France | 1.3% | 67% | – | 401 | 386 | – |
| Germany | 1.3% | 44% | – | 363 | – | – |
| Norway | 1.2% | 26% | 328 | 303 | – | – |
| Portugal | 1.0% | 100% | – | 512 | 502 | – |
| Spain | 1.0% | 93% | – | 547 | 527 | – |
| South Africa | 1.0% | 72% | – | – | 819 | 762 |
| Austria | 0.9% | 76% | – | 344 | – | – |
| New Zealand | 0.8% | 45% | – | 491 | 630 | – |
| Australia | 0.6% | 50% | – | 768 | 775 | 818 |
| Poland | 0.6% | 76% | – | 377 | – | – |
| Thailand | 0.5% | 86% | – | – | – | 636 |
| Total | 94.9% | | | | | |

Sources: the contribution to global pulp production and the share of chemical pulp for the period 1996–2005 based on FAO (2012a); national averages on evapotranspiration estimated by combining data on the global distribution of forest biomes (FAO, 2001) and spatially distributed data on annual actual evapotranspiration (FAO, 2009).

values for forests could be determined by averaging all values of actual evapotranspiration in a country for all locations that are covered with closed forest.

We consider here green and blue water evapotranspiration from forests as a total.
The difference between the use of green and the use of blue water is not as straightforward for forestry products as it is for other (agricultural) products. This difficulty
is related to the process of water uptake by trees. The extent of the root zone of
a fully-grown tree is generally well beyond the rainwater that is contained in the
soil. Trees obtain water from the soil as well as from aquifers. In-depth studies on
forest hydrology for specific cases would be required to make reliable estimates of
the green–blue ratio in the water footprint of wood. In addition, let me make two
more notes on forest evapotranspiration. First of all, meteorological variations can
cause differences in evapotranspiration across years; climate change may even result
in an upward or downward trend over the long term. The forest evaporation estimates shown in Table 8.3 are based on climate averages (for the period 1961–1990).
Second, the evapotranspiration rate from a forest depends on the maturity of the
forest. The table shows average annual evapotranspiration rates from extended areas
of forest, thus averaging out variations in growth stages within forests.

## Wood yields

We assume here that the wood used for the production of wood pulp is harvested at
a rate corresponding to the maximum sustainable annual yield from production forests with wood production as its primary function. The maximum sustainable annual
yield is the maximum annual yield that can be obtained from a forested area over
an extended period of time. Per biome we have estimated the maximum sustainable
annual yield by assuming one typical tree type. We made the following assumptions
for tree types in different forest biomes: boreal forests yield pine; temperate forests yield broadleaves and pine; and subtropical and tropical forests yield eucalyptus.
Estimated wood yields by country and type of tree are summarized in Table 8.4.

Generally, most of the wood will be processed into pulp in the same region as
where the wood is harvested, but not always. Paper mills in Sweden, for example,
use 75 per cent of wood that originates from Sweden itself; the other 25 per cent
is imported from Latvia, Estonia and Lithuania (Gonzalez-Garcia *et al.* 2009).

## The water footprint of printing and writing paper

The water footprint per volume of harvested wood for the main pulp-producing
countries is shown in Table 8.5. The water footprint of final printing and writing
paper is shown in Table 8.6. Country-specific recycling percentages are incorporated in these values. The smallest water footprint for printing and writing paper
is 321 litres/kg (eucalyptus from subtropical biome in Spain) and the largest is
2,602 litres/kg (eucalyptus from tropical biome in the USA). For a standard A4
sheet of copy paper ($80\,g/m^2$) we thus find water footprints of between 2 and
13 litres. If nowhere recovered paper would be used, the lowest water footprint

**TABLE 8.4** Wood yield estimates for the main pulp-producing countries

| Pulp-producing country | Wood yield estimates (m³/ha/year) | | |
|---|---|---|---|
| | Broadleaves | Eucalyptus | Pine |
| USA | 7 | 16 | 6 |
| Canada | 7 | – | 6 |
| China | 6 | 6 | 4 |
| Finland | 7 | – | 6 |
| Sweden | 7 | – | 8 |
| Japan | 11 | 14 | 7 |
| Brazil | 20 | 45 | – |
| Russia | 7 | – | 8 |
| Indonesia | – | 19 | – |
| India | – | 10 | – |
| Chile | 22 | 26 | 19 |
| France | 7 | 16 | 9 |
| Germany | 7 | – | 8 |
| Norway | 7 | – | 8 |
| Portugal | 7 | 16 | 8 |
| Spain | 7 | 16 | 8 |
| South Africa | 11 | 23 | – |
| Austria | 7 | – | 8 |
| New Zealand | 14 | 19 | 15 |
| Australia | 14 | 19 | 12 |
| Poland | 8 | – | 7 |
| Thailand | – | 14 | – |

Source: FAO (2006). For several countries, assumptions have been made as reported in Van Oel and Hoekstra (2012).

**TABLE 8.5** The water footprint of harvested wood for the main pulp–producing countries

| Pulp-producing country | Water footprint of wood (m³/m³) | | | | |
|---|---|---|---|---|---|
| | Pines from boreal biome | Pines from temperate biome | Broadleaves from temperate biome | Eucalyptus from subtropical biome | Eucalyptus from tropical biome |
| USA | 463 | 860 | 752 | 397 | 1,081 |
| Canada | 597 | 600 | 525 | – | – |
| China | 891 | 1,001 | 693 | 1,105 | 995 |
| Finland | 592 | 488 | 451 | – | – |
| Sweden | 413 | 381 | 463 | – | – |
| Japan | – | 859 | 571 | 527 | – |
| Brazil | – | – | – | 214 | 233 |
| Russia | 371 | 434 | 528 | – | – |
| Indonesia | – | – | – | – | 564 |
| India | – | – | – | 455 | 551 |
| Chile | – | 298 | 262 | 222 | – |
| France | – | 446 | 584 | 241 | – |
| Germany | – | 435 | 529 | – | – |
| Norway | 393 | 363 | 442 | – | – |
| Portugal | – | 613 | 746 | 314 | – |
| Spain | – | 655 | 797 | 329 | – |
| South Africa | – | – | – | 356 | 331 |
| Austria | – | 412 | 501 | – | – |
| New Zealand | – | 335 | 351 | 338 | – |
| Australia | – | 662 | 549 | 415 | 438 |
| Poland | – | 539 | 459 | – | – |
| Thailand | – | – | – | – | 463 |

Source: Van Oel and Hoekstra (2012)

**TABLE 8.6** The water footprint of printing and writing paper, taking into account country-specific recovered paper utilization rates

| Country | Water footprint of printing & writing paper (litre/kg) | | | | |
|---|---|---|---|---|---|
| | Pine from boreal biome | Pine from temperate biome | Broadleaf from temperate biome | Eucalyptus from subtropical biome | Eucalyptus from tropical biome |
| USA | 1,115 | 2,069 | 1,809 | 955 | 2,602 |
| Canada | 1,667 | 1,676 | 1,466 | – | – |
| China | 2,015 | 2,266 | 1,568 | 2,501 | 2,250 |
| Finland | 1,988 | 1,641 | 1,515 | – | – |
| Sweden | 1,241 | 1,144 | 1,392 | – | – |
| Japan | – | 1,452 | 965 | 891 | – |
| Brazil | – | – | – | 497 | 540 |
| Russia | 840 | 981 | 1,193 | – | – |
| Indonesia | – | – | – | – | 1,275 |
| India | – | – | – | 1,029 | 1,246 |
| Chile | – | 674 | 591 | 502 | – |
| France | – | 766 | 1,005 | 415 | – |
| Germany | – | 657 | 799 | – | – |
| Norway | 1,121 | 1,036 | 1,260 | – | – |
| Portugal | – | 1,769 | 2,151 | 905 | – |
| Spain | – | 638 | 776 | 321 | – |
| South Africa | – | – | – | 806 | 749 |
| Austria | – | 881 | 1,072 | – | – |
| New Zealand | – | 925 | 969 | 933 | – |
| Australia | – | 1,060 | 878 | 665 | 701 |
| Poland | – | 1,312 | 1,118 | – | – |
| Thailand | – | – | – | – | 809 |

Source: Van Oel and Hoekstra (2012)

would be 753 litres/kg (eucalyptus from subtropical biome in Brazil) and the highest 3,880 litres/kg (eucalyptus from subtropical biome in China). For one sheet of A4 copy paper this means between 4 and 19 litres.

By far the largest fraction of the water footprint of the final paper product relates to water consumption in the forestry stage. We can see this by considering the example of the USA. In the USA, annual industrial production of paper is around 97 billion kg/year. The total water consumption in USA's pulp and paper industry is 536 million $m^3$/yr (the sum of the total evaporation, the water contained in solid residuals and the water contained in products, see Figure 8.1). This gives an estimated water footprint of 5.5 litres/kg of paper (0.03 litres for one A4 sheet). We have to note here that this figure refers to the blue water footprint only; we have not analysed the grey water footprint. Including that component of the water footprint can substantially contribute to the overall water footprint of paper, as was shown in the UPM example.

## The water footprint of paper consumption in the Netherlands

Many countries strongly depend on imports of pulp and paper. For those countries, it is relevant to know the size and location of the water footprints of the imported products. We will consider here the case of the Netherlands. As a basis, we use data on the annual production, import, export and consumption of pulp and paper for the Netherlands (Table 8.7). We could trace the origin of imported pulp and paper based on data from the International Trade Centre (ITC, 2006). We assumed that the paper products consumed within the country are based on domestic and imported pulp according to the ratio of domestic pulp production to pulp import. The recovered paper utilization rate in the Netherlands is 70 per cent (FAO and CEPI, 2007).

The total water footprint of paper consumption in the Netherlands has been estimated to be 3.2 to 4.6 billion $m^3$/yr, of which only 0.1 billion $m^3$/yr refers to water consumption within the Netherlands (Van Oel and Hoekstra, 2012). The remainder, 3.1–4.5 billion $m^3$/yr, refers to water consumption in the countries from which the paper and pulp consumed by the Dutch originates. Most of the imported pulp originates from other European countries (85 per cent), followed by North America (12 per cent), Asia (2 per cent) and South America (0.7 per cent). The range in the total water footprint estimate comes from uncertainty about the biomes from which the imported pulp and paper is derived and the fact that the water footprint of wood varies depending on the type of biome from which the wood is obtained. If we translate the total water footprint to an average water footprint per Dutch citizen, we find a water footprint related to paper consumption of 200 to 290 $m^3$/yr per capita. If countries from which the Netherlands imports pulp and paper did not recover paper as they currently do (Table 8.2) and if also the Netherlands itself did not recover paper, the water footprint of paper products consumed in the Netherlands would be 4.9 to 7.1 billion $m^3$/yr. Using recovered paper has therefore resulted in a water saving of about 36 per cent.

**TABLE 8.7** Annual production, import, export and consumption of pulp and paper for the Netherlands

| Product | Pulp | Newsprint | Printing & writing paper | Other paper & paperboard |
|---|---|---|---|---|
| Production (tonne/year) | 125,350 | 387,700 | 895,400 | 1,987,200 |
| Import quantity (tonne/year) | 1,132,860 | 476,540 | 1,267,890 | 1,498,200 |
| Export quantity (tonne/year) | 322,340 | 259,480 | 1,143,450 | 1,417,900 |
| Consumed (tonne/year) | 935,870 | 604,760 | 1,019,840 | 2,067,500 |

Source: FAO (2012a). Averages for the period 1996–2005.

The water footprint of printing and writing paper on the Dutch market is estimated to be somewhere between 962 and 1,349 litres/kg. When the paper is produced from trees grown in the Netherlands, the water footprint is substantially smaller (two to three times) than when the paper is imported or produced from imported pulp (Table 8.8). The water footprint of a standard A4 sheet of copy paper ($80\,g/m^2$) on the Dutch market is between 5 and 7 litres (7–10 litres if no recovered paper is used).

## Two to twenty litres of water per sheet of paper

When we take into account the various figures found in the global study, the study for paper as consumed in the Netherlands and the UPM case study for a paper mill in Germany, we find a water footprint for one standard sheet of A4 paper ranging from 2 to 20 litres of water. If we would take more variables and uncertainties into account, the range would certainly become bigger. Including the grey water footprint in the industrial stage would increase the numbers. The grey water footprint was only included in the study by UPM. None of the studies presented included the indirect water footprint of paper related to other materials and energy used along the supply chain. The machines, materials and energy being used in harvesting wood and in pulping and paper manufacturing all have their own water footprint, as well as the materials and energy used in transporting wood, pulp and paper. Particularly when bioenergy is involved, the water footprint in transportation can be substantial (see Chapter 6). If we included examples of full recycling, we probably could find lower estimates than 2 litres per sheet of paper.

The two major variables that influence the size of the water footprint of paper and that can be relatively easily influenced are the paper recycling rate and the amount of chemicals in effluents discharged into the environment. A substantial reduction in the claim of paper products on the globe's freshwater resources would be achieved by increasing the paper recovery percentages worldwide. An important step towards reducing water contamination can be made by making the shift to bleaching pulp without chlorine chemicals, which is known as total chlorine-free (TCF) bleaching. In addition, of course, the consumption of paper itself can be reduced. The question remains what priority companies, consumers and governments really give to the issues of paper recovery, paperless offices and pollution prevention and control.

**TABLE 8.8** The water footprint of paper products in the Netherlands

| Origin | Product | Water footprint (litre/kg) | |
|---|---|---|---|
| | | Lower estimate | Higher estimate |
| Paper produced from trees grown in the Netherlands | Newsprint | 369 | 410 |
| | Printing & writing paper | 451 | 501 |
| | Other paper & paperboard | 423 | 470 |
| Imported paper to the Netherlands or paper produced from imported pulp | Newsprint | 829 | 1,144 |
| | Printing & writing paper | 994 | 1,402 |
| | Other paper & paperboard | 848 | 1,267 |
| Average paper as on the Dutch market | Newsprint | 802 | 1,101 |
| | Printing & writing paper | 962 | 1,349 |
| | Other paper & paperboard | 823 | 1,221 |

Source: Van Oel and Hoekstra (2012). For the 'average paper on the Dutch market' it is assumed that pulp is used from imported and domestic sources in the same ratio as they are available (imported + produced). Around 94 per cent of the available pulp in the Netherlands is imported.

# 9

# MAXIMUM SUSTAINABLE WATER FOOTPRINT PER RIVER BASIN

It is inevitable that people have an environmental footprint on the Earth. People use natural resources like land, water and energy and undertake various kinds of activities that bring along pollution. Whether the total footprint of all activities together is sustainable, fully depends on the *size* of the footprint. Consider for example the carbon footprint. The fact that human activities add greenhouse gases into the atmosphere has become a problem because of the *total amount* of greenhouse gases added. The carbon footprint of one activity does not have an impact. It is the total carbon footprint of humanity that has become too big: the average global temperature is likely to increase substantially, with secondary effects on evaporation and precipitation patterns and sea level and tertiary effects on ecosystems and societies (IPCC, 2007). We have a similar size-issue with our ecological footprint, or our 'land footprint'. The ecological footprint is the total bioproductive area required to sustain the various components of our consumption pattern. In 2008, humanity's ecological footprint exceeded the Earth's biocapacity by more than 50 per cent (WWF, 2012). This means that we would need 1.5 Earths to sustain our present way of living. We currently survive on this one planet by over-exploiting it, which can be done temporarily but cannot be maintained in the long term. The concern is not directly the ecological footprint that can be associated with any specific human activity, but our total ecological footprint. With the water footprint, we have the same issue of size.

In the case of the water footprint, the typical unit for evaluation is the river basin (Hoekstra *et al.*, 2011). As we will see later in this chapter, there is also an important global dimension to the water footprint, but let me start with the river basin. Within a river basin, water resources availability is constrained by the amount of precipitation. The precipitation that adds to the water in a river basin will leave the basin again by evaporation or runoff to the ocean. The evaporative flow (green water) can be made productive in crop fields or production forests. In this way, the evaporative flow is not 'lost' to the atmosphere but productively used. The runoff flow (blue water) can be made productive as well, by withdrawing water from aquifers and rivers and using it in industries or households or for irrigating fields. In this way, the runoff flow is not 'lost' to the ocean, but consumed for useful purposes. We can use all the green and blue water available in a river basin in a certain period. Temporarily, we can even use more than that, by depleting groundwater and lake reservoirs but, in the longer term, from a sustainability point of view, we cannot use more than the rate of replenishment. The upper limit to consumptive water use within a river basin is the precipitation within the basin. However, this is really an upper-upper limit, because there are two reasons why the actual upper limit lies substantially lower. One is that we cannot use all green water; the second is that we cannot use all blue water. The 'loss' of water to the atmosphere through non-beneficial evapotranspiration and the 'loss' of water to the ocean are not real losses. These flows are essential for the functioning of ecosystems and of societies depending on those ecosystems.

## The maximum sustainable water footprint in a river basin

The upper limit to the green water footprint in a river basin is formed by the total evapotranspiration from the land that can be made sustainably available for agricultural production or forestry. As a rough indication, about 25–50 per cent of the land has to be reserved as a natural area to sustain biodiversity (Svancara et al., 2005). Besides, areas are needed for living and infrastructure, and some areas, like deserts and steep mountains, are unsuitable for production, so that only a fraction of the land is available for agriculture and forestry. Only the green water flow in this area can be productively employed to produce food, feed, fibre crops, timber, paper, etc. Besides, only the green water in the growing season can be employed. The 'maximum sustainable green water footprint' (or shortly 'green water availability') in a river basin is only a fraction of the total evaporative flow.

The upper limit to the blue water footprint in a river basin is given by the total natural runoff from the basin minus the so-called 'environmental flow requirement'. Environmental flow requirements are the flows that need to remain in the river to sustain freshwater and estuarine ecosystems and the human livelihoods that depend on these ecosystems. The idea that all runoff can be consumed without a price is wrong. Biodiversity along rivers and in river deltas obviously depends on the presence of river water. As a rough indication, about 80 per cent of the natural river flow needs to be maintained in order to prevent major changes in natural structure and ecosystem functions along the river and in its delta (Richter et al., 2012). As a rule of thumb, the 'maximum sustainable blue water footprint' (or 'blue water availability') in a river basin is only 20 per cent of the runoff from the basin.

For the grey water footprint, a similar sort of logic applies. The impact of water pollution depends on the size of the pollution. The 'maximum sustainable grey water footprint' in a river basin is reached when the size of the grey water footprint equals the runoff from the basin. In this case, the anthropogenic load of chemicals to the river has reached the so-called critical load, which is defined as the difference between the maximum allowable and the natural concentration of a chemical in a river × the runoff of the river (Hoekstra *et al.*, 2011). In the USA, the concept of critical load is known under the term 'total maximum daily load'. The essence is that loads that go beyond the maximum or critical load cause an exceedance of ambient water quality standards. When the grey water footprint exceeds runoff, the waste assimilation capacity has been fully used.

## The importance of location and timing

In the case of the carbon and ecological footprints, it makes sense to speak about *global* maximum sustainable levels (Ercin and Hoekstra, 2012; WWF, 2012). This is different in the case of the water footprint. The maximum green, blue or grey water footprint will always depend on location and time. A certain blue water footprint for example may cause little change in one catchment area, while the same sized footprint can cause depletion of water in a much drier catchment area. The same difference can occur over time: while a certain blue water footprint may be considered small during a wet month, it can be considered huge in a dry month in the same catchment area. When we aggregate the blue water footprints of all human activities over all the river basins in the world and over the months in a year, we can speak about the global blue water footprint in a year, but it does not make sense to compare this global annual blue water footprint to the aggregated blue water availability in the world over the year. Water shortage in one basin cannot be crossed against water abundance in another basin; and water shortage in one specific month cannot be crossed against the abundance of water in another month. Water scarcity, water overexploitation and water pollution manifest themselves in specific areas at specific times.

## The geographic versus the product perspective

I have employed above what we can call the 'geographic perspective' on sustainability. In this perspective, we look at the total green, blue and grey water footprint within a clearly delineated geographic area, preferably a river basin or catchment area. The green water footprint is then compared to green water availability, the blue water footprint to blue water availability and the grey water footprint to the runoff volume available to assimilate waste. From these comparisons, we will find so-called hotspots, river basins or smaller catchments within river basins, where the total green, blue or grey water footprint is not sustainable. Obviously, products that are produced in hotspot areas and consume or pollute substantial amounts of water contribute to the unsustainable conditions and are thus unsustainable as well. It is tempting to categorize products into two classes: unsustainable products that are fully or partly produced in areas where maximum sustainable water footprint levels are exceeded (hotspots), and sustainable products that are fully produced in geographic areas where maximum levels are not surpassed. The latter category, however, is suspicious. I will explain this with a simple example.

Suppose the hypothetical case of two river basins, with the same surface. Basin A is relatively dry and has, on an annual basis, 50 water units available, the maximum sustainable water footprint. The maximum level, however, is exceeded by a factor of two. Farmers in the basin consume 100 water units per year to produce 100 crop units. Basin B has more water available, 250 water units per year. Water is more abundant than in the first basin, and water is used less efficiently. Farmers in the basin consume 200 water units per year, to produce 100 crop units, the same amount as in the first basin, but using two times more water per crop unit. A geographic analysis shows that in basin B, the water footprint (200) remains below the maximum level (250), so this is sustainable. In basin A, however, the water footprint (100) by far exceeds the maximum sustainable level (50), so this is clearly unsustainable. The question is now: should we categorize the crops originating from basin A as unsustainable and the crops from basin B as sustainable? From a geographic perspective, the answer is affirmative. In basin A, the water footprint of crop production needs to be reduced, that's it. However, when we take a product perspective, we observe that the water footprint per crop unit in basin B is two times larger than in basin A. If the farmers in basin B would use their water more productively and reach the same water productivity as in basin A, they would produce twice as many crops without increasing the total water footprint in the basin. It may well be that farmers in basin A cannot easily further increase their water productivity, so that – if the aim is to keep global production at the same level – the only solution is to bring down the water footprint in basin A to a sustainable level by cutting production by half, while enlarging production in basin B by increasing the water productivity. If basin B manages to achieve the same water productivity level as in basin A, the two basins together could even increase global production while halving the total water footprint in basin A and keeping it at the same level in basin B.

This example is not a theoretical one. In the real world we can see a lot of semi-arid regions where water is relatively efficiently used, but overexploited, while we see water-abundant regions, where no overexploitation takes place but where water productivities are comparatively low. From a geographic perspective, the weak spots in the whole system lie in the regions with water overexploitation, where the total water footprint is too large. From a production perspective, the weak spots in the system lie in the regions with low water productivities, where water footprints per unit of production are unnecessarily large. In order to move the whole system in a sustainable direction, two things need to happen at the same time: total water footprints need to be reduced in the geographic areas where maximum sustainable levels are exceeded and water footprints per unit of production need to be reduced in those areas where this can be achieved most easily. From a global perspective, sustainability requires that maximum water footprint levels for all individual geographic areas are maintained but, in order to achieve that, water-use efficiencies need to be improved everywhere, wherever feasible, also in regions where water is abundant. From this global perspective, a product cannot be considered sustainable simply because it was produced in an area where maximum water footprint levels are maintained. Given certain global demands for various products and given global constraints to water availability, water footprints per unit of product need to remain within certain limits. It is not easy to establish reasonable limits per product, but more about that will come in the next chapter, in which I will reflect on water-use efficiency and benchmarking. In the remainder of this chapter, I will focus on the geographic perspective.

## The blue water footprint: not sustainable in over half of the river basins

In a recent global study, we demonstrated that, for the period 1996–2005, the blue water footprint in 55 per cent of the river basins studied was unsustainable during at least one month per year (Hoekstra *et al.*, 2012). This means that in these basins, during at least part of the year, generally the dry period, environmental flow requirements are not met.

We analysed 405 river basins that collectively account for 69 per cent of global runoff, 75 per cent of the world's irrigated area and 65 per cent of the world's population. For each river basin and each month, we categorized water scarcity from low to severe based on the ratio of blue water footprint to blue water availability. The blue water availability was calculated as natural runoff minus environmental flow requirements. The latter were assumed at 80 per cent of natural runoff. We defined four levels of blue water scarcity as follows. Low blue water scarcity means that the blue water footprint does not exceed blue water availability. The blue water footprint is thus lower than 100 per cent of blue water availability (lower than 20 per cent of natural runoff). Presumed environmental flow requirements are not violated. These are sustainable conditions. Moderate blue water scarcity means that the blue water footprint is between 100 and 150 per cent of blue water availability (between 20 and 30 per cent of natural runoff). Environmental flow requirements are no longer met. Significant blue water scarcity means that the blue water footprint is between 150 and 200 per cent of blue water availability (between 30 and 40 per cent of natural runoff). Severe water scarcity means that the blue water footprint is larger than 200 per cent of blue water availability (larger than 40 per cent of natural runoff).

Table 9.1 gives an overview of the number of basins and number of people facing low, moderate, significant and severe water scarcity during a given number of months per year. In 223 river basins with 2.72 billion inhabitants (69 per cent of the total population living in the basins included in this study), the blue water footprint exceeds blue water availability during at least one month of the year. For 201 of these basins, with together 2.67 billion inhabitants, there was severe water scarcity during at least one month of the year. This shows that when water scarcity exists, it is usually of a severe nature, meaning that more than 40 per cent of natural runoff is being consumed. In 35 river basins with 483 million people, there was severe water scarcity during at least half of the year.

**TABLE 9.1** The number of basins and number of people facing low, moderate, significant and severe water scarcity during a given number of months per year

| Number of months per year (n) | Number of basins facing low, moderate, significant and severe water scarcity during n months per year | | | | Number of people (millions) facing low, moderate, significant and severe water scarcity during n months per year | | | |
| --- | --- | --- | --- | --- | --- | --- | --- | --- |
| | Low water scarcity | Moderate water scarcity | Significant water scarcity | Severe water scarcity | Low water scarcity | Moderate water scarcity | Significant water scarcity | Severe water scarcity |
| 0 | 17 | 319 | 344 | 204 | 353 | 2,690 | 2,600 | 1,289 |
| 1 | 2 | 55 | 45 | 46 | 18.6 | 894 | 357 | 440 |
| 2 | 1 | 26 | 12 | 49 | 0.002 | 302 | 672 | 512 |
| 3 | 4 | 4 | 2 | 33 | 79.6 | 69.2 | 220 | 182 |
| 4 | 6 | 1 | 1 | 22 | 35.0 | 0.14 | 9.2 | 345 |
| 5 | 18 | 0 | 1 | 16 | 897 | 0 | 97.8 | 706 |
| 6 | 9 | 0 | 0 | 10 | 111 | 0 | 0 | 25.6 |
| 7 | 17 | 0 | 0 | 4 | 144 | 0 | 0 | 88 |
| 8 | 29 | 0 | 0 | 4 | 293 | 0 | 0 | 254 |
| 9 | 29 | 0 | 0 | 3 | 66.8 | 0 | 0 | 20.2 |
| 10 | 52 | 0 | 0 | 0 | 428 | 0 | 0 | 0 |
| 11 | 39 | 0 | 0 | 2 | 296 | 0 | 0 | 1.8 |
| 12 | 182 | 0 | 0 | 12 | 1,233 | 0 | 0 | 93.3 |
| Total | 405 | 405 | 405 | 405 | 3,956 | 3,956 | 3,956 | 3,956 |

Source: Hoekstra et al. (2012)

Of importance when considering the social, economic and environmental impacts of water scarcity are both the severity and the duration of the scarcity. Twelve of the river basins included in this study experience severe water scarcity during all months of the year. The largest of those basins is the Lake Eyre Basin in Australia, one of the largest endorheic basins in the world, arid and inhabited by only about 86,000 people, but covering around 1.2 million km². The most heavily populated basin facing severe water scarcity all year long is the Yongding He Basin in northern China (serving water to Beijing), with a surface of 214,000 km² and a population density of 425 persons/km². Eleven months of severe water scarcity occurs in the San Antonio River Basin in Texas, USA and the Groot-Kei River Basin in Eastern Cape, South Africa. Two heavily populated river basins face nine months of severe water scarcity: the Penner River Basin in southern India, a basin with a dry tropical monsoon climate (55,000 km², 10.9 million people), and the Tarim River Basin in China, which includes the Taklamakan Desert (1,052,000 km², 9.3 million people). Four basins face severe water scarcity during eight months a year: the Indus River Basin, mainly in Pakistan and India, with a population of 212 million people; the Cauvery River Basin in India, with 35 million people; the Dead Sea Basin, which includes the Jordan River and extends over parts of Jordan, Israel, the West Bank and minor parts of Lebanon and Egypt; and the Salinas River Basin in California in the USA.

## The sustainability of green water footprints

Regarding the green water footprint, the general attitude among water practitioners is that there is nothing to worry about, because rainwater evaporation occurs anyway, whether it is from natural vegetation, production forest or cropland. Substituting natural forest by cropland may decrease overall evapotranspiration over the year and thus increase annual runoff, but it may decrease the base flow in the dry period (because forests delay runoff more than croplands). These effects, however, are generally not easily measurable at the scale of a river basin. Replacing natural vegetation by rain-fed cropland or replacing one rain-fed crop by another is therefore generally considered of little relevance from a catchment hydrology point of view. The question around the sustainability of the green water footprint should therefore not focus on the issue of hydrological impact within the river basin. Instead, the question should be around the issue of water allocation. Productive lands with sufficient rain for good biomass growth are scarce. When we employ land and its associated green water resources for one purpose, we cannot use those resources for another purpose. Land and green water allocated to cropland or production forest will no longer be available for natural vegetation. Allocating land and green water to maize that will be fed to farm animals means that those resources will not be available for production of bread wheat. Land and green water given to rapeseed for producing biodiesel will no longer be available to produce food crops. Even though rain is free and evaporation happens anyway, a relevant question is how green water resources are allocated. The allocation question is an economic question, as well as a political one, because water is a public good and basic resource for food. Whether the green water footprint in a particular river basin is sustainable or not, is not so much a question of local impact but of efficient and equitable global allocation. More about this will come in Chapter 11.

## The grey water footprint: not sustainable in two-thirds of the river basins

It has been estimated that, in the year 2000, about two-thirds of the river basins in the world have an unsustainable grey water footprint related to nitrogen or phosphorus pollution (Liu *et al.*, 2012). In those basins, the waste assimilation capacity has been fully consumed and concentrations exceed the ambient water quality standards regarding nitrogen and/or phosphorus. There is no comprehensive reporting of the water quality of the world's rivers encompassing a variety of water quality parameters, but it is clear that water quality deterioration is an ongoing worldwide process, whereby no river basin in the world escapes (Meybeck, 2003, 2004). There are probably few rivers in the world left whereby water quality meets all regular water quality standards throughout the year. Excessive amounts of nitrogen and phosphorus are just one widespread form of pollution. Other widespread forms of contamination are pesticides, metals and pathogens.

## Water footprint caps per river basin

In Chapter 5 about cotton, I argued that the five national governments in Central Asia would need to agree on setting a cap on the blue water footprint in the Aral Sea Basin. Such a cap should reflect the maximum sustainable blue water footprint in the area. In Chapter 7 about cut flowers, I explained the usefulness of setting a cap on the blue water footprint for the Lake Naivasha Basin in Kenya. We can generalize this. Discussing and agreeing on a blue water footprint cap would be a useful thing for *all* river basins in the world, but is obviously most urgent in all those basins where the current blue water footprint already exceeds a maximum sustainable level. In our global study on blue water scarcity per basin, we assumed maximum sustainable blue water footprint levels at 20 per cent of natural runoff across river basins (Hoekstra *et al.*, 2012). With this rough assumption, the blue water footprint in more than half of the world's river basins can be classified as unsustainable. More detailed studies per river basin will need to refine the estimate (Richter *et al.*, 2012).

Whether a river basin falls within one nation or is shared among different nations, agreeing on a blue water footprint cap in a river basin is a political thing, whereby it can be expected that the level of the cap set will depend on negotiations and trading off different interests. For basins in which blue water resources are currently overexploited, it is most realistic to agree on a blue water footprint cap that gradually moves in time from the current blue water footprint level down to a level that can be regarded as sustainable. Over time, the necessary measures can then be taken to increase water-use efficiencies, so that the same levels of production can be achieved at a smaller blue water footprint. Other sorts of necessary measures may include shifting between different crops and – if otherwise impossible to meet the blue water footprint reduction target – reducing production levels altogether.

The idea of a cap on water use is not entirely new. In the Murray-Darling Basin in Australia, for example, a cap on surface water diversions was adopted as a response to growing water use and declining river health (MDBC, 2004). It was agreed that the cap be defined as 'the volume of water that would have been diverted under 1993/94 levels of development'. The question is still whether the cap puts a sufficient limit on water use to make water use really sustainable in the long term. A shortcoming of the cap in the Murray-Darling Basin is that it does not include groundwater abstractions, so that as a result of the cap on surface water diversions, the use of groundwater in the basin accelerated. Another deficiency from my point of view is that the cap manages diversions rather than consumptive use.

The grey water footprint in a river basin needs to be capped as well. This is easier than finding agreement on capping the blue water footprint, because most countries already have ambient water quality standards in existing legislation. Together with natural concentrations and river runoff, this implies a certain critical load per chemical. The maximum sustainable grey water footprint in a catchment area is reached when the total load of a chemical equals the critical load; in this case, the grey water footprint is the size of the river runoff. The challenge here is to rationally translate ambient water quality standards per chemical to critical loads and agree on devising institutional mechanisms that ensure that critical loads are not exceeded. The contribution of diffuse sources of pollution should thereby not be ignored. In most basins of the world, it is still common practice that diffuse pollution (e.g. from fertilizers and pesticides used in agriculture) is not properly regulated. For point sources of pollution, it often happens that effluent standards are not strict enough given the number of effluent disposal licences issued or that illegal wastewater disposals take place. As a result, critical loads are easily surpassed.

I would not argue for setting green water footprint caps per river basin, because it is more straightforward to agree on reserving lands for nature. Indirectly, this means that the green water resources attached to these lands will not be available for crop production or forestry. In fact, by determining which lands can be used for agriculture and for forestry, one simultaneously allocates the green water resources in a basin.

## Downscaling caps from the river basin level to individual users

Agreement on blue water footprint caps and critical loads per contaminant by river basin would be an enormous step forward in managing our global freshwater resources wisely. The problem with overdraft from aquifers and rivers and water pollution is that proper mechanisms to set limits are generally absent. Setting the limits clearly is one step towards better regulation. As a next step, the challenge will be to translate maximum water consumption levels and critical loads to limits for individual users. In international river basins, there will be the intermediate step of translating basin limits to national limits for that basin.

Water footprint caps need to be specified spatially – by river basin but also by sub-catchment – and temporally – for example by month. Specific attention will need to go to issues of inter-annual variability, because a potential trap is that limits are set for an average year, which will inevitably lead to problems in drier years. We could see this for example in the Murray-Darling Basin in Australia, where the overdraft of water in recent years has been partly blamed on that fact that water use permits to farmers were issued based on a too optimistic assessment of blue water availability. Once a blue water footprint cap for a river basin has been set, regular monitoring will be needed to evaluate whether the level of the cap is still appropriate, given changing environmental conditions like climate or improved knowledge regarding environmental flow requirements.

# 10

# WATER-USE EFFICIENCY

Efficient water use is an essential element in sustainable water use. But it is only part of the full story. The emphasis on efficiency makes us talk about less water use per unit of production. A famous slogan in the ongoing debate about freshwater scarcity is 'more crop per drop'. Although this sounds good, it makes us forget that, in the end, it is the total water consumption determining the impact on the environment. There is an increasing number of places on Earth where water resources are used in a very efficient way – with good amounts of crop per drop – but where water resources are depleted very quickly at the same time. The total impact of production on freshwater resources depends on *two* factors: the water use per unit of production and the total production. Everywhere, we can see companies reducing the volume of water consumption per unit of production, but the total volume of production grows often quicker, so that the total water consumption of the company increases. We can also find many catchments in which the water footprint per unit of production decreases, but where total production grows quicker, so that the total water footprint in the catchment effectively becomes bigger. It is thus as important to consider total production of water-intensive commodities as to look at water use per unit of production.

In this chapter, we will first examine what practitioners in the water field mean by 'efficient water use'. The term efficiency is being interpreted in different ways, so it often happens that what can be seen as efficient from one perspective, is not efficient from another perspective. There are three levels at which one can consider the efficiency of water use: the water user level, the river basin level and the global level (Hoekstra and Hung, 2005). In addition, at whatever level water-use efficiency is examined, there are two different perspectives: the physical and economic perspective. Traditionally, water resources managers – often educated as engineers or hydrologists – think in terms of water volumes allocated to different users, so they take the physical perspective. More recently, we see economists joining the debate on water scarcity and they emphasize the importance of looking at costs and benefits of water use. After a critical review of the different efficiency concepts, we will move on to a reflection on the limitations of increasing 'resource efficiency' and on the so-called 'rebound effect'.

## Water-use efficiency from a user point of view

'Water-use efficiency' is generally defined as the volume of a good produced per unit of water used or consumed. The term is used interchangeably with 'water productivity'. In crop growing, water productivity is measured as the amount of crop harvested divided by the water consumption. The latter generally refers to evapotranspiration (of both green and blue water) from the crop field over the growing period. Water productivity in crop farming (tonne/$m^3$) can thus be calculated as the yield (tonne/ha) divided by the evapotranspiration ($m^3$/ha). Water productivity is the inverse of the green plus blue water footprint of the crop. Lowering the 'water footprint' per unit of crop (expressed in $m^3$/tonne) is thus the same as increasing 'water productivity' (tonne/$m^3$). In the case of rain-fed agriculture – in which only green water is consumed – one can talk about *green* water productivity. In the case of irrigated agriculture – in which both green and blue water resources are consumed – we can speak about *total* water productivity by taking the total yield over the total green plus blue water consumed. In this case, one can define *blue* water productivity as the additional yield obtained through irrigation divided by the blue water consumed.

One could make an argument to measure water consumption for crop growing as the water uptake by plants, which is roughly equal to the transpiration by plants – rather than as the total evapotranspiration from the crop field. This, however, is usually not done. The reason is that, even though plants only benefit through the transpiration fraction of total evapotranspiration, it is the total that is lost to the atmosphere. The part of total evapotranspiration that does not benefit the plants can be seen as a loss that has to be accounted as well.

In industries, water-use efficiency or water productivity is generally measured in terms of total production divided by total water abstraction. From a company perspective, it makes sense to look at the volume of abstracted water, for example because it needs a licence for water use or because it needs to pay per $m^3$ of water abstracted. From an environmental perspective, though, it is more useful to look at consumptive water use, the blue water footprint. In this book, when speaking about blue water-use efficiency or productivity in industries, I mean total production divided by the total blue water footprint of an industry, which means production per unit of water consumption, not per unit of water abstraction.

Although the pollution factor is always left out of water efficiency or productivity measures, there is no reason to neglect that factor. In the end, water pollution is also a form of water use that subtracts from other uses. It is therefore worth pursuing efficiency increases in this field as well, which means lowering the grey water footprint per unit of production.

## Zero water footprint in industry

A water user can increase his water-use efficiency by producing the same amount with a lower water footprint, or by producing more with the same water footprint. In both cases, the water footprint per unit of product will decrease. Industries will generally focus on reducing the water footprint at a given production level. Industries can strive towards 'zero water footprint' in their operations. The blue water footprint can be brought down to zero by avoiding evaporation losses. When all water abstracted is returned to the catchment or reused, an industry has no blue water footprint. The grey water footprint can be nullified by avoiding any diffuse pollution and making sure that effluents are treated such that the concentration of any chemical is lower than in the abstracted water. Thermal pollution can be avoided by recapturing the heat from effluents before disposal.

The idea of 'zero water footprint' in industry matches the idea of a circular economy, in which resources are not wasted but reused or recycled. Pollution, thus a grey water footprint, does not fit in a circular economy, because pollution means that valuable chemicals are dispersed into the environment instead of being captured and reused. A blue water footprint does not fit in a circular economy either, because consumptive use within an industry means that the industry has not closed its water cycle, but runs on changing catchment hydrology. There is only one exception in which industries will have to go beyond 'zero water footprint', and this is when they need some water to incorporate into their product. This is the case, for instance, with the beverage industry, which will need water as an ingredient in its beverages. Water consumption that goes beyond water use for incorporation into products is unnecessary. Probably, many bottling plants in the world already have an operational water footprint that does not go beyond the water incorporated into the bottles. This was shown for example by Coca-Cola for their bottling plant in the Netherlands (TCCC and TNC, 2010).

'Zero water footprint' is not to be confused with 'no water use'. The essence of the water footprint definition is that it is about consumptive water use and pollution. Water use in itself is not a problem, as long as water that is abstracted is returned to where it comes from, with the same or better water quality as when it was abstracted. Water use can even be disconnected from interference with the catchment altogether. This happens in the case of full water recycling within an industry, whereby all water required comes from its own effluent. Technologically, there are no obstacles to move towards zero water footprint in all industries (only allowing consumptive water use for water to be incorporated into products). The main challenge will be to mobilize the will and money to achieve it.

## Increasing water productivity in agriculture

The idea of zero water footprint is not applicable to agriculture. Transpiration by plants is an essential element of plant growth. Strategies to reduce the water footprint in agriculture should aim at reducing the non-beneficial fraction of evapotranspiration. This can be done, for example, by specific forms of tillage and mulching of the soil (Jalota and Prihar, 1998). In addition, an important strategy will be to increase yield per unit of evapotranspiration, by adopting good agricultural practices (Poisot et al., 2007). Yields in agriculture are often very low, not as a result of climate, soil or other environmental factors, but as a result of poor agricultural management (Molden, 2007). Since water productivity is equal to yield over evapotranspiration, it can be increased not only by reducing evaporation, but also by increasing yields. There is a tremendous number of things a farmer can do to increase yields, including measures to improve soil structure and fertility and choosing suitable crop varieties and cropping patterns. This requires detailed knowledge of agricultural management in general and of the local context in particular. It is generally the combination of practices that is effective, not one single measure. Part of a strategy to increase yields can also be irrigation. If not done carefully, however, evapotranspiration from the field rises more than yields, resulting in reduced water productivity. In Chapter 3 about wheat, I showed that the global average yield in irrigated wheat production is one-third larger than in rain-fed wheat production, but that the global average water footprint per unit of production in irrigation is slightly larger, not smaller. Irrigation can apparently lead to decreased water productivity, something that sounds counter-intuitive. Usually rain comes irregularly, while irrigation is done on purpose when necessary, so how can water productivity in rain-fed agriculture be larger than in irrigated agriculture? The reason is that the practice of irrigation is often not so optimal from a water resources point of view as one might expect.

## Land versus water productivity in crop growing

Traditionally, the focus in agriculture lies on increasing productivity in terms of yields. Low yields are conceived as undesirable. Problems to be overcome are, among others, insufficient rain and poor soil fertility, which hamper optimal plant growth. Therefore, a substantial effort is made in agriculture to improve poor conditions, by irrigation and fertilizer application. There is, however, generally little attention to the marginal benefits and costs of adding irrigation water and fertilizer. Irrigation and fertilizer application are often done up to the level at which yields will not further increase by adding more water or fertilizer. In this way, farmers get most out of their land. The question is whether this is efficient from a water resources point of view. Let me first explain the inefficiency of full irrigation and after that reflect on the issue of fertilizer use.

'Full irrigation' is an irrigation strategy aimed to maximize production per hectare (land productivity). If land is scarce and water plentiful, this makes sense. If, conversely, water is scarce and land abundant, which is the case in most semi-arid and arid regions, this is not a wise strategy. Better strategies in this case will be deficit or supplemental irrigation (Pereira et al., 2002; Geerts and Raes, 2009). 'Deficit irrigation' is a strategy aimed to maximize production per drop of water. With this strategy, a farmer will apply less water than in the case of full irrigation, because the production per drop will decline after a certain optimum level of water application. After this optimal level, more water will still increase production per hectare (up to a certain level), but at reduced production per cubic metre of water. According to Fereres and Soriano (2007), evapotranspiration under deficit irrigation will generally be somewhere between 60 and 100 per cent of evapotranspiration under full irrigation. This can save a lot of irrigation water. Suppose, for instance, that the highest yield for a certain crop at a certain place can be achieved at an evapotranspiration level of 750 mm, but that 500 mm gives highest water productivity. If rain is sufficient to contribute 250 mm to evapotranspiration, full irrigation will require 500 mm, while deficit irrigation will take only half of that. Yields under the deficit irrigation strategy may be substantially lower than under the full irrigation strategy, for example somewhere between 10 and 25 per cent, but the saved water (250 out of 500 mm) can be applied to other land and thus double the production. Instead of over-irrigating the fields in order to increase production per hectare, one could thus better save the water and irrigate more hectares. Alternatively, the water savings can be taken as real savings from the catchment point of view, by not expanding the irrigated area. This is particularly relevant in catchments where current levels of water abstraction for irrigation are not sustainable.

Deficit irrigation maximizes water productivity (in terms of crop per drop), but not in all circumstances there is sufficient blue water available to supply all farmers with the required irrigation water. Under these conditions, supplemental irrigation can be the solution. In this strategy, a farmer will apply even less water than in the case of deficit irrigation. Supplemental irrigation is a strategy in which small amounts of water are added to essentially rain-fed crops during dry spells (prolonged periods of dry weather) to save the harvest. Growth conditions will be far from optimal, but this is to be accepted when not enough water is available to supply all farmers with the desired amounts of water. The gains of supplemental irrigation can be large, because harvests can get severely damaged or even get completely lost through dry spells (Oweis and Hachum, 2012).

While the blue water footprint of an irrigated crop can be reduced in a substantial way through deficit irrigation, the grey water footprint can be diminished markedly by a more rational application of fertilizers and pesticides. This is done in organic or precision farming, agricultural practices that exclude or limit the use of manufactured fertilizers, pesticides and other chemicals.

## Irrigation efficiency versus water-use efficiency

There is often confusion between the terms 'irrigation efficiency' and 'water-use efficiency'. It is thought that water-use efficiency is increased if irrigation efficiency is improved. However, this is not necessarily the case. The term irrigation efficiency refers to the percentage of water withdrawn from an aquifer, river or lake that will finally benefit the crop (taken up by the plant) (Perry, 2007). Engineers strive to increase irrigation efficiencies by reducing water losses along the way. Losses occur during storage, transport, distribution and application. The overall efficiency of irrigation is often defined as the multiplication of conveyance efficiency and field application efficiency. The first term accounts for the losses between water diversion and application to the field; the second for the losses after application to the field. The conveyance efficiency mainly depends on the length of the canals, the soil type or permeability of the canal banks and the condition of the canals, but also temperature (which influences evaporation). Conveyance efficiency typically varies between 60 and 95 per cent for adequately maintained canals (Brouwer *et al.*, 1989). Bad maintenance can reduce the conveyance efficiency by half. The field application efficiency typically varies from 60 per cent (furrow irrigation) or 75 per cent (sprinkler irrigation) to 90 per cent (drip irrigation). Overall irrigation efficiencies thus range from 20 to 85 per cent, or up to 95 per cent if water is pumped and distributed through a pipe system and drip irrigation is optimized. Global average irrigation efficiency has been estimated at about 35 per cent (Wallace and Gregory, 2002). The losses between diversion and plant uptake refer to non-beneficial evaporation (from storage reservoirs, canals or the crop field), seepage (in any stage) or runoff from the tail of the crop field. Reducing irrigation losses is not the same as reducing the blue water footprint of irrigated agriculture. Since the concept of blue water footprint refers to evapotranspiration, reduction of irrigation loss is equivalent to reduction of blue water footprint only if it concerns reduction of evaporation losses. Seepage and runoff flows remain within the catchment and can be reused. They are not regarded as losses from the catchment perspective. The term 'water loss' as defined by the engineer who designs an irrigation scheme is thus different from the term 'water loss' as defined by the catchment manager who is concerned with consumptive water use (the blue water footprint) within the catchment. The term water-use efficiency (or water productivity) refers to the ratio of yield to total water consumption. In general, increasing irrigation efficiency by reducing non-beneficial evaporation losses will help to increase water-use efficiency; however, increasing irrigation efficiency by reducing seepage losses will not affect water-use efficiency.

Despite the important difference between irrigation efficiency and water-use efficiency, the most efficient irrigation techniques and application strategies will also greatly reduce the blue water footprint. Using drip irrigation instead of sprinkler or furrow irrigation and precision application of water can reduce evaporation substantially, while often increasing yields at the same time (Postel, 1999).

## Water footprint benchmarking

In Chapter 3 about wheat, I showed that the global average green plus blue water footprint of wheat growing is 1,620 litres/kg, but that about 20 per cent of the wheat production in the world occurs at green plus blue water footprints of less than 1,000 litres/kg. In Chapter 5 about cotton, I reported a global average green plus blue water footprint of 3,600 litres/kg of seed cotton, but also noted that the best 20 per cent of cotton production in the world has a green–blue water footprint of 1,820 litres/kg or less. A similar analysis can be made for all crops. Based on the variability of water footprints found across regions and among farms within regions, for each crop, a certain benchmark can be established that can act as a reference and target for all farmers that have water footprints above the benchmark. The water footprint benchmark for a certain crop can for example be chosen by looking for the water footprint that is not exceeded by the best 10 or 20 per cent of the producers. This can be done on a regional basis, in order to account for differences in environmental conditions (climate, soil) and development conditions, but it can also be done on a global basis, given the fact that for each crop there is some reasonable level of water productivity (water footprint) that can be achieved in every location in the world that is suitable for that crop.

Another way of establishing water footprint benchmarks for each water-consuming activity is to identify 'best-available technology' and take the water footprint associated with that technology as the benchmark. In agriculture, precision irrigation using micro-irrigation techniques is much more advanced than using sprinklers, so it can be a choice to set these techniques and the associated water footprint of the crop as a benchmark. In industry, closed water-cooling systems have a smaller blue water footprint (possibly zero) than open water-cooling systems and systems that recapture the heat from warm effluents have a smaller grey water footprint than systems that do not.

Water footprint benchmarks for different water-using processes can be useful as a reference for farmers and companies to work towards and as a reference for governments in allocating water footprint permits to users. Business associations within the different sectors of economy can develop their own regional or global water footprint benchmarks, though governments can take initiatives in this area as well, including the development of regulations or legislation. The latter will be most relevant to completely ban worst practices.

Benchmarks for the various water-using processes along the supply chain of a product can be taken together to formulate a water footprint benchmark for the final product. An end-product point of view is particularly relevant for the companies, retailers and consumers who are not directly involved in the water-using processes in the early steps of the supply chains of the products they are manufacturing, selling or consuming, but who are still interested in the water performance of the product over the chain as a whole.

## Economic water productivity

Until this point, we have approached the concept of water productivity from a physical point of view. The focus was on the quantity of product per unit of water. This perspective is sufficient if the product to be produced is given. If, however, one wants to compare the water productivities of alternative products, it makes more sense to look at the *value* produced per unit of water. Value can be expressed in monetary terms, so that one can compare the water productivities of alternative water allocations in, for example, US\$/$m^3$. But there are also other common denominators that can be useful for comparison. If the goal is to compare the water efficiency of different sorts of food, one can look at efficiency in terms of kcal/litre (see Chapter 4). When the interest is to compare the water efficiency of different crops for bioenergy, one can look at MJ/litre (see Chapter 6). Optimizing physical water productivities (e.g. more crop per drop) is good, but this should be done in a broader context, in which also economic water productivity (more value per drop) is optimized. This means that the water should be allocated to different purposes in such a way that the highest benefit is obtained. The concept of economic water productivity can be applied at the micro-level of the individual farmer, but it becomes even more relevant at the macro-level of water allocation.

## Allocation efficiency from a river basin perspective

At the catchment or river basin level, water-use efficiency refers to the efficiency of water allocation to alternative uses. Water-use efficiency at this level can be enhanced by re-allocating water to purposes with higher marginal benefits (Rogers et al., 1998) and by wisely dividing water over upstream versus downstream purposes. The river basin is the unit in which water conflicts between different users occur. Given the limitations to water availability within a river basin, particularly in the dry period(s) of the year, when water demand is highest, there is the question of how to allocate the water wisely among different users.

One principle in water allocation can be to allocate no more to each individual water user than what he reasonably needs given what and how much he produces. If water footprint benchmarks for different production processes have been established, this can be a good basis for determining what different users really need. Still, however, it may be the case that not all demands can be satisfied given limited water availability. Efficient crop irrigation in the desert, not an uncommon phenomenon, may look good if one looks at the productivity. But if water abstractions are beyond sustainable levels, so that groundwater levels steadily drop, a choice will have to made regarding which users will no longer be permitted to consume water.

The total amount of water allocation in a river basin needs to be based on the maximum sustainable water footprint level in the basin. Choices on which users will get how much of the available water will need to be based on economic and social considerations. The competition will be between different sectors of the economy, like household water supply, services, manufacturing, mining, agriculture and forestry. Within the agricultural sector, the question is between water for food, feed, fuel, fibre or flower, the five-f dilemma. Using economic water productivity (US$/m³) as a criterion for allocation will be helpful only partially, because there may be important arguments – for example food security – to deviate from a purely economic allocation. One can make sure that economic water productivity in growing crops for feed or biofuels is very high, but it distracts from the question whether it is wise to allocate water to such purposes given other fundamental demands – growing cereals, pulses, sugar, starch and oil crops, vegetables and fruits for food.

## Allocation efficiency from a global perspective

One can also look at water-use efficiency from a global perspective. According to international trade theory, efficient water-use patterns follow from the comparative advantage or disadvantage that countries have in the production of different products. Global water-use efficiency can be increased when nations use their comparative advantage or disadvantage in producing water-intensive goods to encourage or discourage the use of domestic water resources for producing those commodities for export. Much research has been dedicated to water-use efficiency at the user and river basin levels, but little has been done on global water-use efficiency. That is also very complex, because freshwater is just one of the production factors in the economy, so that optimum global patterns of production depend on many factors other than water. Besides, global production and trade patterns are strongly influenced by political priorities at the national level, like food self-sufficiency, and by trade barriers and differences in tax and subsidy systems.

The only sort of research done in the area of global water-use efficiency has been done from the physical point of view. When the production of goods that have a substantial water footprint is concentrated in areas where water productivities are relatively high, the overall global water need will be smaller than if the goods were made locally, in the regions where they are consumed and where water productivities are sometimes very low. Until today, five studies have been carried out to quantify the physical water savings as a result of global trade. All studies indicate that the current pattern of international trade in agricultural products results in some global water saving (Oki and Kanae, 2004; De Fraiture *et al.*, 2004; Chapagain *et al.*, 2006a; Yang *et al.*, 2006; Mekonnen and Hoekstra, 2011b). According to the most recent and comprehensive study, the global water footprint of producing agricultural products for export amounted to 1,597 billion $m^3$/yr (in the period 1996–2005). If the importing countries were to have produced the imported agricultural products domestically, they would have required a total of 1,966 billion $m^3$/yr. This means that the global water saving by trade in agricultural products was 369 billion $m^3$/yr. The water saving accompanying international trade in agricultural products has thus been (369 ÷ 1,966 =) 19 per cent. The global water footprint of agricultural production is 8,363 billion $m^3$/yr (Mekonnen and Hoekstra, 2011b). Without trade, supposing that all countries had to produce the products domestically, agricultural water use in the world would amount to (8,363 + 369 =) 8,732 billion $m^3$/yr. The current pattern of international trade thus reduces global water use in agriculture by (369 ÷ 8,732 =) 4 per cent.

The 4 per cent global water saving through trade is a result of differences in water productivities between trading nations. If international trade in water-intensive commodities would adapt more to water productivity differences across countries, international trade could probably result in substantially higher savings. However, if water productivities in the world start levelling, particularly if water productivities increase in import-dependent regions that currently have low water productivities, the global water savings currently brought by trade will disappear.

The benefit of trade in water-intensive commodities partly stems from differences in water productivities, so if these differences vanish as a result of increased water productivities in the regions where productivities are currently still low, the benefit of trade also diminishes. What remains, however, is the fact that water endowments between countries vary greatly and that a number of countries do simply not have sufficient water resources to be food self-sufficient, so that they will have to rely on food imports. This holds for countries in the Middle East and North Africa, but also Mexico, for instance.

## The limitation of increasing efficiency

Increasing water-use efficiency or water productivity is widely recognized as an important challenge for the coming decades, worldwide. Taking it more broadly, an increasing number of governments recognize 'resource efficiency' as an important theme. In Europe, for example, the European Commission formulated 'a resource-efficient Europe' as one of its seven 'flagship initiatives' (EC, 2011). The flagship initiatives are part of a ten-year strategy launched in 2010 by the European Commission to boost growth and jobs. This betrays an interesting dilemma: on the one hand, the goal is growth, on the other hand, sustainability. Concepts like 'resource efficiency' and 'green growth' seem to give an answer to the dilemma. Resource efficiency means less natural resources use and environmental impact per unit of production and consumption. Growth means more production and consumption. The idea is that increased resource efficiency can lead to a decoupling of growth and natural resources use. In reality, it is highly doubtful whether increased resource efficiency can offset the increased demand for resources that is naturally part of growth.

There are practical limitations to improving resource efficiency. A good example is water consumption in agriculture, the sector that accounts for 92 per cent of the water footprint of humanity. In many places there is great potential to reduce water consumption and pollution and thus the water footprint of our food, cotton and biofuels. But there are inherent limitations to reducing water consumption in agriculture, because crop growth is essentially linked to evaporation. Global water consumption has continuously increased over the past century and is projected to keep on increasing during the coming decades (Molden, 2007; FAO, 2011). The reason is not just population growth – more people need more food – but also the shift towards a consumption pattern that is much more water-intensive than in the past. Particularly the global shifts to more meat and dairy and to bioenergy will intensify water demand. During the past decades, water productivities have increased substantially, but the increased efficiency was not enough to have water consumption levels decrease. On the contrary, total water consumption has kept growing during the past decades, despite the efficiency improvements. There is no other basis than ungrounded optimism to assume that water productivity increases in the coming few decades will offset the impact of the growing demands for water-intensive commodities. This is a serious problem. The average blue water scarcity – the blue water footprint divided by blue water availability – experienced by people around the world is estimated to be already 133 per cent (Hoekstra and Mekonnen, 2011). As reported in the previous chapter, a conservative estimate of 2.7 billion people live in river basins where the blue water footprint exceeds the blue water availability by a factor of two or more during at least one month per year. To mitigate water scarcity, water productivity increases are an essential ingredient, but not sufficient. According to a recent study, blue water efficiency, in all sectors combined and as a global average, could be improved by 25 per cent (EC and PBL, 2011). According to the same study, the efficiency gains in water use will not be sufficient to offset the effects of population growth.

The overarching goal should not be increasing 'efficiency' (footprint per unit of production), but reducing the overall footprint. Efficiency increase is one of the means to achieve that, but it needs to be coupled with measures that constrain the continued growth of total demand. Areas of particular attention are the increase in meat, dairy and bioenergy demand, significant multipliers to global water demand. But also other developments are of concern, like the adoption of new techniques in mining, including for example hydraulic fracturing (fracking) to open up shale gas reserves or extracting oil from tar sands. Water use and pollution in mining activities are still largely under the radar of policy makers, probably partly due to the absence of proper statistics, but also because mining activities are not really directly related to daily consumer goods in a visible way.

## The rebound effect

There is another reason to be cautious for an over-optimistic expectation of the environmental gains of increased water-use efficiency. From energy studies, we know a phenomenon that is called the 'rebound effect' (Binswanger, 2001; Sorrell et al., 2009; Terry et al., 2009). Rebound refers to a typical response in the market to the adoption of new techniques that increase the efficiency of resource use. The typical response is that if resources are saved, they become available for additional production, so that in the end the original environmental gain is partly or completely offset. Sometimes, consumption even increases (rather than decreases) as a result of the efficiency increase. This specific case of the rebound effect is known as the Jevons paradox. There are only a few studies on the rebound effect in the field of freshwater use, but there is no reason to assume that it does not occur in this sector (Ward and Pulido-Velazquez, 2008; Crase and O'Keefe, 2009). Imagine those vast areas in the world where land is readily available, but water isn't. If a farmer is used to pumping water for irrigating his land and finds out that he can obtain the same yield with less water, he may well decide to irrigate more land, thus increasing his total production, using more efficient irrigation techniques but in total the same volume of water. It is not extraordinary to assume that water productivity increases in food supply will facilitate an even quicker shift to the production of biofuels.

# 11

# ALLOCATING THE WORLD'S LIMITED FRESHWATER RESOURCES

At the start of the twenty-first century, the average world citizen had a water footprint of 1,385 m³/yr (Hoekstra and Mekonnen, 2012a). We found, however, big differences between and within countries. The average consumer in the United States had a water footprint of 2,842 m³/yr, whereas the average citizens in China and India had water footprints of 1,071 and 1,089 m³/yr, respectively. The global average of 1,385 m³/yr has brought us where we are now: overexploitation of blue water resources in roughly half of the world's river basins and pollution beyond assimilation capacity in at least two-thirds of the river basins in the world (see Chapter 9). We can try to shift the burden to some extent from overexploited to not-yet overexploited river basins to find better regional balances between water consumption and water availability and between water pollution and waste assimilation capacity. In this way we may be able to better accommodate our current global water footprint. It is hard to imagine, however, that an increase of the current global water footprint can work out sustainably.

According to the medium population scenario of the United Nations, the world population is expected to increase from 6.1 billion in the year 2000 to 9.3 billion in 2050 and 10.1 billion by the end of this century (UN, 2011). This means that, if we want to make sure that the water footprint of humanity as a whole will not increase over the coming century, the average water footprint per capita will have to decrease from 1,385 m³ in 2000 to 910 m³ in 2050 and 835 m³ in 2100. If we assume an equal water footprint share for all global citizens, the challenge for countries like China and India is to reduce the current water footprint per capita level by about 22.5 per cent over the coming century. For a country like the USA, it means a reduction of the average water footprint per capita by about 70 per cent. Improved technologies alone will not be sufficient to reach this goal.

## The need to address consumption patterns

There is an urgent need to evaluate the sustainability of current consumption patterns in the light of limited freshwater resources and a growing world population. Since about 29 per cent of the water footprint of humanity relates to growing feed for farm animals (Hoekstra and Mekonnen, 2012a), addressing the level of meat and dairy consumption will be one of the key issues. The second most important issue is probably to address the growth of water use for growing crops for biofuels. Wise water policies for the future will definitely need to include meat and biofuel paragraphs.

There are three criteria to assess whether the water footprint of a community of consumers or an individual consumer is sustainable. First, the water footprint of consumers is not sustainable if some of the goods consumed originate from areas in which water is being overexploited or polluted beyond assimilation capacity. Second, if some of the goods consumed take far more water than what can be reasonably expected, even if this happens in water-abundant regions, this is not sustainable either. The water in water-abundant areas needs to be used productively in order to be able to reduce production levels in overexploited water-scarce areas. The third criterion for sustainability relates to the share that a community or individual takes in the total water footprint of humanity. As we have seen above, in the medium population projection of the UN, there will be no more than $910\,m^3/yr$ for the average global citizen around the year 2050, and no more than $835\,m^3/yr$ around 2100. In the most optimistic scenario, the low fertility variant, the population will still reach 8.1 billion in 2050, with $1,045\,m^3/yr$ for the average global citizen if we do not want to increase the total water footprint of humanity beyond the 2000 level.

How can developing countries like China and India grow economically without enlarging their water footprint per capita or even while reducing it? In India, where meat consumption is relatively low, the government should try and keep it that way. The major challenge will be to reduce water consumption in cereal production. In China, the number-one concern should be meat consumption. In both countries, policies should aim at reducing food waste and developing industries with best-available technology, so that industrial development will not go hand in hand with an industrial water footprint as we can see in industrialized countries. For most of the developing countries, the challenge is threefold: improving water productivities in agriculture; ensuring that industrial developments are based on best-available technology; and staying with or moving towards low-meat diets.

The challenge in the industrialized world is probably even bigger than in the developing world. Taking the UN's medium population growth variant and assuming that all countries will need to move towards a fair share in the global water footprint of humanity, countries like the USA, Canada, Australia, Spain, Portugal, Italy and Greece will need to reduce their water footprint per capita roughly by a factor of three in the period 2000–2050. If those countries will not move towards their fair share, it means that the water footprint of humanity will inevitably increase, because it is hard to imagine that developing countries will compensate. The idea of a 'fair share' is challenging and probably difficult to accept for many countries that currently have a water footprint per capita beyond the global average.

Politically, there are two steps to be taken. First, national governments need to reach a consensus about the need to halt the continued growth of the water footprint of humanity as a whole. In the best case, a consensus is reached on the need to keep the total water footprint of humanity at the 2000 level or bring it back to that level. Not that the current water footprint is sustainable, but to some extent this can be blamed on unfavourable spatial distribution. There is some room for a spatial redistribution of the total footprint in such a way that the burden is shifted from overexploited catchments to other areas that can tolerate some increase. In a worse case, governments reach a consensus about a maximum global water footprint, but accept a further increase beyond the current level. In the worst case, no consensus is reached at all about the need to stabilize the water footprint of humanity. Let me assume that some agreement is reached at least. In that situation, the second step to be taken in international politics will be to reach a consensus about water footprint reduction targets or maximum water footprint increase levels per country.

## International agreement on national water footprint reduction targets

The limited availability of freshwater in the world implies a ceiling for humanity's water footprint. The question for the global community is how this global maximum can be transferred to the national or even the individual level. In other words: what is each nation's and each individual's 'reasonable' share of the globe's water resources? And what mechanisms could be established in order to make sure that people do not use more than their 'reasonable' share? Maximum levels of water consumption and pollution to guarantee a sustainable management of the world's freshwater resources could be institutionalized in the form of an international agreement on 'water footprint allowances' specified per nation. Such a 'water footprint allowance' would be the total water footprint that the consumers within a nation are allowed to have within the international agreement. The allowance would reflect the share that the consumers within a nation have in the total water footprint of humanity. The levels of the allowances per country would need to be negotiated among countries, and will therefore probably lie somewhere between the country's current water footprint levels and the 'fair share' per country based on population numbers.

Similar to the idea of establishing water footprint allowances per nation in an absolute sense, is the idea of agreeing on water footprint reduction targets per nation compared to a certain reference year. If the international community would succeed to reach such an agreement, nations would be responsible for translating the water footprint reduction targets into national policy in order to meet the target. Enforcement could be done in the form of penalties when not meeting the agreed targets. Targets would need to be specified, for example, by water footprint component (green, blue, grey water footprint); they could also be specified by sector or product category. Obviously, water footprint allowances or reduction targets could develop over time and would need to be negotiated on a regular basis, like every ten years or so. The similarity with international negotiations about carbon footprint reductions is clear.

An international agreement on water footprint allowances or water footprint reduction targets per nation would be somehow comparable to the Kyoto Protocol on the emissions of greenhouse gases (UN, 1998). The Kyoto Protocol – which was drafted in 1997 and became effective in 2005 – is based on the understanding that, to prevent human-induced climate change, a maximum is to be set to the volume of greenhouse gas emissions from human activities at the global level. The protocol is an international agreement to cut greenhouse gas emissions, with specific reduction targets by country. The overall goal was a collective reduction of greenhouse gas emissions by 5.2 per cent in 2012 compared to the reference year of 1990. The experience with the Kyoto Protocol is both hopeful and discouraging. The good side of the experience is that the global community has shown that it is able to collaborate towards a common interest, but the downside is that the agreement did not have reach and teeth enough to be really effective: humanity's carbon footprint has continued to increase (Olivier et al., 2012). It would be good if, in the global talks about addressing the global water footprint, lessons were drawn from the experience with the Kyoto Protocol (Ercin and Hoekstra, 2012). Simply adopting the same sort of format, with tradable emission credits, seems to be a bad idea, because the possibility of offsetting offers an escape route away from actual footprint reduction. We have to acknowledge that, after all, the idea of offsetting is not such a good idea as it seemed at the time it was invented. The achievement of the Kyoto Protocol is the establishment of the whole idea of setting concrete footprint reduction targets by nation. With hindsight, however, we can conclude that the mechanisms that were installed to reach those reduction targets are flawed.

## The global dimension of water allocation

Given that the world's available freshwater resources are limited, it is important to quantify how available water volumes are appropriated: for producing certain commodities, for certain people. Because water-intensive commodities can be traded internationally, wise allocation of freshwater resources to alternative purposes is a question with a global dimension. Water-abundant areas often show low water productivities (kg/litre) and thus large water footprints per unit of product (litre/kg). Even though the local environmental impact of water use can be small, one would be mistaken to leave these areas out of the scope of water policy (Hoekstra and Mekonnen, 2012b). An important component of the solution to overexploitation of blue freshwater resources in water-stressed catchments is to increase water productivities (reduce water footprints per unit of product) in water-abundant areas. Particularly the efficient use of the world's green water resources in rain-fed agriculture can help to reduce the need to consume blue water resources (Falkenmark and Rockström, 2004). A mere focus on reducing the water footprints of crops (litre/kg) in water-stressed catchments, as proposed by some scholars (Ridoutt and Huang, 2012), displays a limited perspective on the question of what is globally sustainable and efficient water use.

Water footprints need to be seen from the perspective of equity as well. The fact that consumers in the USA have a water footprint per inhabitant that is 2.6 times larger than for people in China and India, justifies a debate about equitable appropriation of freshwater resources. The world's spatially distributed freshwater resources are accessible from anywhere through trade in water-intensive commodities. The widespread inefficient use, overexploitation and pollution of water must be a concern for all that have a water-intensive consumption pattern, not only for those that directly depend on the areas where the environmental impact of water use is greatest.

Reducing the aggregate water footprint in environmentally stressed catchments deserves priority, but given the competition over the globe's freshwater resources, increasing water productivities (lowering water footprints per unit of product) in non-stressed basins can be an instrument to reach that goal. Especially the increase of green water productivity (lowering green water footprints per unit of product) in rain-fed agriculture in catchments without water shortage can give an important contribution to the solution of the world's water problems elsewhere (Aldaya *et al.*, 2010a). It will help to increase production volumes from water-abundant areas, thus taking away the need to overexploit water for crop production in regions where water supplies are severely limited.

## Water allocation: the producers' and consumers' perspective

There are two different perspectives on water allocation. From the producers' perspective, the question is: how will water footprint permits be divided over competing users? From the consumers' perspective, the question is: how will the total water footprint in the end be divided among final consumers? In the first case, we talk about the direct allocation of water, in the second case about indirect allocation. Usually, when water managers talk about water allocation, they refer to the first type of allocation, the direct allocation of water to different users (producers). It may have become clear in the course of this book that it makes sense to look at the indirect allocation of water as well. If water is allocated to a soyabean farmer who exports the soyabean as animal feed, the water has been indirectly allocated to a meat eater abroad. The question is whether this is a priority in water allocation in the country of the soyabean farmer. The same sort of question can be posed if water is allocated to a maize farmer who produces for the bioenergy market. There are no clear-cut answers to such questions, but questions on indirect allocation need to be addressed. The allocation of water resources within a river basin to different uses needs to be regarded in a broader, national and global context and subject to the question: who will ultimately benefit from the water?

## The three pillars under wise water allocation

There are three pillars on which wise water allocation should rest: environmental sustainability, resource efficiency and social equity (Figure 11.1). The first pillar was addressed in Chapter 9, in which I argued that it is vital to agree on water footprint caps for all river basins in the world, in order to ensure a sustainable water use within each basin. A water footprint cap sets a maximum to the water volume that can be allocated for the various human purposes. Please note that 'water allocation' refers here to granting 'water footprint permits' to specific users. It does not refer to 'water abstraction permits', because it is particularly relevant to regulate consumptive water use and water pollution per user, not gross water abstraction.

The second pillar under wise water allocation is efficient water use. In Chapter 10 I proposed to formulate water footprint benchmarks for all water-using processes, and by considering the various steps in the supply chains of products, also for end-products. In this way, producers who use water, governments that allocate water and companies and final consumers in the end of supply chains, share information about what are 'reasonable water footprints' for various processes and products. When granting certain water footprint permits to specific users, it makes sense for governments to take into account the relevant water footprint benchmarks for the different users.

**FIGURE 11.1** The three pillars under wise water allocation

The third pillar under wise water allocation relates to social equity. Water allocation may be environmentally sustainable and efficient from a resource point of view, but that does not automatically imply that water allocation is fair from a societal point of view. We need some common understanding of what makes the water footprint of a community of consumers fair or reasonably acceptable, given the limited maximum sustainable water footprint per global citizen. As argued in this chapter, we need a political debate at the international level about fair sharing of the world's freshwater resources.

There does not exist a recipe for sustainable, efficient and fair water allocation among water users and final consumers, because none of the three concepts is very strictly defined and trade-offs are possible. Allocation of water is essentially political. It is therefore time that politicians put water scarcity and water allocation higher up on their agendas.

# 12

# GETTING TRADE RIGHT

The recent past has shown a growing interest from both trade and water experts in the relation between international trade and freshwater scarcity. Until today, it has not been very common for water sector specialists to look at the relation between water use in a region and import into or export from this region. Traditionally, in their view, water demand in an area is simply a function of the amount and needs of the water users in that area. At the same time, economists do not generally consider the implications of international trade for the water sector. The reason is that water inputs usually hardly contribute to the overall price of traded commodities. This seems to justify the conclusion that water cannot be a significant factor influencing production and trade patterns. The fact that water inputs are often heavily subsidized by national governments is hereby ignored. Trade specialists also tend to overlook that external effects of water use can be very significant, but are never included in the price of water, and that no country charges a scarcity rent for water inputs even though water is sometimes very scarce. When merely looking at the prices of traded commodities, one will indeed get the impression that water scarcity cannot be a driving force of or limiting factor to international trade.

Water is not usually regarded as a global resource. Whereas in most countries the energy sector has an obvious international component, this is different for the water sector. The international characteristics of water are recognized in the case of trans-boundary rivers, but the relation between international trade and water management is not something that water sector officials think much about. This is probably because water itself is not traded internationally, due to its 'bulky' properties. Besides, there is no private ownership of water so that it cannot even be traded in a market (Savenije, 2002). Water sector specialists forget, however, that water is traded in virtual form, that is in the form of agricultural and industrial commodities (Hoekstra and Hung, 2005; Chapagain and Hoekstra, 2008). Although invisible, the import of 'virtual water' can be an effective means for water-scarce countries to preserve their domestic water resources (Allan, 2003).

One of the principles widely accepted in water resources management is the subsidiarity principle, according to which water issues should be settled at the lowest community level possible (GWP, 2000). When upstream water uses affect downstream uses, it has been recognized that it is necessary to take the perspective of a river basin as a whole, considering water as a river basin resource. Viewing water as a global resource is very uncommon. The Global Water Partnership writes:

> In order to achieve efficient, equitable and sustainable water management [...], a major institutional change will be needed. Both top-down and bottom-up participation of all stakeholders will have to be promoted – from the level of the nation down to the level of a village or a municipality or from the level of a catchment or watershed up to the level of a river basin. The principle of subsidiarity, which drives down action to the lowest appropriate level, will need to be observed.
>
> (GWP, 2000)

There is no word about a global dimension of water governance.

Considering water management from a local, national or river basin perspective is, however, often insufficient. Many water problems are closely linked to international trade (Hoekstra and Chapagain, 2008). As we have seen in Chapter 5, subsidized water in Uzbekistan is overused to produce cotton for export. Chapter 7 showed how Kenya overexploits its water resources around Lake Naivasha to produce cut flowers for export to Europe. And we can provide so many other examples: Thailand experiences water problems due to irrigation of rice for export (Chapagain and Hoekstra, 2011); and Chinese rivers get heavily polluted through waste flows from factories that produce cheap commodities for western markets (Economy, 2004). Not only water problems, but also water solutions, have an international trade component. For instance, various countries in the Middle East meet their demand for food and save their scarcely available water resources through food imports from overseas (Hoekstra and Chapagain, 2008); Mediterranean countries will expectedly experience increased water scarcity due to climate change, forcing them into the direction of increased import of water-intensive products. Apparently, there are more connections between seemingly local or national water issues and international trade than recognized at first sight.

In this chapter, I will start with a reflection on the mutual relation between water scarcity and trade and address two questions: what is the effect of international trade on domestic water resources and, reversely, what is the effect of water availability on international trade? After that, I will describe the water scarcity–export paradox, the counter-intuitive phenomenon that some highly water-scarce regions in the world produce water-intensive commodities for export. Next, I will discuss the need for an international agreement on proper water pricing.

Subsequently, I will reflect on the conflict between product transparency – which is aimed at enabling people to differentiate between sustainable and non-sustainable products – and the non-discrimination principle, which is one of the basic building blocks of international trade agreements. I will then discuss the problem that strong international trade agreements exist, but that international agreements on sustainable water use are absent altogether, so that a legal basis to restrict trade based on mutually agreed sustainability criteria is lacking. Next, I will discuss the idea of an international water label for water-intensive products. Finally, I will reflect on the current trade-negotiation round of the World Trade Organization (WTO) and on the risks and opportunities associated with the intensification of international trade in water-intensive commodities.

## The effect of international trade on domestic water resources

An obvious effect of international trade in water-intensive commodities is that it generates water savings in the countries that import those commodities. This effect has been discussed since the mid-1990s (Allan, 2003; Hoekstra, 2003). The national water saving associated with import can be estimated by multiplying the imported product volume by the volume of water that would have been required to produce the product domestically. The other side of international trade in water-intensive commodities is that it takes water in the exporting countries that can no longer be used for other (domestic) purposes. Besides, the social and environmental costs that are often associated with water use remain in the exporting countries; they are not included in the price paid for the products by the consumers in the importing nations.

In many countries, international trade in agricultural and industrial products effectively reduces domestic water demand (Table 12.1). These countries import commodities that are relatively water intensive while they export commodities that are less water intensive. During the period 1996–2005, Japan, the largest net importer of water-intensive goods in the world, annually saved 134 billion $m^3$ of water through trade (Mekonnen and Hoekstra, 2011b). This volume of water is equivalent to more than three times the water footprint within Japan (42 billion $m^3$/yr) and would come on top of the current water footprint within the country if Japan had produced all imported products domestically. In a similar way, Malta saves, through trade, 0.9 billion $m^3$ of water per year, which is more than ten times the water footprint within its own territory.

People in Malta, but also in countries like Libya, Kuwait, Jordan, Yemen and Israel, thus survive owing to the fact that their water footprint has largely been externalized to other parts of the world. Wise trade partly covers up the water shortages in those countries: the export of goods and services that require little water per unit of foreign currency earned and the import of products that need a lot of water per unit of money spent. Saving domestic water resources in countries with relative water scarcity through virtual water import (import of water-intensive

**TABLE 12.1** Examples of nations with net water saving as a result of international trade, 1996–2005

| Country | Total water footprint within the country (billion m³/yr) | Net water saving due to international trade (billion m³/yr) | | | | Net water saving as % of water footprint within the country |
|---|---|---|---|---|---|---|
| | | Due to trade in crop products | Due to trade in animal products | Due to trade in industrial products | Overall | |
| Malta | 0.09 | 0.6 | 0.3 | 0.005 | 0.9 | 1,059 |
| Libya | 5.3 | 10 | 29 | −0.1 | 39 | 745 |
| Kuwait | 0.57 | 2.3 | 0.94 | −0.09 | 3.2 | 563 |
| Jordan | 1.4 | 6 | 0.9 | 0.15 | 7.1 | 492 |
| Yemen | 7.7 | 11 | 16 | −0.03 | 27 | 354 |
| Israel | 4 | 11 | 2.4 | 0.04 | 13 | 337 |
| Japan | 42 | 123 | 14 | −2.5 | 135 | 317 |
| Korea, Rep. | 20 | 43 | 5.8 | −0.53 | 48 | 248 |
| Cyprus | 0.9 | 1.6 | 0.1 | 0.08 | 1.8 | 182 |
| Lebanon | 4 | 2.3 | 2.4 | 0.2 | 4.9 | 138 |
| Saudi Arabia | 15 | 17 | 3.3 | −0.66 | 20 | 129 |
| Italy | 70 | 35 | 19 | −0.36 | 54 | 76 |
| Morocco | 37 | 27 | 0.3 | 0.1 | 27 | 74 |
| Mexico | 149 | 64 | 19 | 0.13 | 83 | 56 |
| Peru | 26 | 11 | 0.5 | 0.02 | 12 | 46 |
| Spain | 82 | 29 | 0 | 0.91 | 30 | 37 |
| Greece | 18 | 0.5 | 5.2 | 0.84 | 6.5 | 37 |
| Iraq | 36 | 13 | 1.1 | −3.5 | 11 | 30 |
| Iran | 113 | 23 | 0.6 | −0.26 | 24 | 21 |
| Chile | 16 | 2.9 | 0.1 | −0.09 | 2.9 | 19 |
| Egypt | 69 | 12 | −0.5 | 0.36 | 12 | 17 |

Source: Mekonnen and Hoekstra (2011b)

products) thus looks very attractive. There are, however, a number of drawbacks that have to be taken into account. First, saving domestic water through import should explicitly be seen in the context of the need to generate sufficient foreign exchange to import food that otherwise would be produced domestically. Some water-scarce countries in the world are oil rich, so they can easily afford to import water-intensive commodities. However, many water-scarce countries lack the ability to export energy, services or water-extensive industrial commodities in order to afford the import of water-intensive agricultural commodities. Second, the import of food carries the risk of moving away from food self-sufficiency. This plays an important role in the political considerations in countries such as China, India and Egypt (Roth and Warner, 2007). Third, the import of food will be bad for the domestic agricultural sector and lead to increased urbanization, because import reduces employment in the agricultural sector. It will also result in an economic decline and worsening of land management in rural areas. Fourth, in many water-scarce developing countries, where an important part of the agriculture consists of subsistence farming, promoting food imports may threaten the livelihoods of those subsistence farmers and reduce access to food for the poor. Finally, increases in virtual water transfers to optimize the use of global water resources can relieve the environmental pressure on water-scarce countries but may create additional pressure on the countries that produce the water-intensive commodities for export.

The export of water-intensive commodities obviously raises national water demand. In the period 1996–2005, 19 per cent of the water use in the world was not for producing products for domestic consumption but for producing goods for export (Mekonnen and Hoekstra, 2011b). The biggest water users for export can be found in North and South America (the USA, Canada, Brazil and Argentina), southern Asia (India, Pakistan, Indonesia and Thailand) and Australia. Assuming that, on average, production for export does not cause significantly more or fewer water-related problems (such as water depletion or pollution) than production for domestic consumption, roughly one-fifth of the water problems in the world can be traced back to production for export. Consumers do not see the effects of their consumption behaviour due to the distance between areas of consumption and areas of production. The benefits are at the consumption side and, since water is generally grossly underpriced, the costs remain at the production side. From a water resources point of view, it would be wise for the exporting countries in the world to review their water use for export and decide to which extent this is a good policy given the fact that the foreign income associated with the exports generally does not cover most of the costs associated with the use of domestic water. The construction of dams and irrigation schemes and even operation and maintenance costs are often covered by the national or state government. Negative effects downstream and the social and environmental costs involved are not included in the price of the export products as well.

International trade brings along another phenomenon: natural cycles of nutrients such as nitrogen and phosphorus are disturbed through depletion of the soil in some places, excessive use of fertilizers in others, long-distance transfers of food and animal feed and concentrated disposal of nutrient-rich wastes in densely populated areas of the world (Grote et al., 2005). This has already led and will further lead to depletion of the soils in some areas (Sanchez, 2002; Stocking, 2003) and to eutrophication of water elsewhere (McIsaac et al., 2001; Tilman et al., 2001). The surplus of nutrients in the Netherlands, for instance, is partially related to deforesta-tion, erosion and soil degradation in those areas of the world that export food and feed to the Netherlands, for example in Brazil from where a lot of soyabeans are exported as feed for Dutch pigs and chickens. This implies that the nutrient surplus in the Netherlands is not an issue that can simply be understood as a Dutch issue. Dutch water pollution is part of the global economy.

The disturbance of nutrient cycles is not the only mechanism through which international trade influences the quality of water resources worldwide. Meybeck (2004) shows how other substances are also dispersed into the global environment and change the water quality of the world's rivers. Nriagu and Pacyna (1988) set out the specific impacts of the use of trace metals in the global economy on the world's water resources. The regular publication of new reports on global water pollution shows that this phenomenon in itself is no longer news; what is now gradually being uncovered and therefore relatively new is the fact that pollution is not simply 'global' because pollution is so 'widespread', but that it is interlinked with how the global economy works and is therefore a truly global problem. Water pollution is intertwined with the global economic system to such an extent that it cannot be dealt with independently from that global economy. Indeed, pollution can be tackled by end-of-pipe measures at or near the location of the pollution, but a more cause-oriented approach would be restructuring the (rules for the) global economy, with the aim of the sustainable closure of elemental cycles.

## The effect of water availability on international trade

There is an immense body of literature about international trade, but there are only a few scholars who address the question to which extent international trade is influ-enced by regional differences in water availability or productivity. International trade is rather explained in terms of differences in labour productivities, availability of land, domestic subsidies to agriculture, import taxes, production surpluses and associated export subsidies, etc.

According to international trade theory, which goes back to Ricardo (1821), nations can gain from trade if they specialize in the production of goods and services for which they have a comparative advantage, while importing goods and services for which they have a comparative disadvantage. According to the Ricardian model of international trade, countries can best specialize in producing goods in which they have a relatively high productivity. In more precise, techni-cal terms, economists say: countries have a comparative advantage in producing a particular good if they have a relatively high 'total factor productivity' for that good, whereby total factor productivity is a measure that relates output to all input factors (like labour, land and water). An alternative model of comparative advan-tage is the Heckscher-Ohlin model, which was formulated in the first half of the previous century. This model does not look at differences in factor productivity across countries, but at differences in factor abundance and in the factor intensity of goods. According to the Heckscher-Ohlin model, countries can best specialize in goods that use their relatively abundant factors relatively intensively. Neither model is comprehensive: whereas the Heckscher-Ohlin theory states that a country can best specialize in producing and exporting products that use the factors that are most abundant, Ricardo's theory says that a country can best focus on producing goods for which they have a relatively high productivity (output per input). But in any case, the rough idea is clear: production circumstances differ across countries, which gives some countries an opportunity in certain products, while it gives other countries an opportunity for other products, thus constituting mutual gains in trade. From the perspective of water, countries with either relative water abundance or relatively high water productivity (value of output per unit of water input), or a combination of both, will have a comparative advantage in producing and exporting commodities that are relatively water intensive.

A simple example may help to illustrate the idea of comparative advantage. Let's look at two countries and two crops and assume that there are differences in water productivities across crops and countries. We assume – for the sake of easy explanation – that water is the only input factor in production. Suppose that country A can produce 0.3 kg of seed cotton per m³ of water and that country B produces 0.1 kg of seed cotton with the same volume of water. As an alternative to cotton, both countries can produce rice. Assume that country A can produce 0.6 kg of paddy rice and that country B can produce 0.5 kg of paddy rice per m³ of water. From the productivity differences, we see that country A has higher water productivities for both cotton and rice, so we can say that country A has an 'absolute advantage' in both cotton and rice production. More relevant for the opportunity of trade, however, is to look at the 'comparative advantage' of each country. Therefore we have to look at the opportunity costs of water use. If country A applies 1 m³ of water in cotton growing, it produces 0.3 kg of seed cotton, but if it were to use the water for rice growing, it would produce 0.6 kg of paddy rice. We can thus say that, for country A, the opportunity cost of producing 1 kg of seed cotton is 2 kg of paddy rice. Similarly, we can calculate that in country B the opportunity cost of producing 1 kg of seed cotton is 5 kg of paddy rice. Since the opportunity cost of seed cotton is lowest in country A, this country can best specialize in cotton growing and export to country B. Reversely, country B can best focus on rice growing, because in country B the opportunity cost of producing 1 kg of paddy rice is only 0.2 kg of seed cotton, while this is 0.5 kg of seed cotton in country A. We say that country A has a comparative advantage in growing cotton, while country B has a comparative advantage in growing rice. The potential for trade does not only depend on differences in water productivities, but also on water availability per country. Besides, the picture becomes more complex given that there are many countries, not just two, many different products that can be produced, again not just two, and many production factors, not just water. How important water availability and water productivities are in telling what sort of trade makes most economic sense, depends on how scarce water is compared to other production factors.

There is evidence that water scarcity influences international trade. Yang *et al.* (2003, 2007) have shown that cereal imports have played a crucial role in compensating water deficits in various water-scarce countries. They demonstrate that below a certain threshold in water availability, an inverse relationship can be identified between a country's cereal import and its renewable water resources per capita. In the early 1980s, the threshold was at about 2,000 m³ per capita per year. At the end of the 1990s, it had declined to about 1,500 m³ per capita per year. Countries with less water than the threshold cannot do without the import of staple foods. The threshold declined over the past couple of decades as a result of improved water productivities and the expansion of irrigated areas.

It is interesting to remark here that the mechanisms through which water scarcity differences in the world currently influence some of the international trade flows is not the price mechanism. Water in water-scarce areas is generally not priced higher than in water-abundant areas; water is mostly free, or at least priced far below its real value, throughout the world, as a result of which water scarcity is not factored into the price of traded commodities. The mechanism is not through price but through physical constraints: the available water resources in some countries simply fall short to produce the food to survive, so that food imports are inevitable.

The driving force behind international trade in water-intensive products can be water scarcity in the importing countries, but more often other factors play a decisive role (Yang et al., 2003; De Fraiture et al., 2004). International trade in agricultural commodities depends on many more factors other than differences in water availability in the trading nations, including differences in availability of land, labour, knowledge and capital, and differences in economic productivities in various sectors (Wichelns, 2010). The existence of domestic subsidies, export subsidies or import taxes in the trading nations will also influence the trade patterns. As a consequence, international virtual water transfers usually cannot – or can only partly – be explained on the basis of differences in water availability and productivity.

## The water scarcity–export paradox

The relation between water availability and trade can be counter-intuitive. North China, for instance, has a very low availability of water per capita, unlike South China but, nevertheless, there is a very significant trade in food from North to South China (Ma et al., 2006). It was estimated that, in 1999, the total virtual water transfer from the North to the South added up to 52 billion m³. Of course, this intensifies the water problems in the North. A similar case can be found in India, where water has become relatively scarce in the northern states of Punjab, Uttar Pradesh and Haryana. Nevertheless, these states use substantial amounts of water to produce food that is exported to the eastern states of Bihar, Jharkhand and Orissa, which have much larger water endowments than the northern states (Kampman et al., 2008; Verma et al., 2009). During the period 1997–2001, the net virtual water flow from North to East India was 22 billion m³/yr (Figure 12.1). No simple reason will suffice to explain the counter-intuitive situations with respect to the

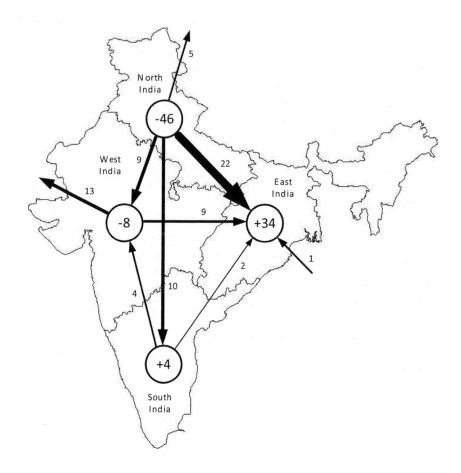

**FIGURE 12.1** The net virtual water flows between four main regions of India in billion
m³/yr, 1997–2001

Source: Kampman *et al.* (2008)

interregional trade within China and India, because various factors will play a role, including historical, political and economic ones. One factor that may play a role as well is that in water-scarce regions the incentives to increase water productivity are greater. As a result of the investments made in productivity, it becomes attractive to produce in those regions, which enhances water scarcity. This may be a factor in northern India, where water productivities are indeed higher than in the eastern states, providing them with a comparative advantage though the water availability in absolute terms is much lower.

Forecasts of how international trade patterns will develop generally ignore water as a possible constraint to production. As a result, some of the scenarios developed predict increased agricultural production in areas where water is already highly scarce or even over-drafted. Liao *et al.* (2008) illustrate this for the case of China by studying the effect of trade liberalization after China's accession to the World Trade Organization in 2001. They show that existing projections of agricultural production and trade, which ignore water as a production factor, are unrealistic. Including water as a constraint leads to projections where cereal imports into China will be much higher than previously thought, and to less optimistic prospects with respect to the increased export of vegetables.

## Water pricing

A major issue when talking about good water governance and international trade is the fact that particularly the international market in agricultural products is heavily distorted. Since 92 per cent of the global blue water consumption occurs in agricultural production (Mekonnen and Hoekstra, 2011b), this is highly relevant for water. The distortion is related to all sorts of direct and indirect subsidies that agriculture receives in all countries in the world, albeit in different forms per country. This issue is widely known, but most discussion is about direct subsidies to farmers and about export subsidies and import taxes. Much less attention is given to the fact that water, an important input factor to agriculture, is generally hugely underpriced. The result is that water is not a factor of importance in the establishment of production and trade patterns. This results in perverse trade flows, where water-intensive crops are exported on a large scale from areas where water is highly scarce and overexploited. There is no chance that free trade will ever contribute to optimal production and trade outcomes from a water perspective if water remains so underpriced.

There is a need to reach a global agreement on water pricing structures that cover the full cost of water use, including investment costs, operational and maintenance costs, a water scarcity rent and the cost of negative externalities of water use (Hoekstra and Chapagain, 2008; Hoekstra, 2011a). Without an international treaty on proper water pricing, it is unlikely that a globally efficient and sustainable pattern of water use will ever be achieved. The need to have full cost pricing has been acknowledged since the Dublin Conference in 1992 (ICWE, 1992). A global ministerial forum to come to agreements on this does exist in the regular World Water Forums (Marrakech 1997, The Hague 2000, Kyoto 2003, Mexico City 2006, Istanbul 2009 and Marseille 2012), but these forums have not been used to take up the challenge of making international agreements on the implementation of the principle that water should be considered as a scarce, economic good. The World Water Forums are not organized under the umbrella of a UN organization. Alternative forums to initiate and negotiate an international water pricing protocol could be UN-Water or the UN Commission on Sustainable Development.

It is not sufficient to leave the implementation of the 'water-is-an-economic-good principle' to national governments without having some kind of international protocol on the implementation, because unilateral implementation can be expected to be at the cost of the countries moving ahead. The competitiveness of the producers of water-intensive products in a country that one-sidedly implements a stringent water pricing policy will be affected and, this, together with the natural resistance of domestic consumers to higher prices of local products, will reduce the feasibility of a unilateral implementation of a rigorous water pricing strategy. An international protocol on full-cost water pricing would contribute to the sustainable use of the world's water resources, because water scarcity would be translated into a scarcity rent and thus affect consumer decisions, even if those consumers live at a great distance from the production site. Besides, it is no more than fair to make producers and consumers pay for their contribution to the depletion and pollution of water. Proper pricing of water would shed a fresh light upon the economic feasibility of plans for large-scale inter-basin transfers, since it would force negative externalities and opportunity costs to be taken into account. As already acknowledged at the Dublin Conference (ICWE, 1992), full-cost water pricing should be combined with a minimum water right, in order to prevent poor people not being able to obtain their basic needs (Gleick, 1999; Mehta and La Cour Madsen, 2005).

## Product transparency versus non-discrimination in trade

Better pricing of water is important, but will not be sufficient (see Chapter 1). As will be argued more elaborately in Chapter 13, the basis for well-informed consumer behaviour, governmental policy and company strategy is product transparency. The 'product-transparency principle' requires that all relevant information about a product is publicly available, including information about the product as it appears as well as information about how the product was produced. When we limit ourselves here to how a product relates to the use of freshwater, relevant information may include for instance answers to questions such as: how much water was consumed to make the product in the different stages of its supply chain, how much water was polluted, what type of pollution, does the water consumption or pollution take place in areas where water is relatively scarce and already polluted beyond acceptable limits, are downstream users or ecosystems negatively affected, could the water consumed have been used for an alternative purpose with a higher societal benefit? Products may often look alike – same colour, smell, feel, taste and quality – but nevertheless they may be quite different. Every product has a unique history. The origin of the ingredients may differ as well as the production circumstances of the ingredients. A beverage like cola contains sugars that can come for instance from sugar beet, sugar cane or maize (high-fructose maize syrup). The crop may be grown with irrigation water from the overexploited Ogallala Aquifer beneath the Great Plains in the United States or under rain-fed conditions in a water-abundant part of Europe. In other words, one bottle of cola is simply not equal to another. Production circumstances can vary among countries, but also within countries; differences can exist between brands, but also within brands and even between different batches of otherwise precisely the same product. From a water-footprint perspective, one may like to discriminate between seemingly similar goods, based on the different impacts the goods have on freshwater resources. In Chapter 5 I showed how the blue water footprint of cotton consumed in the UK can be localized in different regions of the world (Figure 5.1). Among the most important growing regions of irrigated cotton consumed in the UK are Turkey, India, Italy, Pakistan and Morocco. In some of the source regions, like for instance in the Indus Basin in Pakistan, water consumption levels are far beyond sustainable levels. Within the region, some cotton farmers do far better than others. Discriminating in trade between sustainable and unsustainable cotton, however, is problematic.

An important principle used in the context of international trade negotiations is the 'non-discrimination principle'. This principle says that the international trading system should be without discrimination, which means that a country should not discriminate between its trading partners nor between its own and foreign products (WTO, 2008). A key question to be posed in this context is what are the criteria to evaluate whether two goods can be called similar. According to the non-discrimination principle, one may not discriminate between cotton from different countries or between beef from different countries. But what does the principle say if it appears that two seemingly similar products are not similar after all? Discrimination is considered unfair when products are similar, but discrimination is quite natural when products are not similar.

Fair international trade rules should include a provision that enables consumers, through their government, to raise trade barriers against products that are considered unsustainable. In practice, this means that the non-discrimination principle would hold only for similar products that are also considered similar in terms of the existing impacts along their life cycle. It would imply that a country could favour the import of a certain product from a country that can guarantee that the product's water footprint is not located in catchments where environmental flow requirements are violated or where ambient water quality standards are not met. This preference would have to hold – according to the non-discrimination principle – for all countries that can give that guarantee. The favour, however, would not necessarily hold for countries that cannot provide that guarantee. Obviously, a guarantee of sustainability can be provided only when proper arrangements for product transparency are in place.

When arrangements for product transparency in a particular country are in place, it can occur that one batch of a certain commodity from that country fulfils a set of specified sustainability criteria, while another batch does not. In that case, another country may be willing to have free trade with respect to the first batch, but raise trade barriers against the other batch. It seems justified to allow for such arrangements in international trade rules. Countries can either choose to agree on shared sustainability criteria, which can then be included in an international trade agreement, or they can leave the formulation of such criteria to each country separately. The former situation may be preferable, because it creates equity and security on the market, but it will be at the cost of national sovereignty to quickly respond to new developments and adapt criteria. Besides, countries may have highly divergent opinions about what criteria should be chosen. Anyhow, trying to agree on shared criteria for product sustainability can be part of international negotiations. This should be in a different context than the World Trade Organization, because the WTO limits itself to trade negotiations and refrains from negotiations on environmental protection. For environmental protection, the WTO refers to multilateral environmental agreements formulated in other international settings. According to WTO rules, a trade dispute that falls under a certain multilateral environmental agreement signed by two conflicting countries should be settled using the environmental agreement.

## The absence of international agreements on sustainable water use

In the perspective of the WTO, 'free trade' is not at odds with 'green trade'. National governments have negotiated WTO rules voluntarily. Similarly, national governments negotiate and agree on international environmental agreements. If a dispute arises over a trade action taken under an environmental agreement, and if both sides of the dispute have signed that agreement, then they should try to use the environmental agreement to settle the dispute. However, if one side in the dispute has not signed the environmental agreement, then the WTO would provide the only possible forum for settling the dispute (WTO, 2008). Besides, it matters whether an international agreement contains rules that relate to trade or not. As Neumayer (2004) observes, most regional or international environmental agreements do not contain any trade-restrictive measures. As a result, these environmental agreements will be irrelevant, i.e. ignored, when settling a trade dispute. In the case an international environmental agreement is absent and where a trade barrier is raised with reference to *national* environmental legislation, it will again be the WTO who settles the dispute. Historic evidence shows that free-trade rules agreed internationally within the context of the WTO go beyond environmental protection rules set by national governments or international environmental agreements not signed by one of the parties of the dispute. According to the WTO, if trade barriers could be raised with reference to national regulations,

> then any country could ban imports of a product from another country merely because the exporting country has different environmental, health and social policies from its own. This would create a virtually open-ended route for any country to apply trade restrictions unilaterally – and to do so not just to enforce its own laws domestically, but to impose its own standards on other countries.
>
> (WTO, 2008)

Internationally binding agreements on sustainable water use or, more particularly, on 'sustainable water use in the production of goods and services' do not exist. The reason is probably that freshwater is primarily seen as a local resource, to be managed at the level of a nation or river basin at most. As a result, policies for water governance are always shaped in the form of national legislation, supplemented by international agreements on trans-boundary rivers and agreements on a regional level like in the European Union. This means that whenever trade disputes with reference to freshwater protection arise, the dispute will be settled by the WTO and that – with reference to the non-discrimination principle – the outcome will be in favour of free trade and not freshwater protection.

There is no legal basis to discriminate in international trade based on environmental product standards. This is a fundamental imbalance in the area of international agreements. In the WTO, international trade rules do not necessarily go beyond international environmental agreements but, in absence of the latter, the international trade rule of non-discrimination becomes decisive. The WTO agreements say two important things: 'First, trade restrictions cannot be imposed on a product purely because of the way it has been produced. Second, one country cannot reach out beyond its own territory to impose its standards on another country' (WTO, 2008). As many products on the world market have significant impacts on freshwater systems, because their production contributes to the violation of local environmental flow requirements or ambient water quality standards, it is expected that consumers will increasingly request product transparency and it is likely that consumers in some countries will start asking their government to ban imports of products that obviously do not meet domestic sustainability criteria. Yet, it is very unlikely that national efforts to ban products with reference to national standards on sustainable water use will succeed. Reaching greater product transparency, however, must be possible.

## An international water label for water-intensive products

As will be discussed in Chapter 13, a water label on products could be a means to contribute to product transparency. A 'water label' could be a label physically attached to a product, but also digital information about a specific product available through the internet by scanning its barcode in the shop or at home. Furthermore, it could be a simple quality certification showing whether a product meets a certain set of sustainability criteria (a 'yes or no' label), but it could also be a more advanced label with detailed quantitative information on a number of relevant criteria. Introducing such a label would be most relevant for water-intensive products. The label could be introduced first for a few commodities that usually have great impacts on water systems, such as cotton, rice and cane sugar. Given the global character of the cotton, rice and sugar markets, international cooperation in setting the labelling criteria and in the practical application of the water label is a precondition. Consideration could be given to integrating the water label within a broader environmental or fair-trade label, but this would probably create new bottlenecks for global implementation, so that a first step could be to agree on a separate water label.

If one or a number of countries agree on some sort of water-labelling scheme, it is still unclear how current WTO rules would be interpreted if a dispute arose. Consider the case in which a country raises a trade barrier for all countries that do not fulfil the requirements of the water-labelling scheme. Given the decisions made in earlier disputes (consider for instance the so-called tuna–dolphin dispute between the USA and Mexico), the WTO rules are unlikely to lead to acceptance of discrimination of products from another country not fulfilling a certain labelling requirement if that other country has not signed up for the labelling scheme. The WTO stipulates that one country cannot impose its own environmental regulations on another country. However, some commentators have argued that under some conditions it is possible for WTO members to impose environmental regulations on another member (Charnovitz, 2002). Altogether, there is still much ambiguity about the role national environmental standards related to processes and production methods can have in restricting international trade. This underlines the necessity to come to broad international agreements on a water-labelling scheme. Without international agreement, any labelling scheme will be useful for domestic products only and unlikely be effective in restricting trade. If countries agree on an international water label, this label will likely be covered by WTO's Technical Barriers to Trade (TBT) Agreement, which has been designed to ensure that regulations, standards, testing and certification procedures do not create unnecessary obstacles to trade. This means that the labelling scheme should fulfil a set of conditions set by the WTO.

A broad international water label laid down in an international agreement is far from reality. Liberalization of trade in water-intensive products under the WTO makes it more difficult, if not impossible, for countries to take action against products from countries that are considered as undesirable because they either lack transparency or are transparent but do not meet certain domestically defined sustainability standards. Under existing WTO rules, countries have to let products that do not meet production standards enter the country under the same conditions as similar products that do meet those standards. The only remaining choice is that consumers select themselves in the shop. This choice will be hampered, however, by lack of information, because countries cannot impose a labelling scheme on imported products.

## The Doha Development Round

The WTO rules apply to most products but still exclude, or include to a limited extent, services and agricultural products. Because 92 per cent of the water footprint in the world lies in agriculture, concerns with respect to sustainable freshwater use can still be taken into account in the negotiations in the Doha Development Round, the current trade negotiation round of the World Trade Organization, which started in 2001. Trade in agricultural products is one of the key focus areas of the current negotiations. As follows from above, from a sustainable water-use perspective it is key that any new rules on international trade in agricultural products include provisions ensuring that efforts to contribute to more sustainable water use behind the traded products are promoted and rewarded.

## Intensification of trade in water-intensive commodities: risks and opportunities

International transfers of water in virtual form are substantial and likely to increase with continued global trade liberalization (Ramirez-Vallejo and Rogers, 2004). Intensified trade in water-intensive countries offers both opportunities and risks. The most obvious opportunity of reduced trade barriers is that virtual water can be regarded as a possibly cheap alternative source of water in areas where freshwater is relatively scarce. Virtual water import can be used by national governments as a tool to reduce the use of their domestic water resources. This import of virtual water (as opposed to real water, which is generally too expensive) will relieve the pressure on the nation's own water resources. Besides, trade can save water if products are traded from countries with high to countries with low water productivity. For example, Mexico imports maize from the USA, the production of which requires 4.1 billion $m^3$ of water per year in the USA. If Mexico were to produce the imported maize domestically, it would require 12.2 billion $m^3$ of water per year. Thus, from a global perspective, the trade in maize from the USA to Mexico saves 8.1 billion $m^3$/yr (Mekonnen and Hoekstra, 2011b). Although there are also examples where water-intensive commodities flow in the opposite direction, from countries with low to countries with high water productivity, the available studies indicate that the resultant of all international trade flow works in a positive direction.

A serious drawback of trade is that the indirect effects of consumption are externalized to other countries. While water in agriculture is still priced far below its real cost in most countries, an increasing volume of water is used for processing export products. The costs associated with water use in the exporting country are not included in the price of the products consumed in the importing country. Consumers are generally not aware of – and do not pay for – the water problems in the overseas countries where their goods are being produced. According to economic theory, a precondition for trade to be efficient and fair is that consumers bear the full cost of production and impacts. Another downside of intensive international virtual water transfers is that many countries increasingly depend on the import of water-intensive commodities from other countries. Jordan has an annual net import of virtual water of 5.7 billion $m^3$ of water (Mekonnen and Hoekstra, 2011b), which is six times the 0.94 billion $m^3$ of total annual renewable water resources of the country (FAO, 2012b). Other countries in the Middle East, but also various European countries, have a similar high water-import dependency. The increasing lack of self-sufficiency has made various individual countries, but also larger regions, very vulnerable. If, for whatever reason, food supplies cease – be it due to war or a natural disaster in an important export region – the importing regions will suffer severely. A key question is to what extent nations are willing to take such a risk. The risk can be avoided by promoting national self-sufficiency in water and food supply (as Egypt and China do). The risk can be reduced by importing food from a wide range of trading partners. The current worldwide trend, however, facilitated by the World Trade Organization, is towards reducing trade barriers and encouraging free international trade, and decreasing interference by national governments.

The current global trade pattern significantly influences water use in most countries of the world, either by reducing domestic water use or by enhancing it. Future national and regional water policy studies should therefore include an assessment of the effects of trade on water policy. For water-scarce countries, it would be wise to make the reverse assessment as well: study the possible implications of national water scarcity on trade. In short, strategic analysis for water policy-making should include an analysis of expected or desirable trends in international or inter-regional virtual water flows.

International agreements on the liberalization of trade in agricultural products – as negotiated in the WTO's ongoing Doha Development Round – should include provisions that promote sustainable water use in agriculture. As yet, it is unclear what such provisions would look like, since the WTO explicitly refrains from making environmental agreements. An imbalance in global trade regulations will be created as soon as free-trade agreements are effective while sustainable product and sustainable water-use agreements to constrain international trade are not yet existent. This is a serious risk, since there are no international agreements on sustainable water use or sustainable products currently in existence or being prepared.

# 13
## PRODUCT TRANSPARENCY

Public debates about water footprint are sometimes quickly narrowed down to a discussion about the need for a water label on products. Some people like the idea of a label for sustainable water use and argue for the necessity of properly informing consumers and giving them a fair choice. However, there are people who dislike the idea of yet another label, who question whether providing the water footprint as just a number on the label of a product is informative, and who doubt the effectiveness of labels anyhow. I have often been asked whether I am in favour of a water label for products and, if so, what sort of label. As you will understand in the course of this chapter, I am very much in favour of product transparency, which is a much broader idea than product labelling. I also see the usefulness in developing a water label: not one that just shows the water footprint as a number – which can be nice for awareness raising, not beyond that – but one that shows whether the product is based on good water stewardship – which can be a basis for conscious consumer choice.

Before talking about product transparency and more specifically about product labels, I would like to make a step back and reflect on the broader context. The overarching goal in any discussion about the water footprint of things or activities should be to see how we can reduce humanity's water footprint in order to make it sustainable and to develop priorities where and when reduction is most desired. The first logical step is therefore to discuss maximum sustainable water footprint levels per river basin and see how political agreement can be reached about setting water footprint caps per basin (Chapter 9). A second thing is to discuss the efficiency of water use in production and see how regional or global water footprint benchmarks for water-using processes and for final products can be established, in order to have a reference for farmers and companies to work towards and a reference for governments in allocating water footprint permits to users (Chapter 10). A third major discussion should be about our consumption pattern in the light of limited freshwater availability. This discussion should focus on the fairness of the huge differences among the water footprints of people (Chapter 11). Creating product transparency is a means to enable a fruitful discussion about the water footprints of products, so that consumers know how much they contribute to the water consumption, water pollution and water scarcity in different places and so that companies know details about their purchases as well. One may argue that product transparency is important for the sake of transparency itself, but probably more important is that it is difficult to see how we can ever move towards sustainability without product transparency. The water footprint of humanity is equal to the sum of the water footprints of all final consumer goods (whereby goods are interpreted broadly, including services). Without product transparency – information about production circumstances in each step of the supply chain of a product – a consumer will never know how he or she connects to unsustainable water consumption and pollution. With relevant information, consumers can be an active player, a driving force, a partner in moving towards sustainability.

In this chapter, I will first address the question of why product transparency is needed in the context of the broader goal of sustainability. Next, I will pose the question of what precisely companies should be transparent about. Subsequently, I will reflect on the issue of product transparency from different perspectives: final consumers, companies, investors and government. After that, I will discuss the issue of physical product labelling. Finally, I will reflect on the concept of good water stewardship, an umbrella term often used to refer to the overall performance of companies if it comes to their efforts in the direction of sustainable water use in their operations and supply chain and their transparency about those efforts.

## Why product transparency?

It is intriguing that generally we know so little about the composition and origin of our daily consumer products. In a local market, with local products, it is likely that we know more or less the details about the origin of products and production circumstances. Production chains are relatively short and local, and consumers and producers know each other. This is different in a global market. Industrialization and globalization of the economy predictably lead to a situation whereby the background of products becomes obscure. In complex and cross-border supply chains, it is inevitable that information gets lost if no special care is taken to move information about the early steps in a supply chain down along the chain towards the final product. A computer contains various metals that have been mined somewhere (or obtained by recycling the components of old computers). A pair of jeans consists of cotton that must have been harvested somewhere under certain conditions and dyed somewhere else under other conditions. If consumers want to assure themselves that what they buy meets some criteria of sustainability, they will have to know some details about the origin of the product ingredients and the way these were produced and processed. This does not only hold for final consumers, but also for retailers or manufacturers that want to make sure that what they purchase is sustainable. Product transparency is primarily in the interest of the buyers along the supply chain. It also becomes of interest for sellers along the chain if other sellers create transparency and if this starts impacting on buyer behaviour.

The main goal of product transparency is to enable communication along the supply chain, in two directions. Companies at the top of the supply chain supply information about production circumstances to companies further down the chain, and ultimately to consumers. In the other direction, based on this product information, consumers and companies can respond by making choices, asking questions and demanding change. Product transparency creates an incentive for companies to move towards greening their business. If nobody can see good efforts, there will be no reward.

## Transparency about what?

Transparency of a product regarding its water footprint entails a number of things. It means that we know: (1) the size and location of the green, blue and grey water footprint of the various product components; (2) the sustainability of this water footprint; and (3) what smart plan of action is in place to reduce the water footprint when and where necessary. The second point, on sustainability, requires that we know in which river basins the water footprint is located and whether it contributes to an unsustainable level of water consumption or pollution in these river basins (see Chapter 9). It also includes that we know whether the water footprint of the product meets a certain set benchmark (Chapter 10).

The biggest dilemma in product transparency is how information is made publicly available. In order to really understand the size, geographic distribution and sustainability of the water footprint of a product, one may need to collect a whole lot of data, particularly if the supply chain of the product is complex. Making all these data publicly available is cumbersome, but more importantly: what will a huge dataset tell people who are interested in the water footprint performance of a product? Product transparency can be given in two different ways: making available *all factual data* – by giving an account of all details of a full water footprint assessment – or making available information about the *overall performance* – which will be based on a set of clearly formulated and shared criteria.

There are pros and cons to both approaches. The big advantage of providing all the details is that companies that purchase a product in order to further process it, have the necessary information to make their own assessment for their own final product. A beverage company may want to receive the full water footprint accounts from all the sugar refineries from which they obtain the sugar for their beverages. If they do not get that, they will not be able to give a full account for their beverage either, which may be undesirable from the point of view of the beverage company or the clients of the beverage company. A second advantage of full water footprint accounts, with all the factual details, is that it is the ultimate form of transparency. It can be *combined* with information about the overall performance, so the fact that detailed accounts by themselves do not include a clear message regarding overall performance is not a real drawback. The disadvantages of product transparency at the detailed level is that it may require a lot of work for companies to make all detailed data publicly available and that companies may like to keep things confidential from a competitiveness point of view. Inevitably, detailed accounts of a company's water footprint will betray from where it gets its resources.

The great advantage of providing information about the overall performance of a product is that individual consumers are better served by comprehensive information that simply ranks the overall performance of a product on a scale, or, even simpler, tells whether or not a product meets a given set of criteria. The disadvantage is that any factual information is now lost further down the supply chain. Summarizing, it seems that detailed accounts are mostly relevant if it comes to business-to-business transparency and that overall performance information may be sufficient in business-to-consumer transparency. After all, the issue of confidentiality of detailed water footprint accounts cannot be an overriding issue, because in business-to-business transparency, agreements on non-disclosure of detailed data can be made if really deemed necessary.

Establishing a mechanism that makes sure that detailed water footprint accounts can flow down the supply chain is not an easy task. It requires a form of accounting along supply chains that accumulates relevant information all the way to the end point of a chain. Some multinationals already have quite advanced *internal* product management systems, whereby, based on the product code of one specific batch of final product, they are able to tell the full history of that batch: which specific batch of resource 1 was used, which specific batch of resource 2, etc. This enables them to trace the origin of a final product in a very precise way. Such product management systems can also be organized beyond the gate of one company, so that tracing along supply chains becomes possible, but obviously this requires cooperation among companies.

Companies can aim at creating product transparency voluntarily, in the absence of regulations, certification schemes or whatsoever. At present, regarding the sustainability of water use behind products, there are no regulations or certification schemes yet, so the degree of product transparency consumers get is fully in the hands of companies. This is not in our common interest, and also not in the interest of companies that want to move forward in this field. As I said, it is very difficult for one individual company to create transparency about its products just on its own, because it will depend on data to be supplied by companies earlier in the supply chain, from which it purchases its product ingredients or components. Therefore, some sort of governmental regulation and publicly or privately driven certification scheme will be necessary. Since the perceived needs and problems partially differ among stakeholders, let me reflect on the issue of product transparency from different perspectives: final consumers, companies, investors and government.

## The consumer perspective

In order to know what we consume, we will need a form of product transparency that is currently completely lacking. It is reasonable that consumers have access to information about the environmental performance of a product. The individual consumer will have little interest in detailed accounts of the water footprint of a product, including accounts of its sustainability and plans of companies along the supply chain to work on improvements. From a consumer perspective, it is more interesting to receive information in a comprehensive form, in order to know whether a product meets a certain set of sustainability criteria or not. Individual consumers can use this sort of information in choosing between alternative products. However, consumer and environmental organizations may be interested in more detail than just the outcome of an evaluation based on all precise data and some criteria. Knowledge of the full water footprint accounts and company targets and work plans towards improvements, will help consumer and environmental organizations to engage with companies to jointly explore priorities and ways to make positive steps. We therefore need to distinguish between the interest of individual consumers (have a simple basis to make a conscious choice) and the concern of civil society organizations (have a rich basis to call for change).

## The company perspective

There is no such thing as *the* company perspective on product transparency. Companies have divergent views on this. Roughly speaking, there are two kinds of companies. First, there are those that perceive the need for product transparency and struggle to find out what it precisely means, how it can be achieved given internal hurdles and the complexity of some supply chains, and how it can most effectively contribute to consumer communication on the one hand and drive towards sustainability on the other. Second, there are the companies that are critical towards the whole idea, particularly regarding transparency about what happens outside their fence, in the supply chain. Companies in this second category do not acknowledge that they bear responsibility for the full sustainability of their products. They see their responsibility as limited to their own operations. As I will argue in Chapter 14, this view on responsibility is objectionable from an ethical point of view, but also a hindrance from a practical point of view. Companies that acknowledge the positive role they can play in achieving improvements in their supply chain are the companies that actually drive change for the better. Companies that remain within the mode of 'responsibility within the fence' form an obstacle for change. This latter category of companies needs to be captured by governmental regulation and legislation.

Creating product transparency serves the business community as a whole, because proper information about natural resources use and environmental impacts along the supply chains of products is essential in formulating strategies to reduce the pressure on the planet. Water footprint benchmarks can help to formulate smart water footprint reduction strategies. Transparency about the direct and indirect water footprint of a business will also become increasingly important to attract investment funds, because investors start recognizing the critical importance of the risks that water shortages impose on businesses that depend on water (Sarni, 2011).

What is the current state of play in terms of transparency regarding the water footprint of products? I cannot do anything other than provide a snapshot here, because, as I write in 2012, the first time that a company got to know and showed interest in the water footprint concept was in 2007. (For the record: that was the Coca-Cola Company.) Five years is little time when it comes to changes in thought and perception and even less when it comes to changes in activity on the ground. Today, many companies have joined the Water Footprint Network, from different sectors, mostly from the food and beverage, apparel, cosmetic, and pulp and paper sectors. All those companies have started to explore the water footprint of their business, whereby the supply chain gets due attention. No water footprint benchmarks have been developed yet, in any of the sectors. There are many companies with clear goals with respect to the reduction of the water abstractions in their operations, but no company has yet dared to set a zero water footprint target for all of its own operations. Except for the water incorporated into products, this is feasible (see Chapter 10) and probably already common practice among many facilities worldwide. The only thing needed to achieve this is no consumptive use of water and no addition of chemicals to ambient water bodies through effluents or diffuse pollution. Regarding the supply-chain water footprint of companies, the situation is very different. Several companies have started to analyse their indirect water footprint, including its sustainability, but there are no companies yet that have developed a strategy – including smart-formulated reduction targets – to reduce their supply-chain water footprint. I am not pessimistic in this respect, because time has, so far, been too short for companies to reach this stage. It must come, however.

There is a substantial difference between what small and large companies can do. Small companies can aim at sustainable procurement and choose their suppliers wisely. Large companies can do much more. Large firms in the food and beverage sector can put pressure on and support farmers to reduce their water footprint and urge them to provide proper accounts. Support can be in the form of awareness raising, capacity building and investments in better irrigation technology. Supplier agreements can be made with specific farmer groups, whereby specified points of improvement are part of the deal. The same holds for large companies in the apparel sector, which can drive improvements in the cotton supply chain, by cooperating with specific cotton farmers and processing industries and helping them to make the necessary steps to improvement in environmental performance.

## The investor perspective

The possible role of investors in driving towards sustainability is often underestimated. The reason is that we have so clearly seen the reverse role of investors. The general impression from stock markets is that the short-term interest of shareholders in profit is one of the explanatory factors behind the unsustainable behaviour of listed companies. The same sort of impression has been generated by commercial banks, insurance companies and pension funds, that have often put little emphasis on the sustainability of their investments. Fortunately, we can see a gradual shift here, whereby sustainability criteria are slowly entering the world of investments.

A positive sign was when, in 2008, the International Finance Corporation (IFC), part of the World Bank Group, acted as one of the founding partners of the Water Footprint Network. In 2011, at the launch of the Water Footprint Assessment Manual, Monika Weber-Fahr, Global Business Line Leader for IFC's Sustainable Business Advisory, said:

> Water is vital to business: poor water quality or insufficient supply can curtail – or even shut down – activities in business operations and in the supply chain. The method laid out in the *Water Footprint Assessment Manual* fills an emerging and urgent business need for a means of understanding water consumption in operations and in the supply chain, assessing its sustainability, and devising effective response strategies.

In the past few years, the IFC has shown how water-footprint assessment can be a constructive component in creating awareness among companies and driving change towards more sustainable water use, among others by starting initiatives with Jain Irrigation Systems and TATA Group in India and in the apparel industry in Bangladesh.

Another signal of the increasing interest from investors in business transparency regarding water use is the water disclosure initiative by the Carbon Disclosure Project (CDP, 2009). The Carbon Disclosure Project is an independent not-for-profit organization, founded in 2000, that holds the largest database of corporate climate change information in the world, gathered on behalf of institutional investors, purchasing organizations and government bodies. In 2007, the Carbon Disclosure Project extended its work by launching a supply-chain initiative, helping large organizations engage with their suppliers to generate and use high-quality information on the implications of climate change to their supply chains. Several of the member companies asked the Carbon Disclosure Project to help them engage with suppliers on issues related to water. Recognizing the importance of water-related issues, both as a critical part of the wider climate change challenge and as a stand-alone issue, the Carbon Disclosure Project carried out a water disclosure pilot in 2008. In 2012, the fourth annual global water disclosure report was published (CDP, 2012). The report opens with a citation from UPS, the USA-based company in air freight and logistics:

> We have learned from our comprehensive measurement and reporting capabilities for greenhouse gas emissions that transparency is a powerful tool for motivating people and organizations to change behaviour. We are applying the same principle to our near-term and long-term water risk.

The 2012 report shows that, for a third year in a row, an increased number of companies identified water-related risks in their supply chains.

It should be noted here that investors seem to drive business transparency rather than product transparency. For companies that have a small product portfolio, both are more or less the same, but for companies with a large product portfolio, insight into the sustainability of the business as a whole will give little insight into the sustainability of the various specific products of the company.

## The role of government

In creating product transparency, there is an important role for the market (consumers, producers and investors) but for governmental regulation as well. Currently, company efforts to create product transparency are voluntary. In the past, governments have made a lot of regulations for products regarding public health and safety, generally in the form of product standards. Companies have to meet those standards, which is in the interest of consumers. It is reasonable to expect that in the future governments will increasingly pay attention to setting standards regarding the sustainability of products as well. Criteria regarding sustainable water use should be part of those standards.

An additional role for governments lies in enforcing some sort of product transparency in the market. As said earlier in this chapter, one individual company cannot create transparency about its products just on its own, because it will depend on data being supplied by companies further up in the supply chain, from which it purchases its product ingredients or components. There should be some sort of obligation for suppliers to deliver key data on water use to their clients if they demand so. This sort of information can be supplied in different ways. It can be included in a company's annual sustainability report, made available online or as information that goes with the product.

In Chapter 12, I made a case for an international water label for water-intensive products like cotton, rice and cane sugar, with the argument that there is no way to regulate international trade based on sustainability criteria other than through international agreements that include rules allowing specific sorts of trade restrictions. Under the free-trade agreements of the World Trade Organization, a country cannot ban unsustainable products or raise a higher import tax on unsustainable products compared to sustainable products. This would be only possible if an international environmental agreement existed that can supersede the rules of free trade. Particularly governments that put interest in 'sustainable consumption' may like to translate this interest into their trade policy. The UK government, for example, given the fact that about 75 per cent of the total water footprint of the UK citizens lies outside its own territory (Mekonnen and Hoekstra, 2011b), may strive towards more transparency about the underlying water footprint of imported products and even ban or raise barriers against products that violate certain criteria of unsustainable water use. Achieving such a goal will be feasible only if there is international cooperation in this field.

## Should products get a water label?

Let's do the following thought experiment. As a consumer, we can choose to live in one of five worlds. Please rank the worlds in order of your preference:

1   A world in which all products are sustainable. Whatever we take from the shelves in the supermarket or elsewhere fulfils a set of specific sustainability criteria.
2   A world in which many products are not sustainable. All products have an internationally standardized sustainability label that shows the overall performance of the product, covering public health, social and environmental issues. Issues of sustainable water use are integrated in this label.
3   The same as the previous world, but a general sustainability label does not exist. Different labels exist regarding different issues. There are for instance different labels for energy, fair trade and organic food and labels on forest and marine stewardship. The various labels are not attached to all products, but only to products in the most relevant categories. There is also a water steward-ship label for a selection of water-intensive products.
4   The same as the previous world, but without the water stewardship label.
5   A world without labels. There is a full lack of transparency regarding social and environmental issues behind products. Many products are not sustainable, but we have no clue which ones are more or less sustainable.

I listed the worlds such as they reflect my own order of preference. I am curious what your preference is. Currently, we live in World 4. World 3 is about the same as World 4, just with yet another label. If you hate the seemingly unlimited growth in product labels, you are probably not very enthusiastic about the step from World 4 to World 3. I share that feeling, because the unbridled proliferation of product labels seems very costly and ineffective. However, my personal view is that it is all a matter of transition. We are simply not yet ready for an effective and internationally shared comprehensive sustainability label based on shared criteria and international agreement (World 2). Different national and regional labels for separate social and environmental issues are, in my view, an inevitable intermediate station, better than nothing (World 5). The presence of many labels will probably not be so effective in influencing consumer choice compared to just one clear, trusted international sustainability label, but they may nevertheless influence consumer choice to some extent and maybe, even more important, be an incentive for companies to work towards improvements in the various social and environmental fields. From this, it may be clear that I think it would be good if a water stewardship label for products is developed, whereby it is most logical to think about labelling food and beverages and cotton. Greater product transparency in these sectors is a precondition for developing such a label and, in itself, already a huge step forward. Greater product transparency can provide the same sort of market incentive to environmentally innovative and progressive businesses as a physical product label. The label, however, is to involve consumers.

In the world of digitalization, the whole idea of a physical label may become outdated anyway. One can easily imagine that a consumer gets access to product information at different levels of detail by scanning the product code of a good. At the highest level, the consumer would receive information like the price of the product, composition and origin, as well as the performance of the product on a number of issues, including for instance health, energy, water, biodiversity and fair trade. At a more detailed level, a consumer would get more particulars per issue.

Until here, I have consistently spoken about a 'water stewardship label', not about a 'water footprint label'. There is a good reason for that. Earlier in this chapter, when I spoke about product transparency in general, I made a difference between providing all factual data and providing information about the overall performance of a product. Providing full water footprint accounts – including green, blue and grey water footprints of all product components, the sustainability of the water footprint of each product component and a full account of targets and action plans of a company to make future improvements – is not something one would do on a product label. This is part of providing product transparency by other means, for example online or in annual sustainability reports. On a product label, it is more useful to include an overall judgement of the performance of a product, which would be a water stewardship label. Such a label would simply be a stamp, meaning 'produced based on good water stewardship', or it would be a label ranking the degree of water stewardship into a few categories. In-depth knowledge about the water footprint of a product, the sustainability of it and the plans for reduction where necessary would be part of the information used to determine the scores on the various water stewardship criteria.

Some companies have done experiments on putting the water footprint of a product on a product. Raisio, a Finnish food company, was the first company, in 2009, to mention the water footprint on a product. On a package of oat flakes, the company added a logo showing that 101 litres of water were consumed per 100 g of oat flakes, of which 99.3 per cent was in cultivating oats, 0.57 per cent in manufacturing and 0.16 per cent for packaging materials. Based on my arguments above, one may question the usefulness of such a water footprint label. The label itself gives no insight into whether this footprint is good or not, so it does not offer a basis for conscious product choice. It does, however, something else, and I guess that it was also intended for that: it helps create awareness among consumers on the water requirements of food. Looked at from that perspective, the label may be useful. It fits in a whole range of other efforts made by companies and governments to educate people in the area of water. The water footprint as one total number is often used in this context, just for awareness raising. When influencing consumer choice is the aim, however, communicating the degree of good water stewardship is more useful (Postle *et al.*, 2011). That includes a normative judgement (though based on objective criteria), which is more useful as a basis for choice.

From the perspective of a sustainable Earth, a water stewardship product label can be called a success only if it provides an incentive for consumers and producers and takes them on the road to a more sustainable consumption and production pattern. According to UNEP (2005), eco-labels are likely to be most important where initiatives promote sustainable consumption, but only if the customer is the individual consumer. Not all relationships between producers and public or private buyers need to be facilitated through the use of a physical label fixed to the product. Water stewardship can also be measured at the company level, rather than at the product level.

## Good water stewardship

It is not easy to find a good definition of when a company or organization may be called a good water steward. The reason is, of course, that water stewardship intends to be an all-encompassing concept, similar to 'sustainability' but then focused on water. There are a lot of water stewardship initiatives worldwide, but the largest, global initiative is the Alliance for Water Stewardship, which was founded in 2008 by the Pacific Institute, The Nature Conservancy (TNC), Australia's Water Stewardship Initiative, World Wide Fund for Nature (WWF) and Water Witness International. The Alliance for Water Stewardship is designing a water-certification program to foster the adoption of business practices that will improve social and environmental sustainability in water use globally (Richter, 2009).

The International Water Stewardship Standard currently under development by the Alliance for Water Stewardship is meant to be an international standard that defines a set of water stewardship steps, principles, criteria and indicators for how water should be stewarded at a site and watershed level in a way that is environmentally, socially and economically sustainable (AWS, 2012). In the first draft standard, four principles of water stewardship have been formulated: water stewards shall (1) strive to achieve equitable and transparent water governance for all water users within the defined area of influence; (2) strive to achieve and maintain a sustainable water balance, and help to ensure adequate availability for all users at all times within the defined area of influence; (3) contribute to the maintenance of good water quality status in terms of chemical, physical and biological characteristics to maintain ecosystems and ensure adequate water quality for all users within the defined area of influence; and (4) identify important water areas at their sites and within their defined area of influence and strive to protect, manage and restore such areas as necessary. The standard is essentially geographically focused, rather than product or supply chain oriented. Supply-chain criteria, however, may be added in the course of the further development of the standard. Also the idea of developing a water stewardship product label is kept open for the moment.

## A global water footprint standard

Part of business and product transparency is that the same language, definitions and calculation methods are used across sectors and countries. To meet this need, in 2009, about seven years after the first use of the water footprint concept, the Water Footprint Network published the first version of the global standard for Water

Footprint Assessment. Two years later the second version was published (Hoekstra *et al.*, 2011). This standard, which was produced from a process of consultations with organizations and researchers worldwide and subjected to scientific peer review, has comprehensive definitions and methods for water footprint accounting. It shows how water footprints are calculated for processes and products, as well as for consumers, nations and businesses. It also includes methods for water footprint sustainability assessment and a list of water footprint response options. A major challenge for the global community is to further develop a shared language and understanding, because – as has been demonstrated in other fields of environmental accounting – confusion about definitions and methods does not serve the purpose of communication about sustainability.

# 14

# WHO WILL BE THE HEROES OF CHANGE?

Wise water governance is a shared responsibility of consumers, governments, businesses and investors. Each of those players has a different role. It will be in the interplay of actors that things can happen. Players can *discourage* each other to move in the right direction – as currently often happens – but they can also *encourage* each other. Let me first explain how we discourage each other. Most consumers prefer to buy cheap food, clothes and other things, and apparently don't care about the origin of it all. Furthermore, many of the things we buy are, in the end, hardly used or just thrown away. According to a recent study by the Food and Agriculture Organization of the United Nations, consumers in rich countries waste almost as much food (222 million tonnes/yr) as the entire net food production of sub-Saharan Africa (230 million tonnes/yr) (Gustavsson *et al.*, 2011). The fact that consumers do not care about the origin or the fate of products is a clear signal to the market: sustainability is not a relevant factor in producing for the masses. Even though, superficially, people seem to subscribe broadly to the goal of sustainability, actual behaviour is different (Vermeir and Verbeke, 2006). In the race to the bottom, producers are not encouraged to put great efforts in making their operations and supply chain sustainable. Apart from some initial easy gains, reducing water consumption and pollution along the supply chain of products will require investments that need to be covered by final consumers. If final consumers would rather choose the lowest price, it is difficult to see how things will easily move in the right direction. And if then, in addition, governments fail to put proper incentives in place for companies to become sustainable in their operations and procurement, and if investors let short-term gains prevail over long-term sustainability, which companies will still be willing or even able to implement appropriate measures? This creates a negative spiral, because one of the reasons that consumer behaviour does not correspond to the initial positive attitude of most people is the feeling that most products are not sustainable anyway. As Vermeir and Verbeke (2006) put it:

low perceived availability of sustainable products explains why intentions to buy remain low.

So far it's a black scenario. If each player takes his/her own responsibility and acts accordingly, it will bring us into a positive rather than negative spiral. There is sufficient evidence that if consumers take more positive-labelled products from the shelves in the store ('fair trade', 'organic', etc.), those products will get a boost, at the cost of products without the positive label. The growth in sales of fair-trade and organic products during the past decade has been driven by consumers, who are willing to pay more for such products than for conventional products (see for instance Howard and Allen, 2008). It is at the account of governments and business, however, that an increasing number of labels and certification schemes exist. Even though many complain about the large number of labelling and certification schemes and the lack of transparency, and have doubts about the genuineness of some labels, it is doubtful whether many actual improvements on the ground would have occurred without the encouragement provided by some of the labels. Unfortunately, existing labelling and certification schemes hardly include criteria regarding sustainable use of water. Most attention has gone so far into securing public health, good labour conditions, animal welfare, reduced energy use, sustainable forestry and sustainable fishing. Good water stewardship is not yet part of existing labels.

But enough about labels, because this is just one of the many vehicles that can play a role, but not a determining one in itself. The essence is that consumers express preference to sustainably produced products by their actual buying behaviour, whether informed through labels or otherwise. Governments can and should play a key role by providing incentives to consumers to buy such products and to companies to provide them. This can easily be done, for example through lowering the value-added tax for sustainable products compared to non-sustainable products, by taking a leading role in developing meaningful certification schemes and by progressively introducing regulations that force producers to become more sustainable over time. Finally, investors can and should apply social and environmental sustainability criteria when making their investment decisions. Fortunately, there is an increasing interest in this issue among investors. Consumers are also workers, voters and investors of their savings, so that they can exercise their power not only as buyers but also in their own work and by influencing the programmes of political parties, by electing and impelling their government and by lending their savings to banks that apply strict sustainability criteria. It all starts and ends with individuals who, in their various capacities, can and should take responsibility.

Let's review a number of cases that have been discussed in this book, and how different players can take positive measures in the direction of sustainable use of freshwater resources in the world. Chapter 2 about the water footprint of soft drinks has illustrated that – in order to deliver sustainable drinks – beverage companies will need to invest in their supply chain even more than in their own operations. And this will be true for many other companies, particularly companies that draw on agricultural inputs. Chapter 4 about meat has shown that consumers can mitigate problems of freshwater overexploitation and pollution much more effectively by reducing their meat consumption and being critical towards the origin of meat than by installing water-saving devices at home. Chapter 6 on the water footprint of biofuels has illustrated that governments should translate water protection goals towards smart energy policies that account for the implications on water use. Chapter 7 on cut flowers nicely illustrates the potential for cooperation along the supply chain, where consumers in western countries can contribute to a reduced water footprint in flower farming in a developing country by paying a certain premium per flower. Chapter 12 on trade makes clear that governments should also integrate water-protection goals into their trade policy.

## Consumers: creating leverage

It would make sense if consumers (or consumer and environmental organizations) start demanding greater transparency about the underlying water footprint of products, so that one is better informed about the hidden water resources use and associated impacts. This can be a basis for consumers to reduce consumption of certain products or to avoid them altogether. It will also enable consumers to choose between beef with a relative small water footprint and beef with a relative big footprint, or between flowers with a small and flowers with a large water footprint. Of course, the underlying water footprint will be, at best, just one of several arguments to choose between alternative options, but having the choice is better than not having the choice, given that people increasingly value sustainability of products. The advantage of involving consumers is that enormous leverage can be created to establish change in the supply chain. This is maybe best illustrated in the example of cut flowers that was given in Chapter 7.

The positive image of flowers does not match with a negative story about environmental impact. If consumers are willing to pay for flowers without negative impact, it can be achieved at a very low cost for the consumer. In between the flower farmer and the consumer there is a large added value, so that what the consumers pay is much more than what the flower farmers get. If the consumers pay a small water premium that is channelled back to the flower farmers to invest in sustainable water use, the collected funds will be very substantial for the flower farmers and easily sufficient to cover the required investments, for example in drip irrigation and water recycling within the greenhouse. The same holds for all other products where value added along the supply chain is relatively high, which is nowadays the case in a large part of the food and beverage sector. The investments needed to reduce water footprints at field level can be considerable from the farmer's point of view, but they will be very low from the consumer's point of view. The challenge is to change the value chain so that the farmers already create added value to their product, in the first stage of the chain, by applying water-efficient technology. This added value can only be appreciated if there is appropriate communication along the supply chain, so that this added value will be recognized by all players along the chain, including the final consumers.

Consumer awareness is a precondition for change. Companies can play an important role in this field, by explaining why some products are more sustainable than others. The problem, however, is that it is difficult to distinguish between sincere claims and ordinary advertisement, an area where governmental regulation is therefore crucial. It is an area where governments fail at large. We can observe this for example in the field of energy claims made by companies. Many company claims about the energy efficiency or 'carbon neutrality' of their products make little sense, which is highly damaging for those companies that are more genuine and try to reach the consumers with their more sincere claims. The great difficulty for the modern consumer is: what should he or she believe? Selling nonsense is free and unregulated.

## Companies: towards supply-chain responsibility

In order to understand their broader role in society and have guidance on how to act responsibly, companies and management professionals have developed a great number of concepts, tools and strategies. Under the umbrella term of *corporate social responsibility* many companies undertake an effort to make social and environmental objectives an integral part of their business model. Smart social and environmental *key performance indicators* are adopted as a management instrument to measure a company's performance. Many companies raise the flag of *people–planet–profit* or the *triple bottom line* to indicate that their business model includes three pillars: economic, social and natural capital. Concerns about sustainability in the supply chain are addressed under the term *sustainable procurement*, which means that social and environmental criteria, not only economic criteria, are applied when purchasing goods and services. In order to emphasize the financial implications of irresponsible business and an unsustainable use of resources, there is increasing talk about the business risk of not responding properly to social demands and environmental concerns. Companies increasingly recognize that – in addition to the need to meet legal requirements – they need a *social licence to operate*. An important means to make sure that consumers properly appreciate the efforts made by business – and in the best cases also a means to learn and improve – is *community engagement*, the involvement of stakeholders and relevant communities in the creation and implementation of major company decisions. Indeed, the world of business is full of management lingo. The philosophies are generally fine, but let's look at what is under all those nice words, focusing on the topic of water.

One would expect that a company waving the flag of sustainability has some sort of strategy to reduce the water footprint of its products. At present, though, there is hardly any company in the world incorporating water stewardship into its business model. Most companies still restrict their interest in water to their own operational water footprint, leaving the supply-chain water footprint out of scope. For many companies, including all companies in the food and beverage sector and in the apparel industry, the company's supply-chain water footprint is many times greater than its own operational water footprint. Studies carried out by companies like Coca-Cola, PepsiCo, SABMiller and Heineken have shown that the supply-chain water footprint for beverage companies can easily be over 99 per cent of their total water footprint. Nevertheless, all these companies apply a 'key performance indicator' for water that refers to the water use in their own operations only. Investments are geared to better perform in this respect, which means that, under the goal of sustainability, investments are made that aim to reduce that 1 per cent of their total water footprint. It is difficult to imagine that these investments will be most cost-effective if real sustainability is the goal. There is nothing against striving to move from 5 litres of water abstracted per litre of beer to 3.5 litres of water, for example, but the environmental gains will be minimal if the 100 or even 300 litres of indirect water use in the supply chain are not addressed. This is even truer if one realizes that the 5 litres of water abstracted per litre of beer are largely returned to the local system from which the water was abstracted anyway. Only the part of the abstracted 5 litres that is not returned to the local system from which the water was taken counts as blue water footprint (which is defined as the net volume of water withdrawn, not the gross volume). Reducing abstractions from 5 to 3.5 litres will only reduce the blue water footprint if the reduced gross abstraction also leads to reduced net abstraction, which is probably not the case. In short: companies focus on minimizing the wrong indicator.

If it comes to reducing the water footprint, it would be good if companies shift their focus towards their supply chain. This can be painstaking, because most companies have no idea about their supply chain. I asked the chief executive officer of a well-known brand in the apparel industry whether his company could map the fields around the world where all the cotton was grown that goes into the clothes produced by his company. It was just after he had made an impassioned speech about the industry's efforts to green the supply chain. But he had to admit that 'this was still not on the radar'. Admittedly, the cotton supply chain is extremely complex (Rivoli, 2005), but how can a company sell sustainable clothing if it does not even know where and how the cotton is grown? The same holds for companies in other sectors, like the food, beverage and cut-flower sectors. Making supply chains transparent, however, can be a challenge indeed. In the experience I have had, working with and listening to a great number of companies, it appears over and over again that assessing the supply chain of a company is not easy if the real aim is to locate the water footprint. Knowing the precise source of agricultural commodities is important, because the size and local impact of a water footprint will depend on all sorts of local conditions, like climate, irrigation practice and local water scarcity.

Particularly big processing industries, retailers and sector organizations can use their power to effectuate transparency in the supply chain. If there is a will, it is possible. If there is some governmental regulation, it helps. Experiences with organic and fair-trade labels have shown that tracing along supply chains is possible, even if distances are great and developing countries are involved. Big companies can make supply agreements with their suppliers that include conditions regarding a step-wise movement in the direction of a smaller water footprint. Small companies cannot do anything other than choose their suppliers wisely.

## Investing in the long term

Investors can be an important driving force to encourage companies to put water risk and good water stewardship higher on their corporate agenda. Since 2008 or thereabouts, there has been an increasing interest from the investment community in the risks posed by water scarcity (Levinson *et al.*, 2008; Morrison *et al.*, 2009, 2010a, 2010b; Barton, 2010). While this is good in itself, it is also interesting to see how the investment community has caused a reframing of the debate about corporate responsibility regarding water. Until about 2010, business concerns over freshwater were primarily framed under the umbrella of corporate social responsibility. I use the term 'corporate social responsibility' here in the sense of incorporating sustainability principles into the business model, not in the sense of philanthropy (see Crane *et al.*, 2008). The discussion was about internalizing principles of water stewardship into business. Around 2010, we could see a sudden appearance and quick adoption of another frame, that of 'water risk'. As we know, the way a debate is 'framed' influences perceptions and outcomes (Tversky and Kahneman, 1981). When water concerns are part of a good water stewardship agenda, the focus is on sustainability. Framing the question of sustainable water use as a challenge to manage 'water risk' diverts the attention to the economic side of doing business. To some extent, actions undertaken to reduce 'water risk' for the business will coincide with actions required to increase the sustainable use of water. But overexploitation of water resources or water pollution does not always pose an immediate risk for business – since sustainability refers to the long term – and even when it poses a threat, it may be to certain species and communities, which does not necessarily translate into a risk for those that contribute to the threat. Managing water risk for business, in short, is not the same as sustainable water use by business. Nevertheless, we can see an uptake of 'water risk' as a framework of thinking in the broader community, including environmental organizations (Pegram *et al.*, 2009; Orr *et al.*, 2009, 2011; Amis and Nel, 2011).

Investors can play a key role in the shift to a wiser use of the world's scarce freshwater resources. Conceiving freshwater scarcity as a business risk is a good start, but not sufficient. After water resources overexploitation in one region has put further supply from that region at risk, a beverage company can simply source barley or sugar from another region. Mitigating business risk is easier than being socially responsible. Therefore, investors should pursue an agenda that really promotes sustainable development in the long term, for example by applying good water stewardship criteria in any investment decision and by demanding 'water disclosure' from their clients.

## Coherent governmental policy

Water is a public good, so governments cannot withdraw from their responsibility to put proper regulations and incentives in place to ensure sustainable production and consumption. Governments should support consumers, producers and investors in their efforts to move to good water stewardship, for instance by promoting rain-fed and organic and precision agriculture, stimulating more advanced irrigation technology and water-saving strategies, introducing proper water pricing schemes, setting water footprint caps (limits) per river basin, helping different sectors to set water footprint benchmarks and education. But just as important is that governments integrate ambitions with respect to wise water governance into other policy domains, including for example agricultural policy, energy policy, trade policy and tax policy. It does not make sense to subsidize irrigated agriculture in water-short regions, as is common practice in many places in the world. Similarly, it makes no sense to adopt energy policies that unnecessarily aggravate water scarcity. Good water policy includes adopting good agricultural and energy policies. It also means engaging with other governments to work on international agreement on water footprint reduction targets by nation (Chapter 11). In the international context, governments could also try to reach a legally binding agreement on sustainable water use that allows governments to put restrictions on international trade in products that do not meet the production criteria as formulated in such international water agreements (Chapter 12). Furthermore, national governments can – preferably in an international context again – put regulations in place that urge businesses to cooperate in creating product transparency and disclosing relevant information about water use along supply chains (Chapter 13). Finally, good water policy also includes favouring sustainable products above non-sustainable products through national tax policy, which can be done through differentiated value-added tax tariffs.

## Responsibility: can we divide it into pieces?

A common view is that consumers and producers are only responsible for their own natural resources use and associated impacts. In this view, consumers are responsible for their direct water footprint, related to the water use at home. Their indirect water footprint, which relates to the water footprint in the production processes behind the goods and services they consume, is actually caused by the producers of those goods and services, so the producers would be responsible. Similarly, in this view, companies would be held responsible only for their own water consumption and pollution, not their indirect water use. Sustainability reports of companies generally report the water use related to their own operations, leaving out water issues in the supply chain. The same sort of perspective is often applied by governments that only take responsibility for what happens within their own territory. National governments generally feel responsible for the wise use and protection of the water resources within their country, but few governments will feel responsible for what happens outside their territory, even though the citizens of the country may rely on imported goods that obviously relate to unsustainable water use. Properly regulating that unsustainable water use elsewhere would be the responsibility of other nations.

This view on responsibility of consumers, producers and governments is very limited. From a legal point of view, it may be a bit difficult to see how things could be seen otherwise but, from an ethical point of view, it seems odd that consumers would not at all be responsible for consuming unsustainable products, that producers would not at all be responsible for buying ingredients produced in an unsustainable way and that governments would not at all be responsible for regulating the import of unsustainable products. The ethic of the 'everyone is responsible for his own water consumption and pollution' perspective is not consistent with how we look at responsibilities in other but similar cases. Consider the case of buying stolen goods (see also Hoekstra and Chapagain, 2008). The proverb says: the buyer is as bad as the thief. By that we mean that stealing, the act itself, is not good, but neither is buying stolen goods, not because the buyer can be blamed for stealing, but because the buyer chooses to be part of a system where goods are obtained through stealing. Another example is buying goods that depend on work by slaves. We agree that slavery is not good, but I guess that nowadays we also agree that buying goods that have been produced by somebody employing slaves is not good either. I think that, in general, it is fair to say that if producing X is 'bad', buying X is 'bad' as well. Let's not argue, at this stage, over the question of whether both acts are equally bad or that one of the two is worse. The remaining question is whether production based on unsustainable water use or pollution is 'bad'. If so, there is no other way than to conclude that buying goods that depend on unsustainable water use or pollution in their supply chain is not good either. Of course, there needs to be a continued societal debate about what is considered as 'unsustainable'. But whatever is the outcome of the discussion on what is sustainable (good) and unsustainable (bad), the responsibilities to move away from the bad thing will lie with both consumers and producers. Agreeing on this will be of utmost importance for making a shift to wise water governance. This discussion is, of course, not unique to the case of freshwater. Lenzen *et al.* (2007) show how the difficult question of consumer and producer responsibility plays in the fields of greenhouse gas emissions and land appropriation as well.

Even though, from an ethical point of view, the responsibilities of consumers and producers extend beyond their own direct consumption and pollution of water, one could say that, in practice, the most straightforward way would be to make each player accountable for his/her own direct contribution only. If farmers use water in a sustainable manner, if industries process products in a sustainable manner and if consumers use water at home in a sustainable matter, things would be solved. Defining what is 'sustainable' and setting regulations to enforce that activities meet sustainability criteria would be the task of governments. This approach, whereby governments have the role of regulator, setting boundary conditions to water users and polluters, and whereby consumers and producers can use and pollute water as long as it remains within the boundary conditions set, however, has proven not to work in practice. Actually, this is basically the world in which we live. We can see that it does not work from the actual lowering of groundwater and lake levels, the depletion of runoff in rivers and the water pollution beyond accepted water quality standards that we can observe in so many places, also in the most developed countries of the world. One could ultimately blame governments for apparently not putting proper regulations in place, or companies for violating regulations, but the issue is broader. As I started this chapter: it will be in the interplay of actors that things can improve. Consumers pushing both governments and companies will be an essential ingredient that will cause change. Companies pushing their suppliers is as critical. Consumers and companies that take responsibility for the water footprint in their supply chain will ultimately be the heroes of the changes that are necessary.

# REFERENCES

Abdullaev, I., De Fraiture, C., Giordano, M., Yakubov, M. and Rasulov, A. (2009) Agricultural water use and trade in Uzbekistan: Situation and potential impacts of market liberalization, *Water Resources Development*, 25(1): 47–63.

Aizaki, H. and Sato, N. (2007) Consumers' valuation of good agricultural practice by using contingent valuation and contingent ranking methods: A case study of Miyagi Prefecture, Japan, *Agricultural Information Research*, 16(3): 150–157.

Akbar, N.M. and Khwaja, M.A. (2006) *Study on effluents from selected sugar mills in Pakistan: Potential environmental, health, and economic consequences of an excessive pollution load*, Sustainable Development Policy Institute, Islamabad, Pakistan.

Alcamo, J., Döll, P., Henrichs, T., Kaspar, F., Lehner, B., Rösch, T. and Siebert, S. (2003) Global estimation of water withdrawals and availability under current and business as usual conditions, *Hydrological Sciences*, 48(3): 339–348.

Aldaya, M.M. and Hoekstra, A.Y. (2010) The water needed for Italians to eat pasta and pizza, *Agricultural Systems*, 103(6): 351–360.

Aldaya, M.M., Allan, J.A. and Hoekstra, A.Y. (2010a) Strategic importance of green water in international crop trade, *Ecological Economics*, 69(4): 887–894.

Aldaya, M.M., Muñoz, G. and Hoekstra, A.Y. (2010b) *Water footprint of cotton, wheat and rice production in Central Asia, Value of Water Research Report Series No. 41*, UNESCO-IHE, Delft, the Netherlands.

Allan, J.A. (2001) *The Middle East water question: Hydropolitics and the global economy*, I.B. Tauris, London, UK.

Allan, J.A. (2003) Virtual water – the water, food, and trade nexus: Useful concept or misleading metaphor? *Water International*, 28(1): 106–113.

Allan, T. (2011) *Virtual water: Tackling the threat to our planet's most precious resource*, I.B. Taurus, London, UK.

Alwahti, A.Y. (2003) *A taste of vanilla, TED Case Studies No. 686, Trade Environment Database*, American University, Washington, DC, USA.

Amis, M. and Nel, D. (2011) *Managing water risk: Business response to the risk of climate change in South Africa – a synthesis*, WWF, Cape Town, South Africa & Sanlam, South Africa.

ARB (2007) Flowers: Kenya, *Africa Research Bulletin*, 43(11): 17197A–17198A.

Ariga, J., Jayne, T.S. and Nyoro, J. (2006) *Factors driving the growth in fertilizer consumption in Kenya, 1990–2005: Sustaining the momentum in Kenya and lessons for broader replicability in Sub-Saharan Africa*, Tegemeo Working paper 24/2006, Tegemeo Institute of Agricultural Policy and Development, Egerton University, Nairobi, Kenya.

Arnot, C., Boxall, P.C. and Cash, S.B. (2006) Do ethical consumers care about price? A revealed preference analysis of fair trade coffee purchases, *Canadian Journal of Agricultural Economics*, 54(4): 555–565.

AWS (2012) *The AWS International Water Stewardship Standard*, First draft for stakeholder input, Version 03.13.2012, Alliance for Water Stewardship.

Baille, M., Baille, A. and Delmon, D. (1994) Microclimate and transpiration of greenhouse rose crops, *Agricultural and Forest Meteorology*, 71(1–2): 83–97.

Banerji, R., Chowdhury, A.R., Misra, G., Sudarsanam, G., Verma, S.C. and Srivastava, G.S. (1985) Jatropha seed oils for energy, *Biomass*, 8(4): 277–282.

Bartolini F., Bazzani G.M., Gallerani, V., Raggi, M. and Viaggi, D. (2007) The impact of water and agriculture policy scenarios on irrigated farming systems in Italy: An analysis based on farm level multi-attribute linear programming models, *Agricultural Systems*, 93(1–3): 90–114.

Barton, B. (2010) *Murky waters? Corporate reporting on water risk: A benchmarking study of 100 companies*, Ceres, Boston, MA, USA.

Bauer, C.J. (1997) Bringing water markets down to earth: The political economy of water rights in Chile, 1976–95, *World Development*, 25(5): 639–656.

Becht, R. (2007) *Environmental effects of the floricultural industry on the Lake Naivasha basin*, unpublished paper, ITC Naivasha Database, Enschede, the Netherlands.

Becht, R. and Harper, D.M. (2002) Towards an understanding of human impact upon the hydrology of Lake Naivasha, Kenya, *Hydrobiologia*, 488: 1–11.

Becht, R. and Nyaoro, J.R. (2006) The influence of groundwater on lake-water management: The Naivasha case. In: Odada, E.O., Olago, D.O., Ochola, W., Ntiba, M., Wandiga, S., Gichuki, N. and Oyieke, H. (eds) *Proceedings of the 11th World Lakes Conference, 31 October – 4 November 2005*, Nairobi, Kenya, Ministry of Water and Irrigation; International Lake Environment Committee (ILEC), Vol. II, pp. 384–388.

Becht, R., Odada, O. and Higgins, S. (2005) Lake Naivasha: Experience and lessons learned brief. In: *Managing lakes and their basins for sustainable use: A report for lake basin managers and stakeholders*, International Lake Environment Committee Foundation, Kusatsu, Japan.

Berndes, G. (2002) Bioenergy and water: The implications of large-scale bioenergy production for water use and supply, *Global Environmental Change*, 12(4): 253–271.

Bevilacqua, M., Braglia, M., Carmignani, G. and Zammori, F.A. (2007) Life cycle assessment of pasta production in Italy, *Journal of Food Quality*, 30(6): 932–952.

Bianchi, A. (1995) Durum wheat crop in Italy. In: Di Fonzo, N., Kaan, F. and Nachit, M. (eds) *Durum wheat quality in the Mediterranean region*, International Centre for Advanced Mediterranean Agronomic Studies (CIHEAM-IAMZ), Zaragoza, Spain, pp. 103–108.

BIER (2011) *A practical perspective on water accounting in the beverage sector*, Beverage Industry Environmental Roundtable.

Binswanger, M. (2001) Technological progress and sustainable development: What about the rebound effect? *Ecological Economics*, 36(1): 119–132.

Bjornlund, H. and McKay, J. (2002) Aspects of water markets for developing countries: Experiences from Australia, Chile, and the US, *Environment and Development Economics*, 7: 769–795.

Brouwer, F., Heinz, I. and Zabel, T. (eds) (2003) *Governance of water-related conflicts in agriculture: New directions in agri-environmental and water policies in the EU*, Environmental and Policy Series, Vol. 37, Kluwer Academic Press, Dordrecht, the Netherlands.

Brouwer, C., Prins, K. and Heibloem, M. (1989) *Irrigation scheduling*, Irrigation water management training manual no. 4, Food and Agriculture Organization of the United Nations, Rome, Italy.

Bruinsma, J. (ed.) (2003) *World agriculture: Towards 2015/2030: An FAO perspective*, Earthscan, London, UK.

Carter, N.T. and Campbell, R.J. (2009) *Water issues of Concentrating Solar Power (CSP) electricity in the U.S. Southwest*, Congressional Research Service, Washington, DC, USA.

CAWater (2012) *Database Aral Sea*, CAWater-Info, Portal of Knowledge for Water and Environmental Issues in Central Asia, www.cawater-info.net.

CDP (2009) *CDP water disclosure: The case for water disclosure*, Carbon Disclosure Project, London, UK.

CDP (2012) *CDP global water report 2012: On behalf of 470 investors with assets of US$ 50 trillion*, Carbon Disclosure Project, London, UK.

CEC (1988) *European community environmental legislation: 1967–1987*, Document Number XI/989/87, Directorate-General for Environment, Consumer Protection and Nuclear Safety, Commission of European Communities, Brussels, Belgium.

Cepero, E. (2000) La situación ambiental de Cuba al finalizar el siglo XX. In: *Cuba in Transition*, Vol. 10, Papers and Proceedings of the Tenth Annual Meeting of the Association for the Study of the Cuban Economy, Miami, FL, USA.

Chapagain, A.K. and Hoekstra, A.Y. (2008) The global component of freshwater demand and supply: An assessment of virtual water flows between nations as a result of trade in agricultural and industrial products, *Water International*, 33(1): 19–32.

Chapagain, A.K. and Hoekstra, A.Y. (2011) The blue, green and grey water footprint of rice from production and consumption perspectives, *Ecological Economics*, 70(4): 749–758.

Chapagain, A.K., Hoekstra, A.Y. and Savenije, H.H.G. (2006a) Water saving through international trade of agricultural products, *Hydrology and Earth System Sciences*, 10(3): 455–468.

Chapagain, A.K., Hoekstra, A.Y., Savenije, H.H.G. and Gautam, R. (2006b) The water footprint of cotton consumption: An assessment of the impact of worldwide consumption of cotton products on the water resources in the cotton producing countries, *Ecological Economics*, 60(1): 186–203.

Charnovitz, S. (2002) The law of environmental 'PPMs' in the WTO: Debunking the myth of illegality, *The Yale Journal of International Law*, 27(1): 59–110.

CIA (2012) *The World Factbook*, Central Intelligence Agency, Washington, DC, USA.

CIESIN (2005) *Gridded population of the world*, Version 3, Socioeconomic Data and Applications Center, Center for International Earth Science Information Network (CIESIN), Columbia University, New York, USA, http://sedac.ciesin.columbia.edu/data/collection/gpw-v3.

Cooley, H. and Donnelly, K. (2012) *Hydraulic fracturing and water resources: Separating the frack from the fiction*, Pacific Institute, Oakland, CA, USA.

Cornish, G., Bosworth, B., Perry, C. and Burke, J. (2004) *Water charging in irrigated agriculture: An analysis of international experience*, FAO Waters Reports 28, Food and Agriculture Organization of the United Nations, Rome, Italy.

Cosgrove, W. and Rijsberman, F. (2000) *World water vision: Making water everybody's business*, World Water Council, Earthscan, London, UK.

Costanza, R., d'Arge, R., De Groot, R., Farber, S., Grasso, M., Hannon, B., Limburg, K., Naeem, S., O'Neill, R.V., Paruelo, J., Raskin, R.G., Sutton, P. and Van den Belt, M. (1997) The value of the world's ecosystem services and natural capital, *Nature*, 387(6630): 253–260.

Crane, A.G., McWilliams, A., Matten, D., Moon, J. and Siegel, D.S. (eds) (2008) *The Oxford handbook of corporate social responsibility*, Oxford University Press, Oxford, UK.

Crase, L. and O'Keefe, S. (2009) The paradox of national water savings: A critique of 'Water for the Future', *Agenda: A Journal of Policy Analysis and Reform*, 16(1): 45–60.

De Fraiture, C., Cai, X., Amarasinghe, U., Rosegrant, M. and Molden, D. (2004) *Does international cereal trade save water? The impact of virtual water trade on global water use*, Comprehensive Assessment Research Report 4, International Water Management Institute, Colombo, Sri Lanka.

De Pelsmacker, P., Driesen, L. and Rayp, G. (2005) Do consumers care about ethics? Willingness to pay for fair-trade coffee, *The Journal of Consumer Affairs*, 39(2): 369–385.

Dellapenna, J.W. (2000) The importance of getting names right: The myth of markets for water, *William and Mary Environmental Law and Policy Review*, 25: 317–377.

Dennehy, K.F. (2000) *High Plains regional ground-water study*, USGS Fact Sheet FS-091-00, United States Geological Survey, Denver, CO, USA.

Didier, T. and Lucie, S. (2008) Measuring consumer's willingness to pay for organic and fair trade products, *International Journal of Consumer Studies*, 32(5): 479–490.

Dinar, A. and Subramanian, A. (1998) Policy implications from water pricing experiences in various countries, *Water Policy*, 1(2): 239–250.

Dixon, J., Braun, H.-J., Kosina, P. and Crouch, J. (eds) (2009) *Wheat facts and futures 2009*, International Maize and Wheat Improvement Center (CIMMYT), Mexico City, Mexico.

D'Silva, J. and Webster, J. (eds) (2010) *The meat crisis: Developing more sustainable production and consumption*, Earthscan, London, UK.

Dubcovsky, J. and Dvorak, J. (2007) Genome plasticity a key factor in the success of polyploid wheat under domestication, *Science*, 316(5833): 1862–1866.

EC (2009) *Directive 2009/28/EC of the European Parliament and of the Council of 23 April 2009 on the promotion of the use of energy from renewable sources and amending and subsequently repealing Directives 2001/77/EC and 2003/30/EC*, European Commission, Brussels, Belgium.

EC (2010) *Water Framework Directive Implementation Reports*, European Commission, Brussels, Belgium.

EC (2011) *A resource-efficient Europe: Flagship initiative under the Europe 2020 strategy*, Communication from the Commission to the European Parliament, the Council, the Economic and Social Committee and the Committee of the Regions, European Commission, Brussels, Belgium.

EC and PBL (2011) *EU resource efficiency perspectives in a global context*, PBL Netherlands Environmental Assessment Agency, The Hague, the Netherlands and European Commission, Brussels, Belgium.

Economy, E.C. (2004) *The river runs black: The environmental challenge to China's future*, Cornell University Press, Ithaca, NY, USA.

EPA (2009) *National primary drinking water regulations*, Environmental Protection Agency, Washington, DC, USA.

EPZA (2005) *Horticulture industry in Kenya*, Export Processing Zones Authority, Nairobi, Kenya.

Ercin, A.E. and Hoekstra, A.Y. (2012) *Carbon and water footprints: Concepts, methodologies and policy responses*, United Nations World Water Assesment Programme, Side Publications Series No. 4, UNESCO, Paris, France.

Ercin, A.E., Aldaya, M.M. and Hoekstra, A.Y. (2011) Corporate water footprint accounting and impact assessment: The case of the water footprint of a sugar-containing carbonated beverage, *Water Resources Management*, 25(2): 721–741.

Ercin, A.E., Aldaya, M.M. and Hoekstra, A.Y. (2012) The water footprint of soy milk and soy burger and equivalent animal products, *Ecological Indicators*, 18: 392–402.

Everard, M. and Harper, D.M. (2002) Towards the sustainability of the Lake Naivasha Ramsar site and its catchment, *Hydrobiologia*, 488: 191–202.

Falkenmark, M. and Rockström, J. (2004) *Balancing water for humans and nature: The new approach in ecohydrology*, Earthscan, London, UK.

FAO (2001) *The world's forests 2000*, GeoNetwork, Food and Agricultural Organization of the United Nations, Rome, Italy.

FAO (2005) *Livestock policy brief 02*, Food and Agriculture Organization of the United Nations, Rome, Italy.

FAO (2006) *Global forest resources assessment 2005: Progress towards sustainable forest management*, FAO Forestry Paper 147, Food and Agriculture Organization of the United Nations, Rome, Italy.

FAO (2009) *Global map of yearly actual evapotranspiration: Resolution 5 arc minutes, for the period 1961–1990*, Food and Agriculture Organization of the United Nations, Rome, Italy.

FAO (2010) *Global forest resources assessment 2010*, FAO Forestry Paper 163, Food and Agriculture Organization of the United Nations, Rome, Italy.

FAO (2011) *The state of the world's land and water resources for food and agriculture: Managing systems at risk*, Food and Agriculture Organization of the United Nations, Rome, Italy, and Earthscan, London, UK.

FAO (2012a) *FAOSTAT*, Food and Agriculture Organization of the United Nations, Rome, Italy, http://faostat.fao.org.

FAO (2012b) *AQUASTAT*, Food and Agriculture Organization of the United Nations, Rome, Italy, http://www.fao.org/nr/water/aquastat/main/index.stm.

FAO (2012c) *FertiStat*, Food and Agriculture Organization of the United Nations, Rome, Italy, www.fao.org/ag/agl/fertistat.

FAO and CEPI (2007) *Recovered paper data 2006*, Food and Agriculture Organization of the United Nations, Rome, Italy, and Confederation of European Paper Industries, Brussels, Belgium.

Fereres, E. and Soriano, M.A. (2007) Deficit irrigation for reducing agricultural water use, *Journal of Experimental Botany*, 58(2): 147–159.

Ferrara, V. and Pappalardo, G. (2004) Intensive exploitation effects on alluvial aquifer of the Catania plain, eastern Sicily, Italy, *Geofisica Internacional*, 43(4): 671–681.

Galli, A., Wiedmann, T., Ercin, E., Knoblauch, D., Ewing, B. and Giljum, S. (2011) Integrating ecological, carbon and water footprint into a 'footprint family' of indicators: Definition and role in tracking human pressure on the planet, *Ecological Indicators*, 16: 100–112.

Galloway, J.N., Burke, M., Bradford, G.E., Naylor, R., Falcon, W., Chapagain, A.K., Gaskell, J.C., McCullough, E., Mooney, H.A., Oleson, K.L.L., Steinfeld, H., Wassenaar, T. and Smil, V. (2007) International trade in meat: The tip of the pork chop, *Ambio*, 36(8): 622–629.

Geerts, S. and Raes, D. (2009) Deficit irrigation as an on-farm strategy to maximize crop water productivity in dry areas, *Agricultural Water Management*, 96(9): 1275–1284.

Gerbens-Leenes, W. and Hoekstra, A.Y. (2011) The water footprint of biofuel-based transport, *Energy & Environmental Science*, 4(8): 2658–2668.

Gerbens-Leenes, W. and Hoekstra, A.Y. (2012) The water footprint of sweeteners and bio-ethanol, *Environment International*, 40(1): 202–211.

Gerbens-Leenes, P.W., Hoekstra, A.Y. and Van der Meer, T.H. (2009a) The water footprint of energy from biomass: A quantitative assessment and consequences of an increasing share of bio-energy in energy supply, *Ecological Economics*, 68(4): 1052–1060.

Gerbens-Leenes, W., Hoekstra, A.Y. and Van der Meer, T.H. (2009b) The water footprint of bioenergy, *Proceedings of the National Academy of Sciences*, 106(25): 10219–10223.

Gerbens-Leenes, W., Hoekstra, A.Y. and Van der Meer, T.H. (2009c) A global estimate of the water footprint of Jatropha curcas under limited data availability, *Proceedings of the National Academy of Sciences*, 106(40): E113.

Gerbens-Leenes, P.W., Van Lienden, A.R., Hoekstra, A.Y. and Van der Meer, T.H. (2012) Biofuel scenarios in a water perspective: The global blue and green water footprint of road transport in 2030, *Global Environmental Change*, 22(3): 764–775.

Gleick, P.H. (ed.) (1993) *Water in crisis: A guide to the world's fresh water resources*, Oxford University Press, Oxford, UK.

Gleick, P.H. (1994) Water and energy, *Annual Review of Energy and the Environment*, 19: 267–299.

Gleick, P.H. (1999) The human right to water, *Water Policy*, 1(5): 487–503.

Gleick, P.H. (2010) *Bottled and sold: The story behind our obsession with bottled water*, Island Press, Washington, DC, USA.

Gleick, P.H., Wolff, G., Chalecki, E.L. and Reyes, R. (2002) Globalization and international trade of water. In: Gleick, P.H., Burns, W.C.G., Chalecki, E.L., Cohen, M., Cushing, K.K., Mann, A.S., Reyes, R., Wolff, G.H. and Wong, A.K. *The world's water 2002–2003, The biennial report on freshwater resources*, Island Press, Washington, DC, USA, pp. 33–56.

GoI (2008) *National policy on biofuels*, Government of India, Ministry of New and Renewable Energy, New Delhi, India.

Gonzalez-Garcia, S., Berg, S., Feijoo, G. and Moreira, M.T. (2009) Environmental impacts of forest production and supply of pulpwood: Spanish and Swedish case studies, *International Journal of Life Cycle Assessment*, 14(4): 340–353.

Goodland, R. and Anhang, J. (2009) Livestock and climate change: What if the key actors in climate change are cows, pigs, and chickens? *World Watch Magazine*, Nov/Dec 2009, pp. 10–19.

Goria, A. and Lugaresi, N. (2002) *The evolution of the national water regime in Italy*, Euwareness Project, Istituto per la Ricerca Sociale, Milan, Italy.

Grote, U., Craswell, E. and Vlek, P. (2005) Nutrient flows in international trade: Ecology and policy issues, *Environmental Science and Policy*, 8(5): 439–451.

Gunkel, G., Kosmol, J., Sobral, M., Rohn, H., Montenegro, S. and Aureliano, J. (2006) Sugar cane industry as a source of water pollution: Case study on the situation in Ipojuca River, Pernambuco, Brazil, *Journal of Water, Air, and Soil Pollution*, 180(1–4): 261–269.

Gustavsson, J., Cederberg, C., Sonesson, U., Van Otterdijk, R. and Meybeck, A. (2011) *Global food losses and food waste: Extent, causes and prevention*, Food and Agriculture Organization of the United Nations, Rome, Italy.

GWP (2000) *Integrated water resources management*, TAC Background Paper No. 4, Global Water Partnership, Stockholm, Sweden.

Hardin, G. (1968) The tragedy of the commons, *Science*, 162(3859): 1243–1248.

Harper, D. and Mavuti, K. (2004) Lake Naivasha, Kenya: Ecohydrology to guide the management of a tropical protected area, *Ecohydrology and Hydrobiology*, 4(3): 287–305.

HCDA (2007) *Horticulture products export volume statistics*, Horticultural Crops Development Authority, Nairobi, Kenya, www.hcda.or.ke.

Hendy, C.R.C, Kleih, U., Crawshaw, R. and Phillips, M. (1995) *Livestock and the environment finding a balance: Interactions between livestock production systems and the environment, Impact Domain: Concentrate feed demand*, Food and Agriculture Organization of the United Nations, Rome, Italy.

Herrero, M., Gerber, P., Vellinga, T., Garnett, T., Leip, A., Opio, C., Westhoek, H.J., Thornton, P.K., Olesen, J., Hutchings, N., Montgomery, H., Soussana, J.-F., Steinfeld, H. and McAllister, T.A. (2011) Livestock and greenhouse gas emissions: The importance of getting the numbers right, *Animal Feed Science and Technology*, 166–67: 779–782.

Hoekstra, A.Y. (ed.) (2003) *Virtual water trade: Proceedings of the International Expert Meeting on Virtual Water Trade*, Delft, the Netherlands, 12–13 December 2002, Value of Water Research Report Series No. 12, UNESCO-IHE, Delft, the Netherlands.

Hoekstra, A.Y. (2008) The relation between international trade and water resources management. In: K.P. Gallagher (ed.) *Handbook on trade and the environment*, Edward Elgar Publishing, Cheltenham, UK, pp. 116–125.

Hoekstra, A.Y. (2009) Human appropriation of natural capital: A comparison of ecological footprint and water footprint analysis, *Ecological Economics*, 68(7): 1963–1974.

Hoekstra, A.Y. (2010a) The water footprint of animal products. In: D'Silva, J. and Webster, J. (eds) *The meat crisis: Developing more sustainable production and consumption*, Earthscan, London, UK, pp. 22–33.

Hoekstra, A.Y. (2010b) *The relation between international trade and freshwater scarcity*, Working Paper ERSD-2010-05, January 2010, World Trade Organization, Geneva, Switzerland.

Hoekstra, A.Y. (2011a) The global dimension of water governance: Why the river basin approach is no longer sufficient and why cooperative action at global level is needed, *Water*, 3(1): 21–46.

Hoekstra, A.Y. (2011b) The relation between international trade and freshwater scarcity. In: Hoekstra, A.Y., Aldaya, M.M. and Avril, B. (eds) *Proceedings of the ESF Strategic Workshop on accounting for water scarcity and pollution in the rules of international trade*, Amsterdam, 25–26 November 2010, Value of Water Research Report Series No. 54, UNESCO-IHE, Delft, the Netherlands, pp. 9–29.

Hoekstra, A.Y. (2012) The hidden water resource use behind meat and dairy, *Animal Frontiers*, 2(2): 3–8.

Hoekstra, A.Y. and Chapagain, A.K. (2007) Water footprints of nations: Water use by people as a function of their consumption pattern, *Water Resources Management*, 21(1): 35–48.

Hoekstra, A.Y. and Chapagain, A.K. (2008) *Globalization of water: Sharing the planet's freshwater resources*, Blackwell Publishing, Oxford, UK.

Hoekstra, A.Y. and Hung, P.Q. (2002) *Virtual water trade: A quantification of virtual water flows between nations in relation to international crop trade*, Value of Water Research Report Series No. 11, UNESCO-IHE, Delft, the Netherlands.

Hoekstra, A.Y. and Hung, P.Q. (2005) Globalisation of water resources: International virtual water flows in relation to crop trade, *Global Environmental Change*, 15(1): 45–56.

Hoekstra, A.Y. and Mekonnen, M.M. (2011) *Global water scarcity: Monthly blue water footprint compared to blue water availability for the world's major river basins*, Value of Water Research Report Series No. 53, UNESCO-IHE, Delft, the Netherlands.

Hoekstra, A.Y. and Mekonnen, M.M. (2012a) The water footprint of humanity, *Proceedings of the National Academy of Sciences*, 109(9): 3232–3237.

Hoekstra, A.Y. and Mekonnen, M.M. (2012b) From water footprint assessment to policy, *Proceedings of the National Academy of Sciences*, 109(22): E1425.

Hoekstra, A.Y., Chapagain, A.K., Aldaya, M.M. and Mekonnen, M.M. (2011) *The water footprint assessment manual: Setting the global standard*, Earthscan, London, UK.

Hoekstra, A.Y., Gerbens-Leenes, W. and Van der Meer, T.H. (2009) The water footprint of Jatropha curcas under poor growing conditions, *Proceedings of the National Academy of Sciences*, 106(42): E119.

Hoekstra, A.Y., Mekonnen, M.M., Chapagain, A.K., Mathews, R.E. and Richter, B.D. (2012) Global monthly water scarcity: Blue water footprints versus blue water availability, *PLoS ONE*, 7(2): e32688.

Howard, P.H. and Allen, P. (2008) Consumer willingness to pay for domestic 'fair trade': Evidence from the United States, *Renewable Agriculture and Food Systems*, 23(3): 235–242.

Hughes, S., Partzch, L. and Gaskell, S. (2007) The development of biofuels within the context of the global water crisis, *Sustainable Development Law & Policy*, 7(3): 58–62.

ICID (2006) *Experiences with inter basin water transfers for irrigation, drainage and flood management*, Revised draft report of the ICID Task Force on Inter Basin Water Transfers, International Commission on Irrigation and Drainage, New Delhi, India.

ICWE (1992) *The Dublin statement on water and sustainable development*, International Conference on Water and the Environment, Dublin, Ireland.

IEA (2006) *World energy outlook 2006*, International Energy Agency, Paris, France.

IPCC (2007) *Climate change 2007: Synthesis report*, Contribution of Working Groups I, II and III to the Fourth Assessment Report of the Intergovernmental Panel on Climate Change, IPCC, Geneva, Switzerland.

ISTAT (2008) *Annual crop data*, Italian National Institute of Statistics, Rome, Italy, www.istat.it.

ITC (2006) *PC-TAS version 2000–2004 in HS or SITC*, International Trade Centre, Geneva, Switzerland.

Jalota, S.K. and Prihar, S.S. (1998) *Reducing soil water evaporation with tillage and straw mulching*, Iowa State University Press, Ames, IA, USA.

Jenkinson, D.S. (2001) The impact of humans on the nitrogen cycle, with focus on temperate arable agriculture, *Plant and Soil*, 228(1): 3–15.

Jongschaap, R.E.E., Corré, W.J., Bindraban, P.S. and Brandenburg, W.A. (2007) *Claims and facts on Jatropha curcas L.: Global Jatropha curcas evaluation, breeding and propagation programme*, Report 158, Plant Research International, Wageningen, the Netherlands and Stichting Het Groene Woudt, Laren, the Netherlands.

Jongschaap, R.E.E., Blesgraaf, R.A.R., Bogaard, T.A., Van Loo, E.N. and Savenije, H.H.G. (2009) The water footprint of bioenergy from Jatropha curcas L., *Proceedings of the National Academy of Sciences*, 106(35): E92.

Kampman, D.A., Hoekstra, A.Y. and Krol, M.S. (2008) *The water footprint of India*, Value of Water Research Report Series No. 32, UNESCO-IHE, Delft, the Netherlands.

Kellner, K. (2010) *The water footprint of paper products*, M.Sc. thesis, University of Natural Resources and Applied Life Sciences, Vienna, Austria.

Kitaka, N., Harper, D.M. and Mavuti, K.M. (2002) Phosphorus inputs to Lake Naivasha, Kenya, from its catchments and the trophic state of the lake, *Hydrobiologia*, 488: 73–80.

Krier, J.-M. (2005) *Fair trade in Europe 2005: Facts and figures on fair trade in 25 European countries*, Fair Trade Advocacy Office, Brussels, Belgium.

Larijani, K.M (2005) *Iran's water crisis: Inducers, challenges and counter-measures*, 45th Congress of the European Regional Science Association, VU University Amsterdam, Amsterdam, the Netherlands.

Lenzen, M., Murray, J., Sack, F. and Wiedmann, T. (2007) Shared producer and consumer responsibility: Theory and practice, *Ecological Economics*, 61(1): 27–42.

León, L.M. and Parise, M. (2008) Managing environmental problems in Cuban karstic aquifers, *Environmental Geology*, 58(2): 275–283.

Lerman, Z. and Stanchin, I. (2006) Agrarian reforms in Turkmenistan. In: Babu, S.C. and Djalalov, S. (eds) *Policy reform and agriculture development in Central Asia*, Springer, New York, USA, pp. 222–223.

Levinson, M., Lee, E., Chung, J., Huttner, M., Danely, C., McKnight, C. and Langlois, A. (2008) *Watching water: A guide to evaluating corporate risks in a thirsty world*, J. P. Morgan, New York, USA.

Liao, Y., De Fraiture, C. and Giordano, M. (2008) Global trade and water: Lessons from China and the WTO, *Global Governance*, 14(4): 503–521.

Liu, C., Kroeze, C., Hoekstra, A.Y. and Gerbens-Leenes, W. (2012) Past and future trends in grey water footprints of anthropogenic nitrogen and phosphorus inputs to major world rivers, *Ecological Indicators*, 18: 42–49.

Ma, J., Hoekstra, A.Y., Wang, H., Chapagain, A.K. and Wang, D. (2006) Virtual versus real water transfers within China, *Philosophical Transactions of the Royal Society of London B*, 361(1469): 835–842.

Maheu, A. (2009) *Energy choices and their impacts on demand for water resources: An assessment of current and projected water consumption in global energy production*, McGill University, Montreal, Canada.

Mangiti, P.O. (2007) *Will SWAps fix the water sector? Kisima, a forum for analysis and debate on water and sanitation issues in Kenya*, Issue 4 (Jan 2007), pp. 1–3.

Mavuti, K.M. and Harper, D.M. (2006) The ecological state of Lake Naivasha, Kenya, 2005: Turning 25 years research into an effective Ramsar monitoring programme. In: Odada, E.O., Olago, D.O., Ochola, W., Ntiba, M., Wandiga, S., Gichuki, N. and Oyieke, H. (eds) *Proceedings of the 11th World Lakes Conference, 31 October – 4 November 2005*, Nairobi, Kenya, Ministry of Water and Irrigation; International Lake Environment Committee (ILEC), Vol. II, pp. 30–34.

McGuire, V.L. (2007) *Water-level changes in the High Plains Aquifer, predevelopment to 2005 and 2003 to 2005*, Scientific Investigations Report 2006–5324, United States Geological Survey, Reston, VA, USA.

McIsaac, G.F., David, M.B., Gertner, G.Z. and Goolsby, D.A. (2001) Eutrophication: Nitrate flux in the Mississippi river, *Nature*, 414(6860): 166–167.

MDBC (2004) *The cap: Providing security for water users and sustainable rivers*, Murray-Darling Basin Commission, Canberra, Australia.

Mehta, L. and La Cour Madsen, B. (2005) Is the WTO after your water? The General Agreement on Trade in Services (GATS) and poor people's right to water, *Natural Resources Forum*, 29(2): 154–164.

Mekonnen, M.M. and Hoekstra, A.Y. (2010) A global and high-resolution assessment of the green, blue and grey water footprint of wheat, *Hydrology and Earth System Sciences*, 14(7): 1259–1276.

Mekonnen, M.M. and Hoekstra, A.Y. (2011a) The green, blue and grey water footprint of crops and derived crop products, *Hydrology and Earth System Sciences*, 15(5): 1577–1600.

Mekonnen, M.M. and A.Y. Hoekstra (2011b) *National water footprint accounts: The green, blue and grey water footprint of production and consumption*, Value of Water Research Report Series No. 50, UNESCO-IHE, Delft, the Netherlands.

Mekonnen, M.M. and Hoekstra, A.Y. (2012a) A global assessment of the water footprint of farm animal products, *Ecosystems*, 15(3): 401–415.

Mekonnen, M.M. and Hoekstra, A.Y. (2012b) The blue water footprint of electricity from hydropower, *Hydrology and Earth System Sciences*, 16(1): 179–187.

Mekonnen, M.M., Hoekstra, A.Y. and Becht, R. (2012) Mitigating the water footprint of export cut flowers from the Lake Naivasha Basin, Kenya, *Water Resources Management*, 26(13): 3725–3742.

Meybeck, M. (2003) Global analysis of river systems: From Earth system controls to Anthropocene syndromes, *Philosophical Transactions of the Royal Society B: Biological Sciences*, 358(1440): 1935–1955.

Meybeck, M. (2004) The global change of continental aquatic systems: Dominant impacts of human activities, *Water Science and Technology*, 49(7): 73–83.

Millstone, E. and Lang, T. (2003) *The atlas of food*, Earthscan, London, UK.

Mitchell, D. (2008) *A note on rising food prices*, Policy Research Working Paper 4682, Development Prospects Group, The World Bank, Washington, DC, USA.

Miura, A. (2001) *Coffee market and Colombia*, TED Case Studies No. 637, Trade Environment Database, Vol. 11, No. 2, American University, Washington, DC, USA.

Molden, D. (ed.) (2007) *Water for food, water for life: A comprehensive assessment of water management in agriculture*, Earthscan, London, UK.

Molle, F. and Berkoff, J. (2007) Water pricing in irrigation: The lifetime of an idea. In: Molle, F. and Berkoff, J. (eds) *Irrigation water pricing: The gap between theory and practice*, Comprehensive Assessment of Water Management in Agriculture Series No. 4, CAB International Publication, Wallingford, UK, pp. 1–20.

Monzote, R.F. (2008) *From rainforest to cane field in Cuba: An environmental history since 1492*, University of North Carolina Press, Chapel Hill, NC, USA.

Morrison, J., Morkawa, M., Murphy, M. and Schulte, P. (2009) *Water scarcity and climate change: Growing risks for business and investors*, CERES, Boston, MA, USA.

Morrison, J., Schulte, P. and Schenck, R. (2010a) *Corporate water accounting: An analysis of methods and tools for measuring water use and its impacts*, United Nations Global Compact, New York, USA.

Morrison, J., Schulte, P., Christian-Smith, J., Orr, S., Hepworth, N. and Pegram, G. (2010b) *Guide to responsible business engagement with water policy*, Pacific Institute, Oakland, CA, USA.

Mpusia, P.T.O. (2006) *Comparison of water consumption between greenhouse and outdoor cultivation*, M.Sc. thesis, ITC, Enschede, the Netherlands.

Mumma, A. (2005) *Kenya's new water law: An analysis of the implications for the rural poor*, paper presented at the international workshop on 'African water laws: Plural legislative frameworks for rural water management in Africa', Johannesburg, 26–28 January, 2005.

Musota, R. (2008) *Using WEAP and scenarios to assess sustainability of water resources in a basin*, case study for Lake Naivasha catchment, Kenya, M.Sc. thesis, ITC, Enschede, the Netherlands.

Nandalal, K.D.W. and Hipel, K.W. (2007) Strategic decision support for resolving conflict over water sharing among countries along the Syr Darya river in the Aral Sea Basin, *Journal of Water Resources Planning and Management*, 133(4): 289–299.

Naylor, R., Steinfeld, H., Falcon, W., Galloway, J., Smil, V., Bradford, E., Alder, J. and Mooney, H. (2005) Losing the links between livestock and land, *Science*, 310(5754): 1621–1622.

NCASI (2009) *Water profile of the United States forest products industry*, National Council for Air and Stream Improvement, Research Triangle Park, NC, USA.

NCC (2012) *Economics: Market news, stats and analysis*, National Cotton Council of America, Cordova, TN, USA, www.cotton.org.

Neumayer, E. (2004) The WTO and the environment: Its past record is better than critics believe, but the future outlook is bleak, *Global Environmental Politics*, 4(3): 1–8.

Nilsson, C., Reidy, C.A., Dynesius, M. and Revenga, C. (2005) Fragmentation and flow regulation of the world's large river systems, *Science*, 308(5720): 405–408.

Norse, D. (2005) Non-point pollution from crop production: Global, regional and national issues, *Pedosphere*, 15(4): 499–508.

Nriagu, J.O. and Pacyna, J.M. (1988) Quantitative assessment of worldwide contamination of air, water and soils by trace metals, *Nature*, 333(6169): 134–139.

OECD (2006) *Water and agriculture: Sustainability, markets and policies*, Organisation for Economic Cooperation and Development, Paris, France.

Oki, T. and Kanae, S. (2004) Virtual water trade and world water resources, *Water Science and Technology*, 49(7): 203–209.

Olivier, J.G.J., Janssens-Maenhout, G. and Peters, J.A.H.W. (2012) *Trends in global CO$_2$ emissions: 2012 Report*, Background studies, PBL Netherlands Environmental Assessment Agency, The Hague, the Netherlands and Joint Research Centre of the European Commission, Ispra, Italy.

Olsson, G. (2012) *Water and energy: Threats and opportunities*, IWA Publishing, London, UK.

O'Mara, F.P. (2011) The significance of livestock as a contributor to global greenhouse gas emissions today and in the near future, *Animal Feed Science and Technology*, 166–167: 7–15.

Orgaz, F., Fernández, M.D., Bonachela, S., Gallardo, M. and Fereres, E. (2005) Evapotranspiration of horticultural crops in an unheated plastic greenhouse, *Agricultural Water Management*, 72(2): 81–96.

Orr, S., Cartwright, A. and Tickner, D. (2009) *Understanding water risks: A primer on the consequences of water scarcity for government and business*, WWF, Godalming, UK and HSBC, London, UK.

Orr, S., Sánchez-Navarro, R., Schmidt, G., Seiz-Puyuelo, R., Smith, K. and Verberne, J. (2011) *Assessing water risk: A practical approach for financial institutions*, WWF, Berlin, Germany and DEG, KFW Bankengruppe, Germany.

Ostrom, E. (1990) *Governing the commons: The evolution of institutions for collective action*, Cambridge University Press, Cambridge, UK.

Ostrom, E., Burger, J., Field, C.B., Norgaard, R.B. and Policansky, D. (1999) Revisiting the commons: Local lessons, global challenges, *Science*, 284(5412): 278–282.

Oweis, T. and Hachum, A. (2012) *Supplemental irrigation: A highly efficient water-use practice*, 2nd edition, International Center for Agricultural Research in the Dry Areas, Aleppo, Syria.

Owuor, S.O. and Foeken, D.W.J. (2009) *Water reforms and interventions in urban Kenya: Institutional set-up, emerging impact and challenges*, African Studies Centre Working Paper 83, Leiden, the Netherlands.

Peck, J.C. (2007) Groundwater management in the High Plains Aquifer in the USA: Legal problems and innovations. In: Giordano, M. and Villholth, K.G. (eds) *The agricultural groundwater revolution: Opportunities and threats to development*, CAB International, Wallingford, UK.

Pegram, G., Orr, S. and Williams, C. (2009) *Investigating shared risk in water: Corporate engagement with the public policy process*, WWF, Godalming, UK.

Pereira, L.S., Oweis, T. and Zairi, A. (2002) Irrigation management under water scarcity, *Agricultural Water Management*, 57(3): 175–206.

Perry, C. (2003) *Water pricing: Some important definitions and assumptions*, Occasional Paper No. 59, SOAS Water Issues Study Group, School of Oriental and African Studies/King's College London, University of London, London, UK.

Perry, C. (2007) Efficient irrigation; Inefficient communication; Flawed recommendations, *Irrigation and Drainage*, 56(4): 367–378.

Peterson, J. and Bernardo, D. (2003) High Plains regional aquifer study revisited: A 20 year retrospective for Western Kansas, *Great Plains Research*, 13(2): 179–197.

Pimentel, D. and Patzek, T.W. (2005) Ethanol production using corn, switch grass, and wood: Biodiesel production using soybean and sunflower, *Natural Resources Research*, 14(1): 65–76.

Pimentel, D. and Pimentel, M.H. (2008) *Food, energy, and society*, 3rd edition, CRC Press, Boca Raton, FL, USA.

Pimentel, D., Marklein, A., Toth, M.A., Karpoff, M.N., Paul, G.S., McCormack, R., Kyriazis, J. and Krueger, T. (2009) Food versus biofuels: Environmental and economic costs, *Human Ecology*, 37(1): 1–12.

Pitesky, M.E., Stackhouse, K.R. and Mitloehner, F.M. (2009) Clearing the air: Livestock's contribution to climate change, *Advances in Agronomy*, 103: 1–40.

Poff, N.L. and Zimmerman, J.K.H. (2010) Ecological responses to altered flow regimes: A literature review to inform the science and management of environmental flows, *Freshwater Biology*, 55(1): 194–205.

Poisot, A.S., Speedy, A. and Kueneman, E. (2007) *Good agricultural practices – a working concept: Background paper for the FAO Internal Workshop on Good Agricultural Practices*, FAO GAP Working Paper Series 5, Food and Agriculture Organization of the United Nations, Rome, Italy.

Postel, S. (1999) *Pillar of sand: Can the irrigation miracle last?* W.W. Norton, New York, USA.

Postel, S.L., Daily, G.C. and Ehrlich, P.R. (1996) Human appropriation of renewable freshwater, *Science*, 271(5250): 785–788.

Postle, M., George, C., Upson, S., Hess, T. and Morris, J. (2011) *Assessment of the efficiency of the water footprinting approach and of the agricultural products and foodstuff labelling and certification schemes*, Risk and Policy Analysts Limited, Loddon, Norfolk, UK and Cranfield University, Cranfield, Bedfordshire, UK.

Ramirez-Vallejo, J. and Rogers, P. (2004) Virtual water flows and trade liberalization, *Water Science and Technology*, 49(7): 25–32.

Rep, J. (2011) *From forest to paper, the story of our water footprint*, UPM-Kymmene, Helsinki, Finland.

Renner, A., Zelt, T. and Gerteiser, S. (2008) *Global market study on jatropha*, final report prepared for the World Wildlife Fund for Nature (WWF), GEXSI London, UK and Berlin, Germany.

Ricardo, D. (1821) *On the principles of political economy and taxation*, 3rd edition, John Murray, London, UK.

Richter, B. (2009) Sustainable water use: Can certification show the way? *Innovations*, 4(3): 119–139.

Richter, B.D., Davis, M.M., Apse, C. and Konrad, C. (2012) A presumptive standard for environmental flow protection, *River Research and Applications*, 28(8): 1312–1321.

Ridoutt, B.G. and Huang, J. (2012) Environmental relevance: The key to understanding water footprints, *Proceedings of the National Academy of Sciences*, 109(22): E1424.

Riungu, C. (2007) Kenya: Naivasha flower farms win first round in tax war, *The East African*, 13 August 2007, Nairobi, Kenya.

Rivoli, P. (2005) *The travels of a T-shirt in the global economy: An economist examines the markets, power, and politics of world trade*, John Wiley, Hoboken, NJ, USA.

Rogers, P., Bhatia, R. and Huber, A. (1998) *Water as a social and economic good: How to put the principle into practice*, TAC Background Papers No. 2, Global Water Partnership, Stockholm, Sweden.

Rogers, P., De Silva, R. and Bhatia, R. (2002) Water is an economic good: How to use prices to promote equity, efficiency, and sustainability, *Water Policy*, 4(1): 1–17.

Rosegrant, M.W. and Cline, S. (2002) The politics and economics of water pricing in developing countries, *Water Resources Impact*, 4(1): 6–8.

Roth, D. and Warner, J. (2007) Virtual water: Virtuous impact? The unsteady state of virtual water, *Agriculture and Human Values*, 25(2): 257–270.

SABMiller and WWF-UK (2009) *Water footprinting: Identifying and addressing water risks in the value chain*, SABMiller, Woking, UK and WWF-UK, Goldalming, UK.

SABMiller, GTZ and WWF (2010) *Water futures: Working together for a secure water future*, SABMiller, Woking, UK and WWF-UK, Goldalming, UK.

Sanchez, P.A. (2002) Soil fertility and hunger in Africa, *Science*, 295(5562): 2019–2020.

Sarni, W. (2011) *Corporate water strategies*, Earthscan, London, UK.

Savenije, H.H.G. (2002) Why water is not an ordinary economic good, or why the girl is special, *Physics and Chemistry of the Earth*, 27(11–22): 741–744.

Schindler, D. (2010) Tar sands need solid science, *Nature*, 468(7323): 499–501.

Solomon, S.K. (2005) Environmental pollution and its management in the sugar industry in India: An appraisal, *Journal of Sugar Tech*, 7(1): 77–81.

Sorrell, S., Dimitropoulos, J. and Sommerville, M. (2009) Empirical estimates of the direct rebound effect: A review, *Energy Policy*, 37(4): 1356–1371.

Steinfeld, H., Gerber, P., Wassenaar, T., Castel, V., Rosales, M. and De Haan, C. (2006) *Livestock's long shadow: Environmental issues and options*, Food and Agriculture Organization of the United Nations, Rome, Italy.

Stocking, M.A. (2003) Tropical soils and food security: The next 50 years, *Science*, 302(5649): 1356–1359.

Svancara, L.K., Brannon, R., Scott, J M., Groves, C.R., Noss, R.F. and Pressey, R.L. (2005) Policy-driven versus evidence-based conservation: A review of political targets and biological needs, *BioScience*, 55(11): 989–995.

Tang, S.Y. (1992). *Institutions and collective action: Self governance in irrigation systems*, ICS Press, San Francisco, CA, USA.

TCCC and TNC (2010) *Product water footprint assessments: Practical application in corporate water stewardship*, The Coca-Cola Company, Atlanta, GA, USA and The Nature Conservancy, Arlington, VA, USA.

Terry, B., Athanasios, D. and Jonathan, R. (2009) The macroeconomic rebound effect and the world economy, *Energy Efficiency*, 2(4): 411–427.

Thenkabail, P.S., Schull, M. and Turral, H. (2005) Ganges and Indus river basin land use/ land cover (LULC) and irrigated area mapping using continuous streams of MODIS data, *Remote Sensing of Environment*, 95(3): 317–341.

Tilman, D., Fargione, J., Wolff, B., D'Antonio, C., Dobson, A., Howarth, R., Schindler, D., Schlesinger, W.H., Simberloff, D. and Swackhamer, D. (2001) Forecasting agriculturally driven global environmental change, *Science*, 292(5515): 281–284.

Tiruneh, B.A. (2004) *Modelling water quality using soil and water assessment tool SWAT: A case study in Lake Naivasha basin, Kenya*, M.Sc. thesis, ITC, Enschede, the Netherlands.

Tversky, A. and Kahneman, D. (1981) The framing of decisions and the psychology of choice, *Science*, 211(4481): 453–458.

UN (1992) *Agenda 21: The United Nations programme of action from Rio*, United Nations, New York, USA.

UN (1998) *Kyoto Protocol to the United Nations Framework Convention on Climate Change*, United Nations, New York, USA.

UN (2011) *World population prospects: The 2010 revision, highlights and advance tables, ESA/P/ WP.220, Population Division, Department of Economic and Social Affairs*, United Nations, New York, USA.

UNECE and FAO (2010) *Forest product conversion factors for the UNECE region*, Geneva Timber and Forest Discussion Paper 49, United Nations Economic Commission for Europe, Geneva, Switzerland and Food and Agriculture Organization of the United Nations, Rome, Italy.

UNEP (2005) *The trade and environmental effects of ecolabels: Assessment and response*, United Nations Environment Programme, Nairobi, Kenya.

UNESCO (1998) *UNESCO's initiative for the Aral Sea Basin*, Information document, United Nations Educational, Scientific and Cultural Organization, Tashkent, Uzbekistan.

UNESCO (2000) *Water-related vision for the Aral sea basin for the year 2025*, United Nations Educational, Scientific and Cultural Organization, Paris, France.

UNESCO (2003) *Water for people, water for life*, United Nations World Water Development Report, Part: Case Studies, Chapter 19, UNESCO Publishing, Paris, France and Berghahn Books, Oxford, UK.

UNFPA (2011) *State of world population 2011: People and possibilities in a world of 7 billion*, United Nations Population Fund, New York, USA.

Van Oel, P.R. and Hoekstra, A.Y. (2010) *The green and blue water footprint of paper products: Methodological considerations and quantification*, Value of Water Research Report Series No. 46, UNESCO-IHE, Delft, the Netherlands.

Van Oel, P.R. and Hoekstra, A.Y. (2012) Towards quantification of the water footprint of paper: A first estimate of its consumptive component, *Water Resources Management*, 26(3): 733–749.

Van Oel, P.R., Krol, M.S. and Hoekstra, A.Y. (2009) A river basin as a common-pool resource: A case study for the Jaguaribe basin in the semi-arid Northeast of Brazil, *International Journal of River Basin Management*, 7(4): 345–353.

Van Wyk, B.E. (2005) *Food plants of the world: An illustrated guide*, Timber Press, Portland, OR, USA.

Verma, S., Kampman, D.A., Van der Zaag, P. and Hoekstra, A.Y. (2009) Going against the flow: A critical analysis of inter-state virtual water trade in the context of India's National River Linking Programme, *Physics and Chemistry of the Earth*, 34(4–5): 261–269.

Vermeir, I. and Verbeke, W. (2006) Sustainable food consumption: Exploring the consumer 'attitude - behavioral intention' gap, *Journal of Agricultural & Environmental Ethics*, 19(2): 169–194.

Wada, Y., Van Beek, L.P.H., Van Kempen, C.M., Reckman, J.W.T.M., Vasak, S. and Bierkens, M.F.P. (2010) Global depletion of groundwater resources, *Geophysical Research Letters*, 37: L20402.

Wallace, J.S. and Gregory, P.J. (2002) Water resources and their use in food production systems, *Aquatic Sciences*, 64(4): 363–375.

Ward, F.A. and Pulido-Velazquez, M. (2008) Water conservation in irrigation can increase water use, *Proceedings of the National Academy of Sciences*, 105(47): 18215–18220.

WCD (2000) *Dams and development: A new framework for decision-making*, The report of the World Commission on Dams, Earthscan, London, UK.

Wichelns, D. (2010) Virtual water: A helpful perspective, but not a sufficient policy criterion, *Water Resources Management*, 24(10): 2203–2219.

World Bank (2004) *Water resources sector strategy: Strategic directions for World Bank engagement*, World Bank, Washington, DC, USA.

Worldwatch Institute (2007) *Biofuels for transport: Global potential and implications for sustainable energy and agriculture*, Earthscan, London, UK.

World Water Commission (2000) *A water secure world: Vision for water, life, and the environment*, World Water Vision Commission Report, World Water Commission, The Hague, the Netherlands.

WTO (2008) *Understanding the WTO*, 4th edition, World Trade Organization, Geneva, Switzerland.

WWF (2004) *Sugar and the environment: Encouraging better management practices in sugar production*, WWF Global Freshwater Programme, WWF, Zeist, the Netherlands.

WWF (2006) *Drought in the Mediterranean: WWF policy proposals*, WWF/Adena, Madrid, Spain and WWF Mediterranean Programme, Rome, Italy.

WWF (2012) *Living planet report 2012: Biodiversity, biocapacity and better choices*, WWF International, Gland, Switzerland.

Xu, T.Z. (1999) *Water quality assessment and pesticide fate modelling in the Lake Naivasha area, Kenya*, M.Sc. thesis, ITC, Enschede, the Netherlands.

Yang, H., Reichert, P., Abbaspour, K.C. and Zehnder, A.J.B. (2003) A water resources threshold and its implications for food security, *Environmental Science and Technology*, 37(14): 3048–3054.

Yang, H., Wang, L., Abbaspour, K.C. and Zehnder, A.J.B. (2006) Virtual water trade: An assessment of water use efficiency in the international food trade, *Hydrology and Earth System Sciences*, 10(3): 443–454.

Yang, H., Wang, L. and Zehnder, A. (2007) Water scarcity and food trade in the Southern and Eastern Mediterranean countries, *Food Policy*, 32(5–6): 585–605.

Yang, H., Zhou, Y. and Liu, J. (2004) Land and water requirements of biofuels and implications for food supply and the environment in China, *Energy Policy*, 37(5): 1876–1885.

Zwart, S.J., Bastiaanssen, W.G.M., De Fraiture, C. and Molden, D.J. (2010) A global benchmark map of water productivity for rainfed and irrigated wheat, *Agricultural Water Management*, 97(10): 1617–1627.

# INDEX